Along the Side of the Pond

# Along the Side of the Pond

## Memoirs of a Belgian Contemplative

Robert Govaerts

The author / copyright holder can be contacted at r.govaerts@btinternet.com.

Written and typeset in Chicago style. The font style used is Times New Roman 10.5 pts. (main text), 10.0 pts. (preface and acknowledgments), 9.5 pts. (block quotations), 9.0 pts. (copyright page, captions).

All scripture quotations in this book are taken from *The Holy Bible*, Revised Standard Version. Copyright © 1973 by Division of Christian Education of the National Council of the Churches of Christ in the United States of America. Used by permission.

Grateful acknowledgment is given to the following for the photographs that appear in this book in black and white: Lourdes Grotto, Edition A. Doucet, © Sanctuaire de Lourdes; Basilica of Saint Sernin, Toulouse, Editions d'Art Larrey; Cahors, Editions La Clé des Champs; Taizé, photo by Sabine Nitzsche, © Ateliers et Presses de Taizé. All other pictures are from the author's private collection. The map of Belgium and the map of Antwerp and surroundings were produced by the author.

The front-cover photograph was taken by the author in the provincial park Rivierenhof, Antwerp (Deurne), Belgium.

ISBN-13: 979-8645708146

British Library Cataloguing-in-Publication Data: A catalogue record for this book is available from the British Library

Independently published
Millport, Isle of Cumbrae, United Kingdom

*In memory of*
*Frans August Peeters (1914–89) and*
*Carolina Josephina Van Kesbeeck (1930–89)*

# Contents

about my physical and spiritual journey that has included several years in religious communities, my leaving behind of these, and my eventual marriage.

As the title gives away, my story is one of a life lived along the sidelines; there is very little to show for as to what concerns public functions, altruistic acts of self giving, great achievements, or victories. I did make significant efforts towards various achievements and there have been some small victories, but nothing exceptional. The merit of this book is that—besides giving an impression of life in Belgium in the twentieth century—it invites reflection upon the meaning of life, the place of faith, and the relationships that can develop enlightened by this faith. Indeed, central to my autobiographical account is the desire to enter into God's presence and there to partake in a divine union that encompasses a manifoldness of enduring, loving relationships.

R. G.

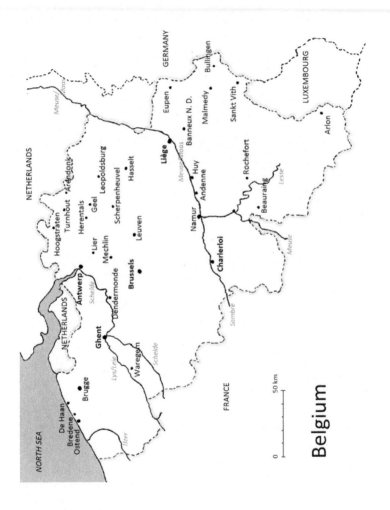

Belgium

NORTH SEA

NETHERLANDS

GERMANY

LUXEMBOURG

FRANCE

De Haan
Bredene
Ostend
Brugge

Hoogstraten
Turnhout Arendonk
Herentals
Lier
Mechlin
Geel
Leopoldsburg
Scherpenheuvel
Hasselt
Leuven

Antwerp
Dendermonde
Brussels

Ghent
Waregem

Eupen
Banneux N. D.
Liège
Huy
Andenne
Namur
Charlerloi

Malmedy
Sankt Vith
Bullingen

Rochefort
Beauraing

Arlon

Meuse/Maas
Schelde
Lys/Leie
Schelde
Ijzer
Meuse/Maas
Sombre
Meuse
Lesse

0    50 km

Antwerp and surroundings

# 1

# Along the side of the pond

THE TIME PERIOD that stretches between our conception in the womb and the breakthrough of consciousness cannot be recalled—at least not unaided—but it does not leave our psyche unmarked. Although the infant is not aware of events that take place during this earliest period of its life, it is not unaffected by it. I received much love in this period, but I was scarred by events that took place around me. In chapters three and six I will dwell upon these events both positive and negative. I start my account, however, with some events that I do recall: instances as yet disconnected from each other as consciousness was starting to break through.

The earliest memory I have is surprisingly not of my mother but of a young girl with long, blond hair. I am lying on my back in a cot, and the girl has a sweet voice and comes over to me. She walks into the room along some white doorposts and bends over the cot. My cot is situated in a corner of the room, and the entry to the room is at the other diagonal end. In subsequent years, this earliest memory would cause me puzzlement. After I registered this very first memory, the girl is gone. Would this very first breakthrough of consciousness have perchance been fraud: a trick played by my young mind?

been better. It is curious that it is just these events that I recall; from all that went on inside the classrooms during my attendance of altogether four years, I cannot remember anything more than what I have mentioned.

# 2

# Manebruggestraat 290

THE HOUSE IN which I grew up was situated at about a kilometer distance from the kindergarten, at the border of the territory of Borsbeek. The address was Manebruggestraat 290. A little history of this street and its curious name may be of some interest.

Manebruggestraat is a street of which the first part runs parallel with a brook called Koudebeek (Cold Brook). Originally, the street name was Oude Baan (Old Road). According to a map of 1812, the old road would have been a section of the way that ran along various villages and hamlets along the eastern side of Antwerp, as far as the town of Herentals, and that connected them with the city.

In the twelfth century, when a need arose for agricultural land, the uncultivated places along the eastern side of Deurne—the township to which the territory of Borsbeek at the time belonged—began to be developed, and farms emerged on them. Between the properties Menegem, Hadrinchoven, and Old Donc, a grounds lay, called Mannincbroek.* The second part of its name *broek* indicates a swampy ground, or marshland. In his history of

---

* The vowel combination *oe* that is used in Dutch names and words is to be pronounced as *oo* in *too*.

Borsbeek, Canon Floris Prims refers to an owner of this land who in 1186 was registered as Henricus de Mannebrucke (the *u* in this name is to be pronounced as *oe*), at the time a councillor of Deurne. In 1260, the name Arnoldus de Manebruc occurs in the registers. So, it is nearby this property that Old Road ran and after which it was much later renamed *Manebruggestraat*. While the road veers away from the Cold Brook in a westerly to southwesterly direction, the brook's overall course is from south to north. About a mile south of the property Mannebrucke, another brook ran into the Cold Brook, this was the Borsebeke, of which *beke* means "brook" and *borse*, "a wild plant that grows on uncultivated land." The brook gave its name to the locality where the village developed, and which became independent from Deurne in 1264. As regards Manebruggestraat, a section of it came to determine the border of the territory of Borsbeek, at a good distance from the old village center.

In 1957/8 my parents built a modest house along Manebruggestraat at the side of the street that was part of the territory of Borsbeek. The border of the village's territory ran along the middle of the street, so that the houses at the other side, those with uneven house numbers, were on the territory of Deurne, which had become a suburb of Antwerp. The house that my parents built was the middle one in a small row of just three that were built around the same time. It had two floors and a flat roof, just as most of the other houses in the street. It was only five meters broad, smaller than the standard six meters, but it was quite elongated. At the front it had a small garden of about five by five meters and at the back a long narrow garden with a sizable workplace at the end of it. There was no garage, but it had cellars under the entire ground floor of the house. The front cellars had windows in them, and these allowed for airing and light to come through along the three steel grids in front of the house. One of the front cellars was a coal cellar, and once a year the coalman would open the metal grid and drop the coal bags through the window opening into the cellar. For each of the three grids, a wooden cover was made covered with felt; these covers were placed over the grids when it rained. The house had concrete flooring, as is customary in North Belgium. The downstairs windows had heavy rolling shutters, which were let down at night, and the glass parts of the doors were covered by metal grids, as were the elongated windows beside them. The garden was enclosed by concrete walls on either side, high enough so that people could not look over them.

Shortly after my parents built their house, a small chocolate factory, owned by Mr. Gartner, was built to the left of the three houses. It was set in about fifty meters from the street, so that it had quite a long drive, place to park cars, and a large lawn in front. The factory building shared the back wall of the workplace at the end of our garden. Along the right side of the three houses, at a distance of about one hundred meters, a beautiful land house presented itself, belonging to Mr. and Mrs. Corluy. They were growers, specializing in tomatoes and lettuce. Hence, large greenhouses stood behind our houses. Beyond these, if I recall it well, largely uncultivated fields were lying. Along the other side of the street, across from our house, a row of houses had been built some years before ours. Overall, the other side of the street within Deurne was more built up, whereas the Borsbeek-side of the street was gradually being built up from about the times when my parents built. The first years that my parents lived there, Manebruggestraat was a cobbled road with an open ditch along the Borsbeek-side, which about fifty meters further ran into the

ing plots, one on which the house stood and an adjacent one, which had a hedge and a small wooden gate at the front, where they had a vegetable patch. Beside them, an elderly couple, Mr. and Mrs. Praet, lived. When I was about ten, Mrs. Praet died. A little time afterwards, however, another lady moved in, Mrs. Van Acker, who was well advanced in years. Her grandson, Johnny, often stayed with them, and he became a member of my class in Primary 5.

Next to them was the house of Frans August Peeters, the policeman. When Walter was a boy of about twelve, he would have seen him setting out on his bicycle so as to perform his policing duties in Deurne. He was married to Joanna Ludovica Beeckman (born June 10, 1915 in Zandvliet). They had five children: Gerard, Eugena, Maria, Walter, and Vera, who were all about a generation older than Walter, my own brother. Their youngest son, Walter, had married Lucienne, the daughter of our next-door neighbors, Mr. and Mrs.

Frans August Peeters

Clessens. Vera, the youngest daughter of Frans and Joanna, lived at the time in the house of her parents with her husband Ward (Eduard). All five children were married. On March 31, 1968, Joanna died at the age of fifty-two from breast cancer. My brother, Walter, who was at the time about sixteen, would have noticed that, in the months after Frans became a widower, he was often aimlessly leaning on the windowsill of the upstairs open window, surveying the movements in the street.

When Walter was about eighteen, and I was a little boy of four, some further profound changes had taken place in the neighborhood and in our family. Frans was now living in our house. The period that these drastic changes had taken place lay just before the time that I reached conscious awareness, just beyond what I am able to recall. Instead, I retained some vague memories of the period not too long after the move of Frans had taken place. I remember a day's outing at the Belgian coast with my mother, Frans—whom I somehow held to be my father—and some of his children with their spouses. As was popular at the time, we rented a large go-cart for a couple of hours on which about eight people could sit. These were pretty heavy vehicles and required a lot of pedaling power. I would, however, have been sitting with my mother at the backseat as passenger. Once the young men that were on the trip had a few beers in them, they tended to get pretty boisterous. The go-carting along the seafront and neighboring streets would have been a pretty hilarious event, which my mother later liked to recall.

Besides that day's outing, Frans (Pa), Ma, and I paid evening visits to—if I am correct—the flat of his son Gerard and Nieke, and the flat of his daughter Maria and Frans. These couples had children with them, and on one occasion, one or two of the girls wanted to get little Bob in the bath with them. Even though I might have been tempted beyond my dislike of wet water, I knew it was nearing the time that we would go home and, moreover, I did not think it behooved to enter into a bathtub full of bubbles and girls on a visit to people whom I did not even know well. I rather stayed along the side of the bath. We went indeed home before the girls had finished their pre-bed bath.

For what concerns Frans's eldest daughter, Eugena: She had been very attached to her mother and, therefore, would have found it rather difficult when her father entered into a new rela-tionship. Moreover, she did not want any contact with her brothers and sisters, so that at that time-period she stayed away from her father whom the others were frequenting.

A new change in situation took place when I was about five. I have in mind an occasion at which Walter was not at home. While I was keeping myself occupied at a table in the living room, at the other end of the room, Pa was sitting in his easy chair, some of his children and their spouses around him. The atmosphere was tense. They were trying to change his mind about something. Pa was holding his hand over his forehead and moved his fingers along from side to side, while he was listening without saying much. I wondered why Ma was not there. To my surprise, I found her upstairs crying on top of the bed. I do not think I had seen that before. I really did not like to see her cry; it devastated me to see my mother cry. I went back downstairs. The hand of Pa left his forehead, he held it slightly raised beside his head, while he pulled up his eyebrows. He had heard enough and made his decision, upon which he and his children, all adult people, stood up. They were clearly very unhappy. He went to the door of the living room, let them out, and they left the house. He went upstairs and comforted Ma.

Another occasion that I remember took place probably not very long afterwards. Something special was going on. In the long elongated living room, the table was being dressed up for a feast and there was some excitement in the air. The only person I remember talking to that day was my grandmother, the "moemoe," that is, my mother's mother. Whereas I called my mother "Ma," my mother would have called her mother "Moe," a word which had become largely old-fashioned in the time of my childhood. It was, however, still our custom to say "Moemoe," or "de Moemoe," that is, with the Dutch article *de* (the). On that conspicuous day, I asked Moemoe what was happening. She then gave the answer, "Your mother is getting married for a second time." I did not ask further, because I thought I understood. It appeared to me a very proper thing that when people love each other very much they get married a second time. I saw my mother and father, that is, Frans, being on very good terms with each other and regularly kissing each other. So, I was happy with that. At the time, it did not occur to me that there would have been a connection between this event and the one I recalled in the previous paragraph. Though both memories have been with me, it is, in fact, only in recalling all this presently that I perceive their likely relation.

Gerard, Maria, Walter, Vera, and their respective families had broken off contact with their father. With them estranged, Eugena decided to return with her husband, Leopold Thomas, and their three daughters, Mia, Ann, and Els, who were all older than me.

Ma and Bobke

Wilrijk on May 20, 1950, and that the place of their residence at the time of my birth was Borsbeek, Manebruggestraat 290. The certificate was made up in the presence of two witnesses, both young workers, one a sailor living in Antwerp, the other a docker living in Broechem, another small municipality in the province of Antwerp. The certificate was made up in Dutch, for that is the official language spoken in this part of the country.

A few days afterwards, I was baptized in the chapel of the ma-

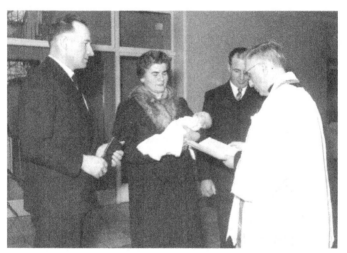

At my baptism with Alfons (left); my uncle Eugène Van Kesbeeck; and his wife, my aunt Irma

ternity hospital. This early baptism does not indicate that my life was in danger; it was customary to do so at the time. Besides me, the two photographs taken at the occasion show the priest, Alfons, and my godparents. The task of godparents had been accepted by my mother's only brother, Eugène Van Kesbeeck, and his wife, Irma. It may be mentioned that the custom in Belgium is not to speak of *godparents*, but rather of *peter* and *meter*, a derivative form of the Latin "pater" and "mater." It is unlikely that there was anyone else present at my baptism, for the photograph does not show Carolina or other family members. It is perhaps rather surprising that my mother would not have been present, but she may still have been recovering. It was, therefore, apparently the father who had the task to register the birth and to bring the child to the chapel for baptism.

For sure, a double blessing was given me in these early days after birth. I had a mother and father, who were Christians; and I was brought before God, enrolled into the Catholic Church, and the Holy Spirit was invoked upon me with oil and prayer.

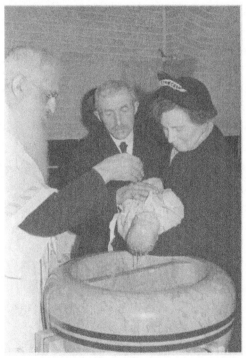

My brother, Walter, at baptism with his grandparents Constant Govaerts and Emma Van Kesbeeck as godparents

Walter received the same blessings fourteen years earlier. He was born and baptized in Saint-Augustine's Hospital in Wilrijk, at a time when Alfons and Carolina were living in nearby Edegem. The one photograph of the occasion shows a priest with a long, white beard pouring water over Walter's head, from where it drips into the large baptismal fount. Walter's godparent along mother's side was Emma Maria Catharina Van Kesbeeck, "de Moemoe"; his godparent along father's side was Joannes Constantinus Govaerts, the father of Alfons. The name that Walter officially received was thus Walter Constantinus Emma Govaerts. It was, at the time, still common practice to give the child three names, often including names that stemmed from the godparents. In the early sixties, it became more common to give to a child two names, while I received just one name, Robert, in 1966. It occurred however also commonly at the time of the birth of Constant and of Emma, around the end of the nineteenth century, that a child received just one name, or two, and so also in the times before and after them. Emma, for example, was the second oldest of fourteen children, and the only one of them who received three names. After the oldest children of a family were born, one ran out of grandparents whose names one wanted to preserve in the progeny, and so the younger ones received just one or two names. Often though, the names of the younger ones were also names that were recurring in that family. Likewise, in the sixties and up to the present, some children have still been receiving multiple names, but such a trend as I suggest, namely, moving away from multiple names, certainly existed. It is probably one of the many manifestations of the sixties in which a tendency occurred to take leave from traditional customs and from what went before. Walter and Robert are, as far as I know, not names that had any particular remembrance to earlier living relatives attached to it.

It is possible, though, that someone of the past was being remembered by my name. When my mother, Carolina, was a girl, often she had to help her mother delivering milk products. Carolina often talked affectionately of the good, old horse that was employed for pulling the cart. It was Bob, the horse. I myself was nearly always called Bob at home, though my official name was Robert. At the time I was born, the first name still had to be an established Christian name. Often official documents and forms would ask for the family name and for the *Christian* name. Much more recently, also this has disappeared, as children are given all kinds of first names.

I was nearly always called Bob. There was, as far as I remember, just one or two occasions when I was called "Robéér!" On both occasions, it was shouted by Ma from the bottom of the staircase while I was upstairs, probably because I did not attend or did not hear prior calls for me to come down for a meal.

But let us move on to consider the years that followed my birth and baptism. Even though Alfons brought me to the chapel for baptism, I have never known him. As far as I know, I have never met him, because he divorced from Carolina before I was fully conscious. The circumstances in which this happened appear to be the following. As I described in the previous chapter, at the back of the long garden of our house, my parents built a largish workplace in large white bricks. The intention of Alfons (who until then had worked for a building company and for a short time had been a truck driver for this company), was allegedly to start a garage together with his brother Urbain, who was a car mechanic, in this workplace. But unfortunately Urbain died shortly before this plan could be realized, on May 14, 1957, at the age of 28. His death was the result of a work accident. This happened when he was working on the large tire of a truck and the hubcap flew from it, hitting him against the forehead and possibly crushing him against the wall behind him as well. After the tragic death of his brother, Alfons could not pursue the plan to begin a garage, the more so because it was Urbain who had the training of a car mechanic. In addition, shortly afterwards, Mr. Gartner built his chocolate factory, which extended behind the rear wall of Alfons's workplace, so that the entry for eventual cars would have become blocked off. Alfons found, instead, work as a bus driver. It is during his work time that he came to know another woman. As far as I heard, she worked at the offices of MIVA, the public-transport company that employed Alfons. The wife is usually the last to find out, and so before things were in the open, it was Walter who had a suspicion of what was happening. At school some friends told him that they had seen his father hand in hand with a woman in the streets of the city of Antwerp.

Alfons did not keep his extra-marital relationship secret for long. For the woman had a car with which, a number of times, she drove Alfons home after work, right to the front door. Ma tried to talk it through with Alfons, but things seemed to have taken a definite turn. She sought help at the local church, which for the Borsbeek-side of Manebruggestraat was the Saint-Johannes-Berchmans Parish. The center of this parish was Tyrolerhof: its wooden chapel, presbytery, and various buildings. Since more and more houses had been built away from the village center of Borsbeek, and since there was a busy road that divided the territory of Borsbeek, a by-parish had been founded in 1948. The priests of a religious order, namely, the Augustinians of the Assumption, had been asked to erect this new by-parish of Borsbeek-West, which received canonical recognition as an independent parish dedicated to Saint Johannes Berchmans in 1957. Two Assumptionist priests took care of the new parish; from the end of 1960, these were Fr. Johannes Berchmans Borghoms, who took on the role of parish priest (replacing Fr. Christiaan Muermans), and Fr. Jacob Jacobs, who was a teacher at a Catholic school in Antwerp and who helped with the various masses. In 1974, other Assumptionist priests took on also the main parish of Borsbeek, dedicated to Saint Jacobus.

Pater Johannes Berchmans Borghoms

Father Johannes came to be known as Pater Pastoor, whereby the first term, *Pater*, referred to the fact that he was an ordained religious within an order, the second term, *Pastoor*, referred to the fact that he was the parish priest. Pater Pastoor was a charismatic man with a compassionate nature; a priest to whom the people could turn with personal troubles. Even though Carolina and her family would at the time apparently not have been regular churchgoers, it was Pater Pastoor whom Carolina asked for help and advice. She asked him to arrange for a meeting with Alfons and talk with him as a last resort. He effectively did this, but it was of no avail.

Alfons moved out and initiated the procedures for a divorce. After he moved out, Carolina was left on her own to look after her children, one still a toddler; and she was left to pay off the mortgage on the house. Earlier, in the period shortly after they built in Manebruggestraat, Ma had been working part-time as a cleaner. With her husband moving out, she needed to find employment as a cleaner again, despite the fact that I was around. Her brother, Eugène, visited her apparently once or twice on his own in this difficult period. After that, he announced to her that he better would not come to visit anymore because the neighbors might think that she had a relationship with another man. In reality though, these neighbors knew well enough that Eugène was her brother.

The only person she could again turn to for help was Pater Pastoor. A few times, when she had to attend a meeting concerning the divorce, he came to the house so as to babysit. Shortly afterwards he made arrangements for me to be taken care of at the kindergarten of Tyrolerhof. I was too young, but it was an emergency measure to help Ma out. A little bed was bought by the kindergarten and a little piss pot was placed in front of Mrs. Lea's desk.

Carolina was at the time of these sad events in her family about thirty-seven to thirty-eight years old and Walter, her eldest son, was about fifteen to sixteen. Many years afterwards, when the house in Manebruggestraat was being vacated for sale, Walter and I went into the workplace at the back of the garden. Along one wall was a row of wooden cages, which Alfons had made for breeding birds, mostly parakeets and finches. It was a long time since they had contained birds. On top of them, two long ladders were lying, a wooden one and a more recent, aluminum one in two parts. I knew these ladders well enough; but on that day, Walter found on top of the cages, behind the ladders, a long cloth bag. I did not really remember the bag. I must have looked at it at an earlier date, but it did not mean much to me, and had forgotten. But it did mean something to Walter. The bag contained fishing rods. I had never gone fishing, but Walter told me that day that when he was a boy, Alfons would take him along fishing. And all these years later, with disappointment, Walter said that our father had given all this up when he left. For Walter, after the separation came about, there was a family divided.

But I better continue the story concerning the time around the divorce itself. A few words that Ma told me about the matter several years later, when I could comprehend it, give an insight that lets us get close to this period and the couple itself. It is about an incident that took place after Alfons had moved out and after initial meetings with the lawyers had taken place. Ma was walking along Herentalsebaan at a time that Alfons just happened to pass by with a bus that he was driving. When Alfons saw her along the pavement, he stopped his bus full of people and stepped out so as to exchange a few words with her. He apparently told her that he realized it was madness that he left her, his wife, and he apologized. As I said, Ma told me this many years later, sorry that he had left her and that these events took place. At no point did she speak of Alfons with hatred but always with love.

Alfons and Carolina had been married in front of civil servants of Wilrijk and in the Catholic Church. Their marriage was legal and valid and as such irrevocable. A Catholic wedding wherein both spouses vow to give themselves to each other for life—until death places them apart—is more than a mere contract. As Jesus is believed to have said, "A man shall leave his father and mother and be joined to his wife, and the two shall become one flesh. So they are no longer two but one flesh. What therefore God has joined together, let no man put asunder (Mark 10:7–9)." When the disciples asked Jesus further about the matter, Jesus replied, "Whoever divorces his wife and marries another, commits adultery against her; and if she divorces her husband and marries another, she commits adultery (Mark 10:11–12)." Jesus speaks of *adultery* even after a divorce, and not of a clean, new beginning, for the reason that a marriage is not simply undone by being declared as such. There is adultery because there is still a marriage. The spouses pronounced their words of self-gift towards each other in the presence of God and the church, and these words and the gift they represent remain. Jesus may well have known the words of the prophet Malachi, "So take heed to yourselves, and let none be faithless to the wife of his youth. 'For I hate divorce, says the God of Israel'" (Mal 2:15–16). Alfons and Carolina had been married for eighteen years, and children had been born from their union. The marriage could not be undone by a retracting of the self-gift or by the official pronouncement of divorce by a judge or lawyer.

I need hasten to say, however, that valid reasons for a husband or wife to separate temporally or permanently from their marriage partner may well exist. Such reasons may be the violent behavior of the marriage partner; or the fact that adultery is being committed, and the partner is living with someone else; or in case all love has come to an end, and the living in each other's presence has become a permanent pain: in these cases, it may indeed be best to continue life away from each other. Jesus himself recognized that when the other partner commits adultery, the breaking up of a marriage may be unavoidable (Matt 5:32; 19:9).

Alfons and Carolina's marriage went well and lovingly for a long time; and it was, therefore, sad that it came to such an ending in its every practicality. There would have been however for a long time premonitions of a strain on the marriage. Whatever other issues were involved, there appears to have been a disagreement about the desirability of more than a single child.

# 4

# My parents and their world (1)

THIS CHAPTER AND the following are a kind of intermezzo to my narrative yet not independent from it and immediately relevant to it. When Alfons decided to give up his marriage and family, matters of faith or their absence would inevitably have played a role. Before continuing with giving more detail about the time-period around my birth and the divorce, it is well to perceive the broader picture as to what concerns these matters.

When Carolina and Alfons had been born, it was into a society that encouraged a religious outlook and living.

Carolina—or *Carlintje* (*Car'lin'tsje* with emphasis upon the second vowel), which is the diminutive form as it would have been pronounced at her home in the local dialect—was baptized in the Parish Church of *Heiligen Petrus and Paulus* (Saints Peter and Paul) at Wommelgem on March 1st, 1930. The house she lived in as a child was at Kandonk Laar, a hamlet at a little distance of about two kilometer bird's eye view from the village center of Wommelgem. Since World War I the population of 't-Laar had steadily been increasing, so as to contain 750 residents in 1935. In that year, around the time that Carlintje was of school age, a chapel and an adjacent school were being built for the locals on property donated by the local landowner. In addition, the community council transformed an existing building into a parish house for the new by-parish that was being dedicated to *Onze-Lieve-Vrouw Boodschap* (literally, Our-Beloved-Lady Message; that is, the Annunciation), and a cemetery was being developed. The little school, containing a kindergarten and two classes for primary school, was served by a religious order of sisters, the Sisters Annunciates. It was, then, a time-period at which new church buildings could be erected, so as to serve as the focal point of a community's life and for giving an own identity to it.

For Alfons's situation I have less particular information, but he was baptized and would have attended services a few miles along the road—that same old way, ultimately towards Herentals, introduced at the beginning of chapter 2—at the centuries-old, late-gothic Parish Church of the *Heilige Pancratius* (Saint Pancras) at Ranst.

Children at the time were admonished to study their catechism and to attend church services. In the catechism they found the common prayers for all the faithful: the Our Father, the Hail Mary, the Glory Be, the Angelus, the Regina Caeli for Eastertide, prayers that were said privately after the Holy Mass, a morning and evening prayer, and prayers intended to be said before and after meals. They learned the Credo, divided in twelve articles of faith; the Acts of Faith, of Hope, of Love and Remorse; the Ten Commands; and the Five Commands of the Church, which were as follows; (I render here an English translation of the catechism in Dutch that came to be used in the Belgian dioceses):

1. Sun- and feast day you will honor.
2. On days of abstinence and Friday forego meat.

3. Keep Lent without blemish.

4. Confess your sins at least once every year.

5. And consume around Easter the Bread of the Lord.

The catechism was taught in the form of question and answer. Not all had to be learned in the first year but, in taking account of their degree of difficulty, spread over the eight years assigned at the time for primary schooling. For several questions, the answers had to be learned by heart in the exact given formulas. For example, the first question to which the answer was to be learned in the first year was, "What is the sign of the Christian person?" The answer: "The sign of the Christian person is the sign of the Cross." The second question for the first year was, "Where is God?" The answer: "God is everywhere: in heaven, on earth, and at all places." The next one was, "Does God know and see everything?" The answer: "God sees everything, even the most secret thoughts; he knows everything, even the future things." They learned with questions and answers that there is one God and three divine Persons: namely, God the Father, God the Son, and God the Holy Ghost. They learned that each human individual has a guardian angel. Further, they learned about the birth, death, and resurrection of Jesus Christ; and so on. In the second school year, they were taught, among others, the following question and answer:

Who has to attend Mass on Sundays and designated feast days?

Those having to attend Mass on Sundays and the assigned feast days are all the faithful that have completed their seventh year and that are not excused because of illness or another valid reason.

One learned that in Belgium these designated feast days are Christmas, Our Lord's Ascension, Our Lady's Ascension, and All Saints.

At a later age, in the fifth year of study, one learned in addition with question and answer that Sundays and feast days are spent profitably by attending not only Mass but also other church services—namely, on Sunday afternoon Vespers and especially Benediction, further also the yearly procession through the fields at which occasion the crops were blessed, and so on—by pious or charitable works, and by finding relaxation in good, clean enjoyment only.

Children were encouraged to venerate the Virgin Mary. Looking once more in the catechism, we find there for pupils of the second year:

> By which devotional exercises shall we venerate the Holy Virgin Mary?
>
> We will venerate the Holy Virgin Mary through the praying of the Hail Mary, the Angelus, and the Rosary; through the wearing of her scapular; and through keeping her feasts.

After the little church had been built at Kandonk Laar, the Angelus would have been rung daily at noon and in the evening. It would, henceforth, have been heard very clearly; not faintly as it used to, when coming from the distant main church of Wommelgem.

For those not familiar with the Angelus, let me describe what it entails: three single strokes of the bell during which the faithful pray, "The angel of the Lord declared to Mary; and she conceived of the Holy Spirit. Hail Mary . . . ;" then the next three strokes at which is prayed, "Behold the handmaid of the Lord; be it done to me according to your word. Hail Mary . . . ;" then the next three strokes, "And the Word was made flesh; and it dwelt among us. Hail Mary . . . ." The bell was subsequently given nine strokes during which is prayed, "Pray for us, O holy Mother of God; that we may be made worthy of the promises of Christ," as well as the concluding prayer:

> Let us pray:
>
> Pour forth, we beseech you, O Lord, your grace into our hearts, that we, to whom the Incarnation of Christ, your Son, was made known by the message of an angel, may by his passion and Cross + be brought to the glory of his resurrection, through the same Christ our Lord. Amen.

It is an exercise in devotion that, as so many others, has largely fallen away in more recent times. In our day and age, the Angelus is heard perhaps only near an abbey church, or in one or other place that forms the exception to the rule. Moreover, a small chapel bell would presently in many locations be much less audible compared to a time when hardly any motorized traffic was about, and when people were not preoccupied in their cars with ears tuned to a transistor radio or the like.

Children received a rosary on the occasion of their First Holy Communion. In Catholic families, parents often prayed the Rosary with their children before bedtime. It was not a situation that Carlintje found at home. She would, however, have received a beautiful white rosary at her First Holy Communion; and, perhaps around that time, in addition, a precious one that belonged to her grandmother.

As regards the prayerfulness of Alfons's parents, I do not have information. It is likely, however, that just as for Carlintje, he would have been admonished to attend liturgical services during the years of his schooling.

On the occasion of their Solemn Holy Communion, also called Confirmation by the Holy Spirit, children tended to receive a beautiful missal with gold edges, which contained all the readings and prayers of the Mass. The liturgical texts were printed in two columns, with the Latin at one side and a Dutch translation beside it. Carlintje did her Solemn Holy Communion in May 1941; Alfons did his, May 1942. Carlintje received a thick leather-bound book, printed in 1940, that is not only a missal but also a vesperal, containing the prayers of vespers for all Sundays and feast days, and various other prayers. This book, which I still treasure, bears witness that it has been well used. The pages containing the ordinary of the Mass, that is, the daily recurring prayers of the Mass, have been so often consulted that some of them are crumpled and torn at the edges.

Even though a certain obligation was placed upon her for attending the Mass and other church services, especially Benediction on Sunday afternoons, and even though she had to help with the work at home, Carlintje would devote herself generously to the prayers. It meant, though, that from her early childhood onwards, little free time was granted her. At home they earned their living by delivering milk and dairy products with horse and cart, even into the city of Antwerp, and they grew potatoes. Carlintje had to help with the milk round. School was at the time to be attended on Saturday mornings as well: hence, six days of the week. On Sundays: even then they drove out with the horse cart to sell milk products. It was, moreover, not a happy home—an aspect we will revisit later onwards—so that besides the friendships with other children, faith and prayer were for her almost all she could hold on to in life for mental support.

During World War II both the chapel at Kandonk Laar and the church in the center of Ranst suffered considerable damage from bombardments. Ma told that often they had to leave the class-rooms and take shelter in covered ditches. As a result, she learned only a few things at school: in fact, not much beyond basic literacy and numerical skills, and the catechism.

Ma related to me that during wartime the church was full of people and that it was a time of fervent prayer. During her child-hood, she had been collecting whatever prayer cards she could lay her hands on; and during the war years, she gave some of these to people who eagerly asked one, and who unfailingly were grateful to her for it.

She did not tell much about her classroom experience, except for the following incident. She liked to talk. School and the company of classmates would have been for her a time away from the tense atmosphere that could prevail at home and a respite from physical work. The sister in charge of the classroom had admonished her to keep quiet. Soon after, however, she was again found talking. Again an admonishment; and then the sister got angry. While Carlintje was once more in conversation with a neighbor, the sister grabbed a chair and in fury smashed it on her head. Everyone was instantly quiet, and the nun was ashamed that in her rage she might have caused serious harm or even have killed the girl. It is, in fact, surprising that neither was the case; her rather profuse hair may have served her well in the incident. Even though it was an irrational explosion, it appears to me pretty certain that the sister would not have dealt thus with most of the children under her care, even if they misbehaved; but she would have had in her mind that with Carlintje, who was born into an irregular union, she could get away with it. It can be seen as characteristic of Carolina that when she told me the anecdote, decades after it happened, she made no criticism or voiced any bad feelings concerning the sister; she merely said that she had been laughing and talking and had upset the good nun. It may, however, be noted that once, when I asked her whether she ever had considered becoming a nun, she confided that the religious life had not attracted her as a possible choice of life; despite her innate devotion, she never desired to become a nun.

Mid May 1942, Carlintje moved with Emma, her mother, and with Eugène, her brother, to Wilrijk, near to where Emma's parents and other relatives were living. (Emma's parents lived at Boomsesteenweg 854, next to them lived Emma's older sister Lien (Florentina Carolina) with her husband August Luyckx at the corner of Oudebaan that leads to Fort 7, and next to them lived the family Fret, just in Oudebaan; Emma and her two children went to live at Boomsesteenweg 837, diagonally across from them and next to the pub De Groene Jager, which was managed by Mr. Mariën, known as "de Groene," together with his wife, known as "Mie Wal," and with whose daughter, Virginie, Emma's younger brother Henri had married.)

Carlintje would continue her primary education at the Catholic school run by the Sisters of the Christian Schools of Vorselaar that was located just off the Boomsesteenweg beside the Parish Church *Saint Jan Vianney*. Maria Fret, a close friend she made in those days, who was at school with her, and who lived nearby her home, recalls that Carlintje was very quiet at school and was never punished. In this school also, the siren warning of approaching bombers would often have sounded, upon which they all had to take shelter in the cellars of the school or in the refectory.

A few months after she finished school, namely, on September 4, 1944, the British 11th Armored Division under command of General-Major Roberts and the 3rd Royal Tank Regiment under

Neighbors:

Back row: Emma, Stinne Torfs, Mie Wal, Maria Fret, Carlintje;

Middle row: Hortance (daughter of Mie Wal), Roza (daughter of Stinne), Lisa Embrechts (a servant at the nearby castle);

Front row: Gilberte (disabled little daughter of Stinne), two children of Lisa.

command of Colonel Silvertop liberated Antwerp with help from the local resistance. It was, however, not the end of the war. For several weeks, war would be waged around Antwerp with the withdrawing German forces (because the British forces could not cross the Albert Canal). And in the six months following liberation by the Allied forces, Belgian towns were targeted by unmanned rockets (V1 and the more advanced V2-Bombs). More than two thousand such rockets, the majority of the V2 type, fell in a ten-mile radius around Antwerp. In the meantime, on December 16, 1944, the Germans launched the Ardennes Offensive with a quarter million soldiers in an attempt to retake the country and aimed to reach Antwerp. Their advance was stalled at the

Meuse near Dinant; in a fierce battle with American, British, and Belgian forces that lasted six weeks, they were pushed back. By February 4, 1945, Belgium was reported to be free of German troops. The end of the V-weapons was April 1945. VE-Day was May 8, 1945.

Against all this background, people carried on as they could. Following her primary schooling, Carlintje would have liked to go to the local vocational school Saint Ursula and attend the classes to be a seamstress, together with Maria Fret. Maria continued her schooling, but Carlintje had to start full-time employment. She took up work at the large factory of Gevaert in Mortsel, developing reels of camera pictures in the dark halls.

It was not much more than a year since the catastrophic April 5, 1943, when a heavy American bombardment took place over Mortsel. The target of the air raid was the former Minerva car-factory, which had been transformed into a plant of the German company *Erla Werke* that made and repaired airplanes; the plant in Mortsel was used by the Luftwaffe for repair of its Messerschmitt fighter planes with the aid of Belgian employees (collaborators). The air raid carried out by eighty-three bombers missed its target considerably, because they were seriously hindered by the German fighter planes after their two accompanying squadrons of spitfires had to return above Ghent, for it was the end of their range, and they were left unaccompanied. Only four or five of the six hundred bombs fell on target, the rest fell on the district *Oude God*, causing many civilian casualties and enormous damage to residential areas. More than three hundred employees of Erla died as well as more than six hundred other civilians, including over two hundred children in the neighboring schools. One bomb fell on the dark halls of Gevaert, killing more than forty girls working there. A few weeks after the bombing, Erla was restored to full capacity. The details of this disastrous bombardment, the heaviest ever in the Benelux, have been gathered by the war historian Pieter Serrien in his book *Tranen over Mortsel* (Tears over Mortsel; 2008; second edition, 2013).

As for Carlintje, the female supervisor at Gevaert apparently did not like her, and due to that she was eventually dismissed. She would, however, have anticipated the criticism awaiting her at home for being out of work and for not earning her contribution, and so she immediately started looking for another job, which she found the same day just across the road from Gevaert at a much smaller factory, making chandeliers.

After the war, Emma and her brother Henri went working in the brickyard near to where they were living, which was owned by Mr. and Mrs. Van den Bosch. Before and after her hours at the brickyard and in the weekends, Emma went, moreover, to work as housekeeper in her boss's house.

Carlintje kept up friendship with Maria Fret and various other young people that lived in the neighborhood. Around 1946 Maria received a bicycle from her parents. Upon this, Carlintje asked Emma for a bicycle; and since Maria came to testify that she had indeed received a bicycle, Emma had to give in. From then onwards both girls were able to go cycling to various places on Sundays.

They cycled to Kandonk Laar, so that Carlintje could show her friend where she had lived.

Going further afield they cycled to Scherpenheuvel (also known as Montaigu; the name refers to the sharp hill that characterizes this place and that can be seen from miles around in a largely flat landscape). It is the place of the cult of Our Lady of Scherpenheuvel, which is traceable to a miracle-working wooden statuette of the Virgin, discovered attached to an oak tree on top of the hill. A small wooden chapel was erected beside the oak tree in 1603. After three great miracles took place around that date, devotion became very widespread; many replicas of the statuette were made, carved from the ancient oak, which was cut down in 1604. It became the national shrine of the Spanish Netherlands and a large basilica was built by the archdukes Albrecht and Isabella during their reign. Many people from around Antwerp and Brussels, and further afield, have since these early years been journeying there on pilgrimage. About forty-five years after Ma and Maria cycled there, at some time after Ma had died, I cycled there as well, as a little pilgrimage on my own.

Other places that the two friends cycled to included Linkeroever, that is, the newer part of Antwerp situated along the other side of the Schelde (or Scheldt), the river that coming from Northern France runs through Belgium, through Antwerp, and towards the North Sea in the Netherlands. The Saint-Anna tunnel—known as the *Voet-gangerstunnel* (Pedestrians tunnel)— allowed pedestrians and cyclists to cross from one side to the other. This tunnel of 572 meters long had originally opened in

Maria Fret (left) and Carlintje (right)

*40*

1933; but in 1944 the retiring German troops had blown up the entrance building of the tunnel at Linkeroever, as well as its lifts and escalators. Only a few years afterwards would the tunnel have reopened, shortly after which Carlintje and Maria would have made the crossing with their bikes.

They cycled also to Bornem (still within the Province of Antwerp, but further southwest), since one of Maria's brothers was in a relationship with a girl who lived there with her family on a farm.

They also came in Kontich (only a few miles from Wilrijk), so as to visit Saint-Rita Church. This church and the surrounding monastery of the Augustinian Order had been built only about ten years before; the church was dedicated

Front of an old prayer card of Carolina; the reverse side contains a prayer to Saint Rita

in 1937. Saint Rita of Cascia (1381–1457) has been a very popular saint, known as the saint for hopeless cases. From childhood onwards, Rita excelled in virtue. She was a devoted wife and mother, despite harsh treatment by her husband. Through her consistent love, he eventually was struck by remorse; nonetheless,

said it was fine this time. Ma quickly found out that Madam treated her sons similarly. During the time that she worked there, one of them had arrived home late one evening and had forgotten his key; he rang on and spoke through the intercom with his mother, but she did not let him inside and he had to find a bed for the night elsewhere. Carlintje quickly found, however, that the lady was not bad, and that though she was being dealt with sternly, she appreciated that she did this with everyone. In the end Carlintje felt that she was almost as a daughter in the household; and of all the places at which she would work, it was the one she liked most.

At her home this aspect of being a daughter would have had a wry taste for Carlintje. As she expressed much later onwards, she felt she had never known a normal daughter-mother relationship. An expression of this is found even in her birth certificate issued by the Registry Office of Wommelgem, which has a curious addition of April 1946, that is, when Carlintje was sixteen. Translated, it states:

> Comment: The child mentioned in juxtaposed birth declaration no. 16 [of 1930] has been recognized by Emma Maria Catharina Van Kesbeeck on April 24, 1946, in the presence of the registrar of Wilrijk. Wommelgem, April 25, 1946. Registrar, (signed Ed. Peeters)

Eugène's birth certificate received a similar comment on that date, that is, when he was twenty. People had advised Emma to go to the Registrar and provide this statement, because they thought that when she would be needy, her children would then be legally obliged to provide for her. It did not bode well with these children, however, for they themselves had been working since childhood and received minimal education. Eugène would

Brother and sister, Eugène and Carolina

give his wages to Emma until the day he married at the age of nearly thirty in 1955.

In June 1949, Emma, Eugène, and Carlintje moved to Neerland 15, which was a little street with a dead end, along the same side of the Boomsesteenweg, in line with Oude baan, (a tiny bit closer to Hof Ter Beke), in a former farmhouse besides the brickyard and owned by the same people. A few months later, in November 1949, they moved again to another nearby address (namely, Kleine Doornstraat 140, right across from Laaglandweg).

Eugène worked as a railway employee, repairing the tracks. Those doing this kind of job were called *piochers*, from the French *une pioche* (pick-axe). By attending evening classes, he would eventually become a signalman, and much later, sub stationmaster at Lier station.

Carlintje did not have a happy home, and Alfons apparently did not have a happy home either. They decided to marry.

Emma paid for the white blouse and the smart, black outfit that Carlintje would wear at the wedding and emptied Carlintje's bank account. Besides this, in that period before the wedding, Ma had been saving up from her pocket money and bought a little cupboard. But when Eugène saw it, he thought it had been bought with household money, and he smashed it to pieces. Ma explained that this had not been the case: Eugène had been using his pocket money for smoking and for playing billiard with his friends, but she had been saving up the little she could.

Perhaps it can be mentioned here, in continuity of this poverty and these losses inflicted upon her, that a little before that time, when she was eighteen, all of Carlintje's teeth were pulled out. She probably had rather bad teeth from childhood onwards; and when a few fillings would have been required, the dentist just pulled them all out and fitted dentures. It is a deplorable practice that may seem incredible to us today. As such, it can be noticed that any pictures taken after that time, usually, have Ma smiling with a closed mouth; though it must be said, such was the custom more generally.

Another thing that may be mentioned is that as regards sexual education she was totally ignorant up till the wedding. Ma told me later, when reminiscing, that she long thought that she could get pregnant by kissing a man.

Alfons and Carolina married May 20, 1950, when they were both twenty years old. The wedding service took place in the small Parish Church of Saint Jan Vianney, situated along the Boomsesteenweg. This church, dedicated in 1927, had sprung from the old mother church *Saint Bavo*. It is in the marriage register (in the *Liber patrimonialis*) of this mother church that I found, indeed, their wedding recorded. Eugène Van Kesbeeck and Jos Govaerts, the oldest brother of Alfons, acted as the two witnesses, and the ceremony was conducted by J. Segers, a curate of the parish. Only a few family members were present at the service, not even Maria Fret; there was no feast afterwards and probably no honeymoon. They were very poor; but Alfons vowed to Carolina that if need be they would break their last slice of bread and share it: they would stick together through thick and thin.

Alfons and Carolina at their wedding

# 5

# My parents and their world (2)

THE PREVIOUS CHAPTER situated my parents in their youth within a Flemish society around Antwerp. It was a time when new parish churches and chapels were emergent in various places that they were acquainted with, namely, in Kandonk Laar, in Wilrijk, in Kontich, and (as we saw in the first chapter) in Borsbeek-West as well. They grew up amidst fields and animals; though they also knew the suburbs of the city and Antwerp itself; they were confronted with the devastation of war and with material poverty. As we saw for Carolina, and so perhaps also for Alfons, from childhood onwards they had to help provide. Let us in this chapter continue to depict their particular situation within the church and society to which they belonged, following the time of their wedding.

At first they rented a small apartment in Edegem (at the top floor of Vrijwilligersstraat 24), a town bordering Wilrijk. Alfons had still to do his military service, and as such he would not have been able to provide a proper wage. They were poor. Carolina did what she could with each penny, and her saved-up Fort stamps (*Fort zegeltjes*) were at times nearly all she had for buying food. (Fort was a Belgian producer of foodstuffs that were being sold in groceries throughout the country; various brands provided stamps that one stuck in a booklet for ensuring customer loyalty, prior to the electronic age and the point system on customer cards of various retail chains.) In this difficult period following their wedding, Moemoe apparently gave them twenty thousand Belgian francs (between six- and seven-hundred dollars); of which Carolina later, when Alfons was working, gave ten thousand back.

Their first born, Walterke, arrived in 1952. Around that period, Alfons worked as a truck driver for a building company. It would not have been so easy for Carolina with a small child to attend church services; and Alfons may, perhaps apart from his primary school days, not have had the habit to practice regularly. Devotion would likely have been practiced in the home, privately. In these early years of their marriage, they came, however, to possess a Sacred-Heart-of-Jesus plaster bust (about 45 cm or 18" wide), which they probably bought.

The tenant below their flat would have caused them much disturbance, because of his anti-social, alcohol-related behavior. Because of this, as soon as they were able, they moved to a new address. In 1953 they found a roof above their head in another flat, at the top floor of a house, with the owner living below them. This new address was situated in Borsbeek (along Herentalsebaan, nearby the busy corner with Frans Beirenslaan, across from the ironware dealer Crollet), quite near to Kandonk Laar.

It is at this address, or perhaps at the previous one, when Walter was still a toddler, that an incident took place that Ma related many years later. She was alone at home with the infant, and a thunderstorm arose. She was standing by the window at the rear of the flat, and she would have been in a prayerful mood for she feared thunderstorms; it made her realize her smallness and vulnerability within the world. Suddenly, lightning came down and a fireball entered into the room through the window. While she stood speechless, the ball moved relatively slowly round the entire room, hovered even a few moments right above the cot in which Walterke was lying and then, without having burned or touched anything, went as it came. A quick search on the internet shows that this kind of phenomenon does indeed occur and that numerous similar experiences have been reported over the centuries. Ball lightning is usually associated with thunderstorms but lasts considerably longer than the split-second flash of a lightning bolt. The diameter of the ball can range roughly between one centimeter and a few meters; most commonly they are between ten and twenty centimeters. The event can last from one second to over a minute with the brightness remaining fairly constant over that period and resembling that of a domestic lamp. It appears that they tend to move most often in a horizontal direction at a few meters per second, but they may also remain stationary or wander erratically in various directions. Some have been reported to appear within buildings, passing through closed doors and windows. Some have entered and left within airplanes without causing damage. Its disappearance is generally rapid and may be silent or explosive. They often leave a smell of burning sulfur. They can be harmless or lethal; move through solid masses without effect or cause great damage. Scientific data about the phenomenon are still rare and several hypotheses have been proposed. Just as for the wartime bombings, which impacted in unpredictable manner, so also this event of natural origin, interesting in itself, which can be harmless or lethal, confronts our contingency, the haphazard quality of our creaturehood. It shows that our existence takes place amidst powers transcending our humanity. Whatever the eventual scientific explanation of ball lightning, are any other than material factors involved? Can such happening and its outcome not be affected by someone's relationship with God, or the absence thereof, or by one's guardian angel? Perhaps the ball lightning entered into Carolina's life as a visiting presence that warned her never to abandon the spiritual. Walterke still received the Holy Scapular at his baptism and was dedicated to Mary; and perhaps this protection under the cloak of Our Lady served him well in his cot.

Another thing that may not escape our attention concerning these years in my parents' lives is that at some point they acquired a copy of Eugene Sue's *Les Mystères du peuple* (The Mysteries of the People) in a Dutch translation of 1952, published in three volumes by Climax – St-Denys-Westrem; (the English translation of 1904 is available online at Hathi Trust Digital Library). It is a historical novel of the romantic genre that depicts a proletarian family through the centuries, starting in Gallic Brittany in the first century BC, along the invasion of Romans and Franks, taking the reader to Palestine at the time of Christ, passing along the Middle Ages and the time of the Crusades, and leading towards the French Revolution and the uprisings in Paris of 1848. Sue (1804–57) was the son of a distinguished surgeon in Napoleon's army and the godson of Empress Joséphine. He became a surgeon himself. After his father's death in 1829, he inherited a considerable fortune and settled in Paris. From then onwards he developed a literary career as a novelist. He turned away from the aristocratic classes; and under the influence of Felix Pyatt, a republican journalist, he became attuned to the socialist ideas of the time. With his boxing teacher, he frequented the working-class areas of the city, which brought him in touch firsthand with the struggles and miseries of the people. These influences prompted him to write some novels depicting the harsh life of the lower classes of the people and the injustices inflicted upon them by the higher classes and the clergy. *Les Mystères du peuple* (1849–56) was suppressed by the censor in 1857, but this did not prevent it becoming very popular among the working classes. Indeed, the inside of the cover of the Dutch translation claims that for decades this novel was the only one to be found in laborer's houses, and it presents itself as "the greatest people's novel of all times." I read the novel about twenty-eight years ago—all of its more than two thousand pages—at a time when I was a novice in religious life, and found it very interesting for all the world history contained in it. The ideological, romantic element manifests itself in his presentation of a noble, unsullied, and courageous spirit possessed by individuals that represent the various generations of the family of Gallic origin and by those supportive of the Reformation, in contrast to the sneaky and malignant characters that make up most of the Catholic establishment in the book. I do not doubt that sad truth is revealed in his pages, but it is told too one-sided.

Assuredly, the several gripping and very informative stories that make up this series-novel have the potential to influence readers in their attitude to church and religious worship. At the time I read it, I made copious notes—as I did with most things that I read—which I have not kept in my many wanderings; but taking a look once more at the book let me quickly find several pages that give a flavor of the anti-Catholic aspect. Although it takes us away from my main story line, from my family in the 1950s, along a dark alleyway into history, I think it is needed to devote in this chapter some pages to looking into the novel. I am, of course, only picking out a few extracts that are of my choosing, yet doing so helps in building up an informed impression of what would have been my parents' mindset or, at least, an influence upon it.

In perusing, for example, the story *The Monastery of Charolles*, at the beginning of volume two of the Dutch version, I find interesting that he writes of the Rule of Saint Benedict: "The Rule of Saint Benedict, which at the time [early sixth century] was observed in a large number of Gallic monasteries, appeared to Brother Loysik [the superior of the monastery of Charolles that observed its own agreed rule] on account of some of its statutes as mortal or demeaning of one's conscience, reason, and human dignity." It is a pity that the Dutch text is heavily abbreviated and does not include explanation of the statutes referred to. One of the statutes being objected to in the unabbreviated text is from the Rule chapter 33, which includes that, "monks may not have the free disposal even of their own bodies and wills." Monastic tradition in general does indeed extol the renunciation of one's own will as a fundamental ascetical practice based on the example of Christ. This own will is to be subjected in obedience to the abbot and the rule. For Saint Benedict, the abbot takes the place of Christ. As a consequence, the abbot and the superiors are so extolled, they should be so holy, and the own will of those subject to the abbot is seen in such negative light that one wonders about the existence of a middle ground, about the place of dialogue. The Rule of Benedict lacks some realism and when not approached in an enlightened manner, it becomes indeed demeaning.

As regards the community of the old monk Loysik, it is presented as living a very austere life and as closely embedded in the local village community. The old monk was each year entrusted with a good amount of money that were donations of the people, so that he could go to the city, namely, Chalon-sur-Saône in the region of Bourgogne-Franche-Comté in eastern France, and buy slaves. These could then become free members of the village community at Charolles. He always regretted, however, to find "that the ecclesial slaves were too high for his purse. The bishops always sold them at double the price of any other." It sounds awful that, as it is presented in this text, ecclesial slaves would have existed at all. Some information about this is provided in the *Catholic Encyclopedia* (under Slavery and Christianity). As explained there, the fact is that the church became a large proprietor of estates that were endowed to it and that with these estates came serfs, who were attached to the soil for its cultivation. Serfdom—which was to be an improvement to slavery as such—had originated when a Roman law of the middle of the fourth century forbade slaves to be removed from the lands to which they belonged. This law was often suppressed thereafter by barbaric rulers; but it was upheld by the church, which itself remained under Roman law. The ecclesial serfs appear to have been, in general, better off than their counterparts owned by lay proprietors. A council of the sixth century (Éauze, 551) enjoins upon bishops that they must exact of their serfs a lighter service and must remit to them one-fourth of their rents. In numerous other councils of the catholic church in Gaul, Spain, Italy, and Britain, rules were decreed that were concerned with the treatment and protection of slaves. And despite the inalienability of all ecclesiastical property, which had been established by several councils, the serfs on church property could be enfranchised. Were those on church property less likely to become freedmen than those of lay proprietors? I am not sufficient an historian to know the answer; but it appears that, overall, they were better protected and that, eventually, their living conditions came closer to that of being free peasants. Nevertheless, it seems reasonable to say that the church maintained feudalism as the organizational system of society, in which masses of people made up the lowest class of poor, hard-working serfs, and in which prelates, abbots, and privileged ecclesiastics moved with pomp among the higher classes and obtained great wealth and worldly power.

Turning towards the story *The Pilgrim's Shell* or *Fergan the Quarryman*, further down in volume two of the Dutch translation, I propose us to look at some pages in Part 3 of the story entitled "The Commune of Laon," which tells about this emergent town-commune in northern France in the year 1112 and following. It is about the transition away from a feudal society, according to which human society was divided into clerical orders, the military, landowners (often descendants of former conquerors; in France, of the Frankish conquerors), and poor serfs who worked the land; a society in which the clerical and feudal powers held a firm grip on the people. The passage that I quote is situated in the story at the time that the bell rings out from the new belfry of the recently completed town hall; at that precise moment all the surrounding churches start ringing their bells so as to drown the sound, just as it had been arranged by the bishop (who is named Gaudry in the story): "'Oh, those priests, those priests!' exclaimed Colombaic. 'Always spiteful, always hypocritical, until the day that they deem themselves strong enough to be merciless. Ring, ring on, ye black-gowns! Ring with all your strength! The canting bells of your churches shall not silence our communal belfry! Your bells summon the people to servitude, to imbecility, to renunciation of their dignity; the belfry calls them to the fulfillment of civic duties and the defense of liberty!'"

Some pages later I find a passage that struck me at my first reading, some twenty-eight years ago: "It was disgraceful to hear the prelate talk about that infamous right of the bishops of Laon, who, before the establishment of the commune had the right to demand *first wedding night of the bride*—a galling shame that, occasionally, the husband managed to redeem with a money payment." Searching a few online resources confirm that the bishop at the time was indeed Gaudry (de Roye), also called Waldric. He had been royal chaplain from 1101 and was Bishop of Laon from 1106 to 1112; besides this, he was Lord Chancellor and Lord Keeper of England from 1103 to 1107. He appears effectively to have been covetous, violent, and envious. His election was contested, but it was upheld by the pope. During his time as bishop, he had someone murdered and another imprisoned and the eyes gouged out. According to the narrative of Sue, in 1112, Gaudry offered the French King, Louis the Fat, a great sum of money, so that the latter would undo the former agreement— for which the commune members had formerly paid a great sum—that allowed for the foundation of the commune. King Louis eventually took the money of Gaudry and ordered the town hall and the belfry to be immediately destroyed and demanded total submission to Gaudry, in view of the rights that he suppos- edly received from God as bishop. It led to a revolt and Gaudry was massacred by the citizens of Laon in the cellars of his palace, were he had hidden in a barrel. King Louis subsequently de- stroyed the commune and put another bishop in place; years later the commune was re-founded. This story seems effectively to have been narrated in keeping with the main parameters of the account of the Benedictine historian and theologian Guibert of Nogent-sous-Coucy (1055–1124) provided in his *Monodiae* (Solitary Songs, commonly referred to as his Memoirs) of 1115. To Sue's merit, his story features, in common with Guibert, the figure of Anselm of Laon (d. 1117), a French theologian who was archdeacon at the main church of Laon, and whom he describes as a true disciple of Christ. Now, as regards the alleged bishops' right upon the first wedding night: such right is more broadly referred to as *droit du seigneur* (French, right of the lord) or *jus primae noctis* (Latin, right of the first night). Although this legal or customary right of the feudal lord is indeed referred to in various literary sources of mainly later centuries, it appears that no evidence exists that such right has been exerted in Europe or, in particular, at Laon; it is not mentioned by Guibert. But again, I am not an historian with great knowledge of the period. Did Sue have another source informing about this? I would be surprised if he did. Guibert appears particularly well informed about the situation at Laon and does not mention it in his quite rounded account. Sue makes this exercise of the droit du seigneur by Gaudry an added motif for his being killed by his assailants, but it is exactly in this respect that he deviates from the account of Guibert. Sue's merit is, however, that he provides an account that empathizes with the ordinary people and that gives a vivid impression of their plight. Altogether, at most it can be proffered that it is not quite excluded that the droit du seigneur has been exerted by Gaudry; certain is, however, that he behaved terribly and that he came to his deserved end.

After all this, only brief mention can be made of what is found in volume three. It takes the reader into, among others, the time of the Reformation; relates about the scandal of the sale of indulgences; Ignatius of Loyola and the Jesuits; and so on.

At the beginning of the story *The Pocket Bible* or *Christian the Printer*, almost half way in the third volume of the Dutch version, which is a considerably abbreviated translation, I select for us the following few lines from a dialogue between Christian and his wife, placed in 1534: "'Alas! my friend, what woman, what mother would not share the reform ideas, seeing that they reject auricular confession? Did we not find ourselves compelled to stop our daughter from attending the confessional on account of the shameful questions that a priest dared to put to her and which, in the candor of her soul, she repeated to us?'"

I myself have, fortunately, as a schoolchild never been subjected to the obligation to undergo confession every few weeks; which for many children is undoubtedly a frightening experience. It would, moreover, have been true that in these foregone centuries and up to Vatican II, if not thereafter, some priests would have asked shameful questions. Many young people have undoubtedly been put off for life from the Catholic Church and its clergy. As regards myself, it is in my early twenties, when I attended a pre-Easter penitential service in my home parish at which individual confession was reintroduced, that I first received the sacrament of reconciliation.

But let us now return to the 1950s when my parents were married for a few years and Walter was a small boy. For with these chosen extracts, I hope to have sufficiently provided an impression of this novel, which undoubtedly would have been an entertaining and powerful reading that stimulates thought about the church.

In 1958 Walter received his First Holy Communion in the Saint-Johannes-Berchmans Parish, which had become an independent parish only the year before. The kindergarten that I would attend at Tyrolerhof on the parish grounds had as yet not been built; building works would start a few months later. Walter attended instead the kindergarten for one year in Saint-Rochus school in Deurne-South, situated near Saint-Rochus Church in Sint-Rochusstraat. (The school has in the meantime been renamed De Octopus.) Walter did his primary schooling here too. Since this was—and still is—a school run by the local government and not by the church, religious education in the Christian faith was an optional course; it was possible to choose non-confessional moral education instead. As such, Walter attended during the first year of his primary education the classes in religion, but from the second year onwards he chose the non-confessional course. He announced his choice at home to his parents, and though he was still but a little boy, they apparently asked no questions about it and made no protestations. Moreover, since Alfons and Carolina were no longer practicing their faith by attending church services, nor did Walter, apart from the special occasion of his First Holy Communion.

Nonetheless, at the age of seven or eight, Walter joined the Chiro of the nearby Pius-X Parish in the old district Silsburg at Deurne-South. At around that time, Pius X was a new independent parish, which had been founded as a by-parish of the Saint-Rochus Parish, because the main parish church was at some distance. Its youth movement grew out of the Chiro from its mother church. Chiro is a Christian-inspired youth movement in the Flemish part of Belgium. The name Chiro is formed by the Greek letters chi ($\chi$) and rho ($\rho$), which are the first two letters of *Christos*, the Anointed One. The Feast of Christ the King was one of the highpoints in the year of the group; so that in the Chiro-ideal the members became knights and handmaids of Christ. On that day and on some other days the group members attended Mass. Playfulness was central, especially in the outdoors; and the idea of instilling religion by providing a lived experience of it instead of through instruction.

The fact that Walter joined this group may be a reason why his parents, and especially Carolina, acquiesced when he chose non-confessional moral education at school. After he had been with it a year or so, however, the Chiro of Pius-X Parish was stopped and they began a scouts group instead. Conceivably, a reason for this happening was the changes that took place within the over-arching Chiro movement: among others, the start of mixed groups, and the policy for this to become the norm. As regards the Chiro, even today it is the largest youth movement in the Flemish part of Belgium; since about the 1980s it has become more pluralistic in its outlook, without wanting to abandon the Christian values. As regards Walter at Pius-X Parish, he remained a member of the scouts until he was about eleven.

In the meantime, Alfons, Carolina, and Walter had moved to their newly-built house in Manebruggestraat. It was there that in the course of 1961 Pater Pastoor would have rung on at the door. Since his appointment as parish priest in November 1960, he had given himself the task to visit all people of Borsbeek-West, church-goers and non-church-goers alike, within a year. Of course, at some doors, especially those of ardent socialists, he had no success in gaining access. It is more than likely that he came in contact with the still young family of non-regularly-practicing Catholics at Manebruggestraat 290.

In the early 1960s, as material prosperity within society increased, the spiritual dimension of life was being pushed to the background. Yet in light of the Cold War and the risk of nuclear power being unleashed, more than ever, prayer and spiritual renewal were needed, as well as spiritual warfare against the powers of evil. Overall, throughout the twentieth century, considerable technological advances have been made, but these have not been matched by a comparable advance in humanity's moral behavior or spiritual awareness. This has placed human life continuously in a very precarious position. The Cold war is long since over its peak, but an enormous amount of nuclear and more conventional weaponry is by several nations still kept ready for immediate use if needed. The threat and risk remains.

In the spring of 1964 Walter made his Confirmation in the faith and received his Solemn Holy Communion in the wooden chapel of the Saint-Johannes-Berchmans Parish. He would still have been given a missal: a custom that came to an end after the Second Vatican Council.

Interior of the wooden chapel of the Saint-Johannes-Berchmans Parish – view towards the entrance and the back. One of the statues is of the patron saint of the parish; the other is of Saint Rita, before which candles are burning. It is for this statue that the parish was widely known as the parish of Saint Rita. It is the one statue that was transferred to the new parish church built in the early 1970s. The Paters dedicated at least monthly, on a- Thursday, a Mass in her honor, which Ma used to attend.

Soon afterwards, Walter completed his primary schooling. Since he proved himself a capable student, Alfons wished to register him at a good school for his secondary education. He tried at Xaverius College in Borgerhout (Antwerp), which was situated just outside the city center of Antwerp. Walter would have been able to cycle it. The school is a well-known Jesuit college; a Jesuit monastery forms part of the complex of buildings and several of them taught at the time in the college. The registration attempt was unsuccessful. Alfons did not take it lightly, however, and in his frustration accused them of elitism, saying to them that if he had not been a simple workman but instead a man with a position, they would not fail to take his son. The non-acceptance would have been a factor that made Alfons more distrustful of the integrity of the church as an institution and of its representatives. It is difficult to say whether Alfons's grudge was reasonable in this particular case without more information about the registration process and the number of places that would have been left available at the time that Alfons made the application. In any case, Walter went to the Royal Athenaeum of Deurne instead. At the time, it was a public school with a very good reputation as well. Eight years after Walter completed his secondary schooling there, I would start attending at the first class of the same school.

In the meantime, around the time that he had changed from primary to secondary, Walter had left the Scouts of Pius-X Parish and had joined a korfball club, again in Deurne-South, at Arena-Weide. The *weide* (meadow) was and still is situated besides a former military fort ("Het Fortje") that was part of a belt of seven forts built in the mid-nineteenth century around Antwerp, which not many years later was replaced by a new, larger belt of twelve forts (Carolina during her youth lived first nearby Fort 2 of Wommelgem, situated besides Kandonk Laar, and later nearby Fort 7 of Wilrijk, situated not far from the Boomsesteenweg). In 1966, Het Fortje van Deurne (the only one extant of the first belt of seven small forts) was transformed into a sports arena, and hence the name of Walter's former sports club, where he met his girlfriend, Sonja, whom I have known around for as long as I have known Walter.

On the world scene, concerning the Roman Catholic Church, the Second Vatican Council was in its last year. It had been opened by Pope John XXIII on October 11, 1962, and would be closed by Pope Paul VI on December 8, 1965. In its aftermath, several guidelines were introduced for, among others, a liturgical renewal. In the church's worship, the emphasis shifted from God in the highest, that is, the God who transcends everything, to God who dwells among us, that is, the God who is immanent in his creation. The high altars of many churches were dismantled; and in its stead, plain tables were brought in. Though officially the normal rite still had the priest facing towards the east during Mass with the congregation behind him, in practice the extraordinary rite, in which the priest faces the people, became used on a daily basis. The normal rite came in disuse in most parishes. It resulted not only in a simplified adornment of the churches but also in a simplification of the ritual itself. The priest's vestments became more sober. The Mass was curtailed of much of its solemnity. Although Vatican II introduced opportunity to perceive the created order and the entirety of life as sacred, in actuality, secularization increased its hold in which an awareness of sacredness within and without the liturgy was much less experienced and often lost altogether. Except in a few monasteries, Mass was no longer served in Latin but in the vernacular. Before the council, the people observed silence in church before and during the liturgy, while the Mass servers gave the set phrases in response to the priest's prayers; whereas now, the entire congregation was encouraged to participate in prayers, which to some extent took on the form of dialogue. While in itself this transition is not a bad thing, churches have too often become places not of Spirit-filled silence but buzz halls filled with petty talk. The exchange of a few words is not to be totally banned, but it is the unrestrained talking without any awareness of sacredness that gives away the spiritual poverty. Solemn vespers and benediction on Sunday afternoons was cancelled. In many churches the statues of saints were removed to a less conspicuous place or were destroyed, just as if it was a new iconoclasm, not now by the Protestants but by the Catholics themselves. This also meant that the link with the communion of saints across the ages became less visible, and the church that encompasses heaven and earth would be experienced too much as a social society in the here and now. Of course, devotion of saints was not completely obliterated and some churches, especially old buildings, still contain sacred statues and images. A good number of faithful still possess devotional pictures, and so on. The situation varies also considerably between one country and another. Certainly, the outcome of Vatican II is not merely negative, for it was inspired by the need for a new attitude of the Roman Catholic Church to the other churches and it consolidated openness to the world. Unfortunately, the way things were implemented meant that the much-needed renewal of the church coincided with a further demise of it. It is well to point out, though, that this diminution of the church in much of continental Western Europe, was taking place well before Vatican II. Already in a book of 1956 (*L'Église en état de mission*), Monsignor Léon-Joseph Suenens, later Cardinal Suenens, lamented the "growing dechristianization of the masses" and the "apostasy of the masses" and pleaded for the urgent need of participation in missionary activity of all the faithful so as to stem the tide (English translation, *The Gospel to Every Creature*, London: Burns and Oates, 1956, pp. 1, 106).

Curiously enough, the years that Vatican II took place coincided with the time period that the hippie countercultural movement took place and blew over the ocean from the United States, to Britain and continental Europe. Hippies rejected established institutions; they sought to replace the dominant mainstream culture marked by middle-class values. They opposed nuclear weapons and the Vietnam War. In their search for new meaning in life they embraced aspects of eastern philosophy, were often vegetarians, and tried to tread lightly on the earth. They championed the use of psychedelic drugs, because they believed it expanded their consciousness; and they championed free love and sexual permissiveness. Later onwards the term *flower power* came to be used as a reference to the hippie movement in general. In the late 1960s it was a symbol of their passive resistance and non-violence ideology. They often embraced the symbolism by dressing in clothing with embroidered flowers and vibrant colors.

In Belgium, Walter got the tail-end of the movement's high day. He and Sonja were just too young; they just escaped from possibly becoming hippies, even though Sonja had long blond hair, and Walter had an old, broad hat that he wore over his longish hair that at times was turned red from his holiday work in the nearby fireworks factory; and even though in the late 60s, they once had a party in Manebruggestraat with a number of friends and lots of confetti at which they played their Beatles singles. But overall they would very much turn their course of life towards taking up their place into the mainstream culture of their times.

In the wake of Vatican II, in light of the changing cultural climate, many expected that the church would be open to the use of artificial contraception. Then, in July 1968, Pope Paul VI presented his encyclical *Humanae vitae*, "On the Regulation of Birth." It caused an outcry; many were perplexed about it, including bishops, theologians, priests, and many of the laity—and presently, over fifty years later, it is still a thorn in the flesh of many. A Study Commission that had the task of gathering opinions on the new questions regarding conjugal life, and in particular on the regulation of births, had already been instituted by Pope John XXIII in 1963. Several councils at diocesan level had likewise been considering the matter and made judgments. The encyclical took stock of all these and was the pope's reply.

A few lines in the document that are central to it are these:

> God has wisely disposed natural laws and rhythms of fecundity which, of themselves, cause a separation in the succession of births. Nonetheless, the Church, calling men back to the observance of the norms of the natural law, as interpreted by her constant doctrine, teaches that each and every marriage act (*quilibet matrimonii usus*) must remain open to the transmission of life (par. 11).

The pope provides reference to, among others, the encyclical *Casti Connubii* (1930), "On Christian Marriage," of Pope Pius XI.

In the section on illicit ways of regulating birth (par. 14), he mentions "the direct interruption of the generative process already begun, and, above all, directly willed and procured abortion, even if for therapeutic reasons" and "direct sterilization, whether perpetual or temporary, whether of the man or of the woman." He continues: "Similarly excluded is every action which, either in anticipation of the conjugal act, or in its accomplishment, or in the development of its natural consequences, proposes, whether as an end or as a means, to render procreation impossible." Still further on the same subject, he adds the qualification: "even when the intention is to safeguard or promote individual, family or social well-being."

In the section on the licitness of recourse to infecund periods (par. 16), the pope argues:

> The Church is coherent with herself when she considers recourse to the infecund periods to be licit, while at the same time condemning as being always illicit, the use of means directly contrary to fecundation, even if such use is inspired by reasons which may appear honest and serious. In reality, there are essential differences between the two cases: in the former, the married couple makes legitimate use of a natural disposition; in the latter, they impede the development of natural processes. . . . The use of marriage . . . during infecund periods to manifest their affection and to safeguard their mutual fidelity. By so doing, they give proof of a truly and integrally honest love.

These last phrases show that Pope Paul VI envisaged the marriage and sexuality as being not only for the sake of begetting children but also as instrumental for living a Christian life of love.

Finally, I note in the paragraph addressed to scientists (par. 24): "It is particularly desirable that, according to the wish already expressed by Pope Pius XII (in 1951), medical science succeeds in providing a sufficiently secure basis for a regulation of birth, founded on the observance of natural rhythms."

In my assessment, I find this document to provide, overall, a clear and valuable instruction. I am of the opinion, however, that despite the pope's teaching and that of the church more generally regarding the direct interruption of the generative process already begun, extreme circumstances may exist in which it is not illicit. But they have to be truly extreme; for I certainly find unjust and most inhuman, legislation that allows for conveyor-belt abortion on demand. Further, while the teaching of the pope regarding artificial birth control is a clear guideline for Christian couples, I would not exclude circumstances may exist in which a well-balanced conscientious decision favoring the use of artificial birth-control may be defensible. Such perception is effectively in accord with the teaching of the church (see, for example, *Gaudium et spes*, 16; *Catechism of the Catholic Church*, no. 1776, 1782).

With this we have reached the time of the divorce of my parents, about which I provide more details in the coming chapter.

Saint-Johannes-Berchmans Parish Church – the church that replaced the wooden chapel as place of worship

It may still be noted that during that same year, 1968, land was bought for the building of a new, modern church adjacent to the wooden chapel of the Saint-Johannes-Berchmans Parish. The building works started in October 1970 and it was completed in March 1972. They built a hexagon construction with a flat roof; large, clear-glass windows; and red brick walls on the in- and outside. It is entirely in keeping with the prevalent interpretation of Vatican II: a basic, wooden table for altar; a plain, white cross above it; hardly any adornment. It has a carpet and plastic chairs; no possibility for kneeling during prayers. The church contained a new statue of Our Lady in sand color at the back, to which people showed, generally, little interest; but there still was kept along the back an older, colorful, life-size statue of Saint Rita, which came from the wooden chapel, before which candles were always being burned by the people. Years later, modern pen-drawings illustrating the Stations of the Cross were hung up along the walls. The wooden chapel became meeting place for youth groups of the parish.

Walter married Sonja in this new building in 1977. Though neither of them ever practiced their faith regularly, they still valued the sacramental marriage and they had their children baptized.

During my upbringing, I would go every Sunday with Frans and Carolina to Mass in this new building. Devotion would come only much later. Even though there have been many scandals, which was emphasized by *The Mysteries of the People*, and as there still are in our day; and even though many of the clergy may be in the power of the devil; fortunately, they have not stolen away my devotion, my relationship with God.

The fact is that faith cannot be merely an individual experience. The scriptural texts, the prayers we know, and the Creed have been passed on to us from the early church onwards. The Eucharist as a reenactment of the Last Supper is a community event; Christian faith is lived out as members of a community. The Roman Catholic Church is the church that was the only one significantly present in Belgium when I grew up and it is the Catholic faith that I have become acquainted with. It is the church of my parents (and I mean here Frans and Carolina) and of numerous saintly men and women. Nevertheless, even in our present age, I am of the opinion that some aspects of Catholicism need a thorough revision, about which more detail towards the end of this book.

I end this chapter with Luke 4:29–30. These scriptural verses conclude the story of Jesus visiting his hometown Nazareth. During the visit he read and preached in the synagogue, but he found little faith in him among the people that knew him. It even came to a confrontation: "And they rose up and put him out of the city, and led him to the brow of the hill on which their city was built, that they might throw him down headlong. But passing through the midst of them he went away." These verses tell me that even when we have good intentions, if we do not take care, we may be vulnerable to being thrown down a cliff by other people or by malicious powers. This is what happened to Alfons. But Jesus went between them. When following Jesus and letting ourselves be guided by him, we too may go between those assailing us and enter life, truth, and the community of love. The same I consider to be the case beyond the veil of death. When we close our eyes, others will await us on the other side: either, people who want us to join their number will push us and lead us away from the light of God into deepening darkness and perdition, amidst multitudes tearing at each other with gnashing teeth; or, we will be out of reach to them and be assisted by an angel or someone sent from heaven and the holy spiritual powers unto the throne of light, that is, the throne of God, and into the communion of saints. We will not enter thereupon unaccompanied. Starting here and beyond death, in the vastness that lies beyond the material, we will not find our way without assistance; but assistance and peace and light awaits those that desire life in God; Jesus is the way; the Spirit is the helper.

Carlintje undoubtedly prayed the Graduale prayer given in her missal for June 21, feast day of Saint Aloysius of Gonzaga, which includes verses from Psalm 70:

It is you, O Lord, who are my hope,
my trust, O Lord, since my youth.
On you I have leaned from my birth,
from my mother's womb you have been my help.
My hope has always been in you.

V/ And you have taken me up because of my innocence:
And confirmed me into your presence for all eternity.

# 6

## Indelible blessings and scars

For more than fifteen years, Alfons and Carolina were a loving couple; then Alfons entered into a relationship with another woman. It led to their divorce at a time when I was still very young so that I never knew Alfons. It was, however, not only Alfons whom I did not know. In the foregoing pages I have been telling about my brother, Walter; but the reader will recall my first memory with which I began these memoirs: indeed, the memory of a girl with blond hair was not mere imaginings, for there was an older sister too. Sadly, as a result of the divorce of our parents, we were being separated; and I did not know Jenny. She was not a part of my early childhood; only a vagueness at the very back of my mind remained. Some more background information is called for, which I try to provide here.

Alfons had envisaged that his marriage with Carolina would ideally result in a single child. This envisaged child, their first, Walter, was born in 1952. Then a few years later, Carolina had a miscarriage. Again some years later, in 1961, a second child was born, namely, Jenny. Alfons would have gone along reluctantly, but he made it clear to his wife that three would be too much for his liking. As it happened, no further child was born for some years; but then, in the spring of 1965, Carolina conceived again.

This picture of 1964 or '65, taken in Wilrijk during a visit to the moemoe, shows Carolina, Walter, and Jenny. It would have been taken by Alfons.

Ma seldom talked about the past, but it was dropped to me several years later that Alfons did not want the third child to be born. He would have preferred for her to try get rid of the embryo. Ma was uncertain about what to do. She loved her husband and did not know what was best. She would have prayed about it, and then it happened that a calm certainty came to her, which she ascribed to Christ. In her inner turmoil, a word was spoken into her soul that made her confident that it was good to keep the child.

For Ma, a few children were a blessing, and she found that she was particularly being blessed to receive these children. She often quoted the saying that receiving a boy and a girl is a king's dream; and then in addition, she got another boy. She had herself lacked the support of a number of siblings and had felt alone, whereas she had known among her friends larger families of which the children were happy. But Alfons had other thoughts,

This picture that is taken at Emma's house (Boomsesteenweg 821, Wilrijk) shows Alfons, Carolina, Emma, and Jenny. The photograph was taken by Walter. It shows to all appearances a rather relaxed and happy family.

other worries perhaps. Perhaps he considered that the size of the house did not allow for a larger family; who knows?

At the time that I was born, Carolina was thirty-six, and so it was rather unlikely that it would come to a very large family. Certainly, if they were to continue at the same rate, a fourth child might have been born to them.

At the time that Alfons initiated the divorce procedures, he had moved out and was living in Antwerp, Jan van Rijswijcklaan 156. Carolina continued living in their house in Borsbeek, Manebruggestraat 290. As for the children, Walter and I were living with Ma, and Jenny with Alfons. I was still a toddler, and so it is perhaps not too surprising that I was living with my mother. Jenny was about six to seven years old. It is well attested that psychology takes its part; and that it tends to make girls of that age more attached to the father than to the mother, who at that age is actually rather seen as a concurrent for what concerns the father's attention. So, it is not too surprising that Alfons knew to lure the girl away from her mother. I remember that Ma told me, years afterwards, of the occasions that she went to look for Jenny at Alfons's address in Jan van Rijswijcklaan. Alfons would have opened the door and would then call inside for the girl, soon coming back with the information that the girl did not want to see her. It occurred a few times and was utterly devastating for Carolina. Surprising to me was that Ma also recalled that Alfons wanted to obtain custody for me. I consider that the motive for this was

Jenny and Ma standing at the front door of the house in Manebruggestraat. The occasion is Jenny's first Holy Communion. It is perhaps the last picture of Jenny from her early childhood with us.

probably that without it, he would not have had much chance to claim the value of half the house: for it was the dwelling of the mother, a toddler (I), and a teenage boy. In this scheme, however, he did not succeed. I was fortunate that I was assigned to the mother and that he was not granted visiting rights for me. Ma informed me that she did not wish the system of children being moved about continually between both parties. It would have made life impossible.

Carolina would have wished to have all three children with her, but that was not possible because of the said situation, which was exploited by Alfons. She considered fighting the case before court, but a lawyer advised her not to go this route. For his experience told him that in the given case the girl would want to be with her father, would rebel, and Carolina would have to let her go in the end anyway. He advised her that the cost of the case would have required her to sell the house and that she would in the end not really gain. He thus advised her to let happen what needs to happen; that the girl would return to her mother before the age of fifteen. It was a message that was hard to take for a loving mother, but she believed that the lawyer spoke with experience and she followed the advice that was given her, which left her with a morsel of hope for the future.

Concerning the material side of the divorce settlement; each kept the savings account that they had under their respective names, and they kept their clothing and so forth. The furniture and movables were estimated to be worth 37,365 Belgian francs and they were entirely granted to Carolina, except that Alfons wanted a few pair of sheets and a blanket that he was using. Their dwelling was estimated to be worth 600,000 Belgian francs. Part of this needed still to be paid under a mortgage agreement; a bill was, moreover, outstanding to the gas company, the Antwerpse Gasmaatschappij, for the costs of connecting the house to the grid; and a *street tax* was outstanding to Borsbeek Council. Alfons granted this property entirely to Carolina, upon whom fell henceforth the responsibility for the outstanding costs. The agreement included, furthermore, that Alfons remained the owner of his share in the farm that belonged to his parents, which was situated in Vaartstraat in Ranst. Each would receive, in addition, the family allowance for the child/children that they were assigned to have under their care. And each was given responsibility for the savings account/accounts of the child/children under their care: that is, Carolina was to take care of the savings accounts of Walter and myself; whereas Alfons was to take care of the savings account of Jenny.

During the period that stretched between the drawing up of the divorce settlement and the pronouncement of the divorce, that is, during the period of procedures, Alfons was required to pay a maintenance contribution to Carolina for the sum of 3,000 Belgian francs, payable on the first day of each month. In view of this, Alfons did not demand a share in the house in Manebruggestraat so as, instead, to obtain relief from any financial responsibility for Carolina, Walter, and I after the divorce would be finalized.

The split between the two partial households was thus destined to be complete, except for the fact that, after Alfons's parents would come to die and their property sold, each of the children would have right upon a share in this. As it was, Alfons's mother had died only a few months earlier, on March 17, 1968; whereas his father, Constant, was still alive.

The divorce settlement was signed on November 18, 1968. Both spouses declared that they chose the procedure to be completed at the law-court-of-first-instance in Antwerp. On the occasion that both were sitting in front of a lawyer's desk, Alfons was asked for the reason that he wanted a divorce. The reason he gave was that Carolina had gotten pregnant for a third time (not counting the miscarriage).

Before the pronouncement of the divorce in the law-court, in the leading up towards it, the spouses were requested to attend a few more times at a meeting, but Ma no longer attended each of these.

For some time after the separation, Walter and I lived alone with Ma in the house in Manebruggestraat. This would have been for a time period of perhaps less than a year. At some point, Frans the policeman from across the road would knock at the door, and a new relationship would develop. Before the time that the divorce was conclusively pronounced, Frans and Carolina had entered into this new relationship.

The idea of a new relationship, and so soon, would initially not have been evident for Carolina. She was a Christian believer, and she still esteemed the teachings of the Catholic Church. She knew it was not normally permitted to enter into another relationship or to remarry. But having wrestled with the problem for some time, she would once more have received inspiration. She ascribed it to Holy Mary that in a dream it was clarified to her that an exception was being made for her.

At around this time, an event took place that would strongly affect me in the years thereafter. I was at the time still unawares. It was late in the evening. There were at home in Manebruggestraat Ma, Walter, I, and two friends of Walter (whom he came to know from Arena-weide korfball club), namely, Jackie and Ludo Van Roey. Frans was not there and was in his house across the road with his daughter Vera and her husband, Ward. Suddenly, Walter announced that he was seeing a man in the veranda at the back of the house. This caused not a little stir. As I described earlier, the house was surrounded at the back by concrete walls, and so it could not just be a figure passing by and looking through the window. It required some climbing over the wall, and the man was apparently seen already inside the veranda. Ma took me upstairs and ordered Walter and his friends to lock themselves inside the small bedroom at the first floor at the front of the house together with me. The boys grabbed kitchen knives and excitedly took up their posts. Ma then decided to get Frans from across the road. But she needed the keys of his house, which were kept in the large cupboard downstairs, whether in the veranda itself or not, I do not recall this detail, though she surely told me. It took her ages to overcome her fear and make the journey to the cupboard. Eventually she got the keys out of it without encountering the alleged intruder. She ran across to the house of Frans and quietly opened the front door; all were already asleep; probably, Frans was on duty early in the morning. Ma crept upstairs and tried to remember which of the doors gave access to Frans's bedroom. She opened the correct door and woke him up. Frans was not easily disturbed or afraid. He took his pistol and followed Carolina out of the house and across the road. He surveyed the scene and went round the house, into the back, into the garden, and into the workhouse at the back. He encountered no one and after calming down Ma went probably back to his bed. Whether it was after this incident that she wanted him to stay with her during the night in the house I do not know, but it may have been a factor that led them to move on with taking their relationship further.

The entire, alleged-intruder incident is rather curious. If Walter truly saw someone, it is not impossible that it was a tramp. The timing of it, though, makes me consider another more likely alternative: Could it have been an acquaintance of Alfons who was sent to spy out who was present in the house, or who was sent with some other purpose? It will have to remain unanswered. I have recalled this incident at length because throughout my childhood I have been plagued with an inordinate fear. It is well possible that at this incident, when I was a toddler of perhaps one and a half, I underwent a shock that set itself deeply into my mind. In all likelihood, I was affected by the panic, the fear, and the excitement around me. In the years ahead, when I was brought to bed at around eight o'clock, while the rest of the family was still downstairs, much misery was involved. I would sit upright in bed for hours watching the door and watching whether the shadow cast by the bedside light in the nearby room was unmoving. Eventually these shadows did seem to move. I often called out for help from my parents downstairs from fear. Often also, I tried to call out but was so paralyzed by fear that hardly any sound came from my throat. I often imagined during these hours to be beset by evil beings that were after me. When eventually I exhaustedly lay flat in the bed, I huddled under the blankets. With my ear pressed against the pillow or against the mattress, I heard my own heartbeat. This sounded to me as the footsteps of the evil beings, so that I hardly dared to breathe under the blankets, for they were upon me. Often when my mother came upstairs around ten as she went to bed, she found me thus under the blankets soaking from sweat, so that my pajamas had to be changed to dry ones. These years of childhood, I would without hesitation call the most dreadful of my life. Carolina and Frans found that this fear was worse on the occasions that I had watched an episode of Doctor Who; in which, as far as I remember, usually featured darkness and alien beings that wanted to inflict harm. So, it was found better that I did not watch these programs.

Eventually, Alfons and Carolina were pronounced as being divorced. Ma told me years later about the occasion. When they were gathered in the law-court, after the pronouncement, the judge made a special point of congratulating Carolina. He con-gratulated her for the fact that various accusations had been made against her by her former husband and that none had stood up to truth; that she was an exemplary woman and that she could not be blamed for anything. Subsequently, the judge turned to Alfons and declared to him that he should be utterly ashamed for divorcing such a woman and for doing this to her and to his children.

All this took place in my first years, before I had come to a clear conscious awareness. Since I am talking about scars, let me explain how, besides some mental scars, I arrived at having a physical scar that is rather unrelated to the foregoing. It apparently happened when I was playing bus with Walter in the living room in front of the hearth. The fireplace consisted of beautiful blue granite stones over a width of about one and a half meter reaching to the ceiling; in front there was a large, flat slab of the same kind of stone: rather rough and with sharp corners. On top of it stood a large coal stove. On the occasion, Walter and I had placed in front of the hearth various wooden chairs one behind another so as to simulate a bus. As I was jumping about, I fell with my chin right at one of the edges of the large blue stone. The result was that my lower front teeth pierced through my chin. The family doctor was called for, and he had to stitch the punctured skin. Before starting, Dr. Van de Kerckhove would have been quite wary, because he knew me from previous occasions as a rather big screamer. As I was told, no sedation was involved, yet I did not move or give a peep and cannot recall the event whatsoever. The doctor called it a miracle.

On July 20, 1971, the second wedding took place in the town hall of Deurne, (which at the time was still an independent municipality; in later years Deurne came to be part of greater Antwerp, and the town hall would become a district's house of the city for public services). The witnesses who signed at the wedding were

Frans's brother-in-law Jan Wouters, who was the husband of his eldest sister, Marie, and Carolina's brother, Eugène. Those waiting for their return to the house in Manebruggestraat included Moemoe, Walter, Sonja, and I. Whether other people were invited and were present for the meal at the long table in the living room, I do not know.

At the weddding of Frans and Carolina. They are pictured here with their witnesses Jan (with his wife Marie) on the right and Eugène (with his wife Irma) on the left before leaving the town hall.

Tragedy and disillusionment would have taken its toll of Ma and leave their scars on her heart, but life carried on. And though I have spoken of dread in my childhood experience, I was fortunate to receive various blessings. Besides the blessings of life, baptism, parental love, a great older brother, and a kind moemoe, and so many other gifts, there came also the gift of my first Holy Communion. I was, however, not a child who took to church matters with great fervor. Things to do with God had still to be sorted out (and still to some extent, no doubt); and church matters

# 7

# Grandparents and ancestors (1)

O F MY FOUR grandparents, Moemoe is the only one whom I have known. I mentioned that my mother, Carolina, was an illegitimate child; and therefore, apart from her mother, "de Moemoe," and apart from her brother, Eugène, I have had few contacts with her side of the family. She never spoke about her father or her grandparents. Moreover, because of the divorce of my parents, I never met Alfons; and therefore I have not had any contact with the Govaerts-family either. Walter, being fourteen years older than me, did of course know Alfons quite well and has known his grandparents; and he has met his uncles and aunt along that side of the family during his youth. Along mother's side, he apparently has had no more contacts than me, and he also never heard anything about her father or about ancestors.

Uncle Eugène outlived my mother and Moemoe, and I regularly had conversations with him. He was a man who had never been able to reconcile himself with the fact of being an illegitimate child. Throughout his long life, it was a topic he regularly alluded to and about which he was extremely sensitive. Even though he would visit Moemoe as long as she lived, he could hardly hide his grudge against her for, among others, this very reason. I have never known him to call her anything else than "mens" (a word that has no parallel in English, but one may perhaps more readily recognize the German equivalent, *Mensch*). From him also, I have never heard anything about his father. In fact, when he spoke about the early years of his life, he sometimes referred to "de drij," that is, dialect for *de drie* (the three): that is, Moemoe, himself, and Carolina.

I obtained some information from the records of Saint-Bavo Parish in Wilrijk, by requesting some genealogical research from a representative of the district Wilrijk, and with the help of local-history groups, especially of Wommelgem, who kindly had their specialist explore the township's archives for me. Through the responsible priest of Saint-Jan-Vianney Parish in Wilrijk, I was brought into touch with my mother's friend of her youth, Maria Fret (married name De Wever), and with my mother's cousin Maria Van Uffel (born Van Kesbeeck). In my address book I had copied, moreover, some names and addresses from Ma's address book after she died in 1989, even though they did not necessarily mean much to me. One such entry referred to a family De Bruyn living in Hemiksem. This appeared to be the address of another cousin of my mother, namely, Louisa Carolina Luyckx, who had married Jozef De Bruyn. Through Maria Fret, I was brought into contact with Louisa, who still lived at the same address and who has been very helpful as well.

I pursued details also of an incident that Ma related during lunch, when we sat at table: Once, when she went to see a doctor, this doctor noted her name during the consultation, and he observed to her surprise that he was her cousin via her father. Ma mentioned in relating this incident that her father was married and had a family, and that, in addition, he had an extra-marital relationship with Moemoe. The doctor invited Carolina—and undoubtedly also her husband—to his house for a meal with his family. The reason she recalled this event and wanted to tell it was that she very much appreciated that this family made her welcome and were friendly to her. It meant a lot to her. Long after both my parents had died, I recalled this story and wondered whether it would be possible—some sixty years after my mother met him—to retrace this doctor and thus obtain some information about Ma's father and the entire circumstances of her upbringing. I did not recall any more details about the circumstances of the story as told by my mother. But at the time, just after it took place, she had told it to her friend Maria Fret; and Maria recalled that it was during the time that Ma was pregnant with Walter, and thus while she was living in Edegem. Eventually, with the help of the local-history group, I did find the name of the doctor concerned. It was Dr. Frans De Voogt, who was family doctor in Edegem. Dr. De Voogt died in 1970, but one of his sons followed in his footsteps and has continued the practice in Edegem, namely, Dr. Patrick De Voogt. It is through him that I obtained some contact with the family of Carolina's father and a little more information. As regards the visit of Ma and, probably, Alfons around end 1951 or begin 1952, it can be noted that Dr. Frans De Voogt practiced as a family doctor since 1938 and only married in 1952; I consider it therefore likely that they actually met with his parents, that is, with a sister of Carolina's father, namely, Maria Josephina De Weerdt, and her family.

About the Govaerts-family, I obtained information with the help of the local-history group of Ranst, through what Walter recalled, by means of a few old photographs, and as contained in the document of the divorce settlement of Alfons and Carolina.

Conceivably, this chapter and the next one could have remained unwritten in my autobiography, yet I am interested to try to organize into a coherent account the few elements of information that I obtained about my grandparents and their immediate relatives. They are facts that were just out of reach and out of sight during my upbringing; but that were not, therefore, necessarily absent or without significance. Even though details remain out of sight, for some concern incidents that happened about a hundred years ago, and even though few people may be interested in them, they provide, among others, insight into the conditions, especially, of Ma's upbringing; and they may even tell something about my internal wiring, that is, my character, and about that of my siblings. Let me start with Moemoe.

Emma Van Kesbeeck was born at Wilrijk in 1897 as the second daughter of Jozef Van Kesbeeck (1870–1946), who was known as "den Teppe," and Theresia Clementina Van Herck (1876–1953), known as "Mance." Both parents of Emma had themselves been born at Wilrijk. There were in total fourteen children born to them. It was the time of large families and a time at which several of the children would not survive for long. Those who survived and lived into adulthood would be remembered by their offspring, by nieces and nephews, and perhaps still by grandchildren. Of those who died prematurely, the memory would be kept by the parents and perhaps vaguely by the eldest children and would disappear with them. Their names would not have been mentioned long after they lived. Even the younger siblings would not have known all the children that preceded them. In faith we can confirm that this does not imply that these children are absent from the realm of eternity in God's presence. It is a consideration that can let us appreciate the value of children's baptism for those of us who believe in God. Let us take a little time to recall these names.

Emma and her siblings were: Florentina Carolina, who was known as Lientje, born November 10, 1895 (baptized the same day), died November 4, 1954; Emma Maria Catharina herself, born April 14, 1897 (baptized the 18th), died September 23, 1996; Franciscus Josephus, known as Jef, born December 29, 1898 (baptized on January 1), died in Hoboken on April 3, 1962; Maria Theresia, born December 30, 1900 (baptized the same day), died December 16, 1905; Carolus, born November 19, 1902 (baptized on 23rd), died November 11, 1904; Philomena, born December 27, 1903 (baptized the same day), died August 16, 1904; Franciscus, born January 18, 1905 (baptized the 22nd), died April 21, 1905; Augustina Clementina, born February 16, 1906 (baptized the 18th), died September 18, 1906; Maria, born September 24, 1907 (baptized the 29th), died November 11, 1907; Louis, born April 19, 1909, died in Duffel on December 3, 1971; Henri Maria, known as Rik, born March 8, 1911 (baptized the 12th), died February 23, 2004; Maria, born April 8, 1914 (baptized the 12th), died June 29, 1914; August Albert, known as Gust, born May 28, 1915 (baptized on 31st), died October 18, 2009; Paulina, born December 31, 1917, died February 2, 1918. The little girl Paulina was called after Teppe's own little sister Paulina Van Kesbeeck (born July 31, 1880), who was the youngest child in a series of ten, all with names almost identical to Teppe's own children.

I note that between August 1904 and November 1907, that is, in a span of three years and months, six children died: four babies less than eight months old, one boy just under two years old, and one girl just under five years old. What a sadness it must have brought to the parents and family. Later onwards they lost two more baby girls: Maria in 1914 and Paulina in 1918. Moemoe's parents were truly acquainted with grief.

Of those that lived into adulthood, the only one I have met besides my grandmother Emma is her youngest brother, whom I knew as Uncle Gust. I have visited him and his wife, Aunt Jeanne (Van Hoeydonck), with Ma and Pa during my childhood. Years later, in 1996, Uncle Eugène asked me to drive him to them, since I still had their address, so as to inform them of the funeral arrangements for Gust's sister Emma. Again, in 2010, in my chase for information, I looked up Aunt Jeanne in the nursing home, which happened to be but weeks before she died (October 21, 2010). In my childhood, in the early 1970s, I accompanied my parents also on visits to the widow of Jef, (that is, the brother of Moemoe born just after her), namely, Aunt Adèle (Verbert) (born 1901), in Hoboken. I remember her as a kind old lady, who seemed to spend her days playing patience (or solitaire). She died at the age of eighty.

Around the same time that I visited Aunt Jeanne, I looked up Maria, the daughter of Uncle Rik. Maria informed me that she—who lived all her life in Wilrijk (born 1934)—had known six of those fourteen children of Teppe and Mance: besides her father, she knew Lientje (the eldest), Emma, Jef, Louis, and Gust. The names of those six that survived are confirmed by the census of 1920 and by the information held by the municipality.

When Moemoe's parents celebrated their golden wedding in 1945 in Wilrijk, it is Lientje, Jef, Louis, Rik, and Gust who with their own respective families feature on the photograph that was taken. The only ones living of the family who are missing when the photo was taken are their daughter Emma (Moemoe) and her two children, as well as Alfons (born August 3, 1918), a son of their oldest daughter Lientje, who at the time was still in Germany. The fact that Moemoe and her children apparently did not participate in the celebration is curious, given that she had regular contact with her parents and that she lived next door to De Groene Jager, where the family gathering took place. Most likely, her absence at the golden wedding was related to the way her own life went; she tended to keep away from all gatherings.

Staying with the golden wedding, I would like to mention that featuring on the photo as well were, most probably, Mance's elder sister, Maria Theresia (Mie) Van Herck (1875–1950), and her husband, Carolus Joannes Verbeeck (b. 1874). They had ten children: The first of these was called Lien (Carolina Catharina; 1900–21), just as the first child of Mance and Teppe was called Lientje (Florentina Carolina); remembered with this name was Mie and Mance's mother, Carolina Catharina Verbeeck (1840–1918). Lien would die at the young age of twenty-one. One of Mie's and Louis' sons was Ludovicus Carolus (Louis) Verbeeck (1910–98) whom I sometimes visited with my parents on his farm in Aartselaar. When we visited him, he would get out a bundle of papers with schematic drawings indicating the position of various heavenly bodies and with various calculations, on the basis of which he made precise predictions of various future cataclysms. He would tell my parents that on such and such a date in one of the years ahead they better keep their car in the garage because hailstones the size of a fist were to be expected. It was curious to have him show these large sheets with careful drawings and calculations on a kitchen table and be all animated about it, while he would be wearing wooden clogs, for he was a farmer, and a heap of potatoes reaching the ceiling was not far off. Such was Louis Verbeeck, the philosopher of Aartselaar. (His drawings I saw again some ten years ago, when I visited the local-history group in Aartselaar, by whom they are being kept.) Finally, the tenth and youngest of the children of Mie and Louis was being called Emma Josephina (1918–2003); so it is well possible that Moemoe, then twenty-one, acted as the godmother.

Josephus and Theresia Clementina, the parents of Moemoe, at their golden jubilee in 1945. Behind the golden couple stands their eldest daughter, Lientje. Her husband, August Luyckx, is the older gentleman on the left side of the photograph near the top. Behind Lientje at the right side on the photo stands her brother Jef and his wife, Adèle (Verbert), with their son, Jos, between them, (he would marry Lisette Volckaerts, and they had two children, Willy and François); their daughter, Alphonsine is the third person to the left of Jef; her husband, Marcel Peeters, is seen left of her on the photo, (they had a daughter, Yvonne). Behind Lientje at the left side, we find her brother Louis. Their brother Rik is at the very left of the picture, with his wife, Virginie (Mariën), beside him. Their two children are at the front: namely, Maria, in front of the golden couple, and Jos. The youngest son of the golden pair, Gust, is standing on a chair and towers above the others; his wife, Jeanne (Van Hooydonck), stands two rows below him besides the older woman. Their daughter, José, is the little girl at the front (who would die at the age of thirty-two); their son, Robert, was not yet born (and he would die at fifty). The elder woman is probably Mance's elder sister, Maria Theresia (Mie); the elder gentleman along the right is most likely her husband, Louis (Carolus Joannes) Verbeeck. The teenage girl besides Lientje is Annie

Heyneman, an officially adopted daughter of hers, (Annie had lived with her mother, Renée/Renate Heynemann, along Boomsesteenweg right across from the family Luyckx prior to her living for seven years with the family Luyckx: her mother, Renée, was an only parent whose partner (not Annie's father) had died just prior to them getting married and who subsequently decided to go working in Germany, since she had no income; later in life Annie became Annie Verbeeck). Those not yet mentioned are offspring of Lientje and August with their spouses: Emma (Luyckx), the eldest daughter, born in 1915, is seen standing in front of the window along the right side; her husband, Isidoor Delvaux is seen at the right of her behind Jef, (they would have one daughter, Arlette, born in 1946). Joseph Luyckx, born in 1916, stands one row below between Alphonsine and Louis; his wife, Bertha (Mampaey), stands in front of him, (they received two children, Roza and Anita). Frans Louis Luyckx, born in 1917, is found standing along the back besides Gust Van Kesbeeck; his wife, Anna Catharina (Dethal) is standing partly behind Lientje, (they had one son, Roger); Frans Louis died in 1955 from tuberculosis, aged thirty-eight, less than a year after the death of his mother, Lientje. Leontine (Tin) (Luyckx), born in 1924, is seen along the back in the middle of the window; she would marry Georges Bellemans, and they had twins, Vera and Christine; Tin kept in close contact with Moemoe. Louisa Carolina Luyckx, the youngest daughter of Lientje and August, born in 1934, is the girl at the front who holds her arm around Jos; she would marry Jozef De Bruyn in 1955. Louisa, Jos, and his sister, Maria, are still alive.

Returning to the six children of Mance and Teppe that lived into adulthood, I note that Lientje was the first who died and this at the age of fifty-eight, a few days short of her fifty-ninth birthday. She died only a year after her mother. Lientje was the godmother of Emma's daughter, my mother. Ma's godfather was her grandfather Jozef, "den Teppe." As such, she received the name Carolina Josephina. Just as Lientje, her aunt and godmother, Carolina Josephina would sadly but reach the age of fifty-eight and die a few weeks short of her fifty-ninth birthday. I already

Edegem. Let me try to analyze and make explicit what this piece of information entails.

Maria Fret recalled that Isidoor Emiel and his brothers were well known among the farmers' community in Wilrijk. Indeed, Emiel's oldest brother, Frans (born 1860), living in nearby Hemiksen, was married to Joanna Maria Verbeeck, likely of farmer's stock; and his second brother, Isidoor (born 1877), was living in Wilrijk with his family (until March 26, 1920, after which they moved to Hove) and was into farming. Denise De Weerdt heard from her father as well that Emiel and his family lived on a farm in Wilrijk. Indeed, her father, Frans, and his brother, Jules, were both born in Wilrijk, presumably at home, (for the building of Saint-Augustine's Hospital was only begun in 1938). Beyond this, the various branches of the larger family De Weerdt included several farmers in the region Wilrijk and Aartselaar.

Maria Van Kesbeeck received the account that Emma went working as housekeeper at the farm of Isidoor Emiel De Weerdt. There he would have made advances towards Emma; even while his wife knew about it. This account is collaborated by the one told me by Denise De Weerdt. Denise added that as Emma became pregnant, Emiel sold the farm and left his pregnant wife and family.

Is it feasible that Emma was doing some work at this farm of De Weerdt? And how can we reconcile this with her being employed at an address in Borgerhout from end May onwards? Perhaps Petronella needed an extra pair of hands to help her out because she was pregnant. It is, of course, speculation, but it could be envisioned that Emma was taken on towards the end of March and that already in April Emiel was making advances towards her. Given that the situation would have become untenable between the two women, Emma may have left the job begin May and have looked for other work, which she would have found in Borgerhout. The relationship with Emiel would nonetheless have continued. It is well possible that she was already pregnant when she left the farm, whether she knew or not.

Emiel turned away from his family. Did they own the farm in which they lived? The accounts received from Denise De Weerdt and from Maria Van Kesbeeck would seem to suggest this. Dr. De Voogt, whom I mentioned at the beginning of this chapter, heard as well from his relatives that Isidoor Emiel had at some point "ran off" with money from an expropriation, though he does not know details about the property concerned. What is certain is that with him leaving with whatever money as was the case, the farm could not be continued. Emiel moved to Landbouwstraat 66, in Antwerpen, which is situated very nearby the house at Boomsesteenweg 360 in which the family Van Kesbeeck was living at the time, and he became a laborer. We can imagine that from then onwards Emma would have moved with a tram between her work and Emiel's place.

After Emiel left Maria Petronella and their children, his relatives were heavily scandalized by what he had done to her. I already related that Emiel had two older brothers, but he also had two sisters. While Emiel had married Maria Petronella on January 25, 1911, his two sisters married on February 15 of the same year, both on the same day. Maria Josephina (born 1879) married Dr. De Voogt—at whose family home my mother later was invited— and Carolina Hortensia (born 1886) married Jozef Mattheessens, who would become the mayor of Hove (from 1926 until 1941). After Emiel abandoned his family, Hortensia lent money to Maria Petronella so that she was able to buy a house in Edegem (Herfstlei 70). It is therefore in Edegem that Alice would be born.

forces were not able to stop the speedy advance of the German forces. On May 18, the German troops marched into Wommelgem; they also entered the center of Antwerp: it was the beginning of an occupation that would last for more than four years. It would make life more difficult. For Emma and Emiel, it would have been rather disastrous. Already in the autumn of 1940, strict regulations would have been in force for the production of milk and butter. Nearly all milk had to be transported to Antwerp for distribution and processing. Many horses were confiscated. Given these facts, no dairy round of selling door to door would have continued as it did before. Moreover, from the autumn of 1941, it was forbidden to transport or to sell any potatoes to private individuals; from then onwards this had to take place through a local centre of the National Farmers and Nutrition Coorporation. According to the town's archives, Emiel was working at the time as a farmhand; whether he had been doing this for most of the twenty years that he lived with Emma at Kandonk Laar, I cannot say for certain.

In May 1942 Moemoe leaves Emiel definitely, moving with her two children for a second time from Wommelgem to Wilrijk: this time to Boomsesteenweg 837, which was just across the road from her parents and sister. In chapter four, I gave some details about their life there in the years following.

One incident that I want to recall here of the post-war years in the life of Ma that is related to all the foregoing and that she would never forget is the following: When she was sixteen, seventeen, or eighteen, she was once walking across the Bist, the large town square in the center of Wilrijk, when she suddenly heard shouting from behind her, "Bastard! Bastard!" She turned around as did many people, and she saw two sisters of the family Verbeek who were farmers in Boechout, who were indeed shouting at her. She knew them well enough; both were older than her, and they were laughing in her face. They used the word that was shouted to her in its primary meaning of *an illegitimate child*. Carolina did not say anything but turned back around and continued crossing the square with a red face, feeling shamefully a thousand eyes on her. As she related all these years later, she would have disappeared into the ground if it had been possible.

In these post-war years, Eugène would be in relationship with his first girlfriend, Tinneke Aerts, who lived not far from them along the Boomsesteenweg. He also fulfilled his military service. Carolina found that the girl was as a sister to her; unfortunately, it was not to last. Though Eugène was made welcome in the family Aerts, he felt ill at ease among his girlfriend's several brothers; apparently, (so he told me), his preoccupation with his own irregular descent haunted him. My further consideration is that the good young lady, one of many in a simple workers' or farmers' family, certainly would not have been expected to inherit great financial means but would not have loved Eugène the less for it, nor for anything to do with his birth certificate.

In the course of 1949, Emma, Eugène, and Carolina moved two times to another address within the same area, as I detailed in chapter four.

In May 1950 Carolina married; and two years later, in May 1952, Emma and Eugène moved once more to another address along the Boomsesteenweg, to number 821, again very nearby the brickyard. The little house had become available when René and Rosa Lievens (a niece of Virginie Mariën) moved house.

Then, Eugène became engaged with Irma Verbeek who lived with her sisters at her parents' farm in Boechout; indeed, incredibly, one of the sisters whom Carolina about eight years earlier had encountered at the Bist. It makes me wonder: Did he or did he not know about that deplorable encounter—he who was so sensitive to being slighted for his birth-situation? Apart from being married to Irma, would he really, knowingly, have wanted to be in close contact for his entire married life with a sister-in-law who had derided his own sister? I don't know the answer, but I do not exclude that Carlintje told him several years earlier, when they were living under one roof, about what happened to her.

Whatever exactly was going on, Carolina and Alfons were at the wedding that took place in June 1955. Unlike the much more sober event of Carolina's wedding, several family pictures were taken. It amazes me to see these pictures with Ma quietly standing, alert and smiling, right behind the ones that had disparaged her in public. Though bodily among them, at what a different spiritual level she stood compared to them.

For some time Eugène lived with his new wife at the farm in Boechout along the Lispersesteenweg. Some time afterwards they built a spacious land house opposite the farm; and the second sister, who insulted Carolina, built an identical house neighboring it, a little further along the same road: both on land from the farm. Eugène and Irma would have one son, Herman.

I once asked Ma whether it was Irma—who became her sister-in-law and my godmother—who had derided her. She said that it was the other sister. While because he was her only brother, we would visit Eugène and Irma's house, we never came near to the house of the other sister. Carolina never felt welcome with Irma though; whereas the other sister, she considered as evil.

But a few words more about Moemoe. For a couple more times, she would change address within Wilrijk: in April 1966 she moved to Oudebaan 262; and in July 1969 to Krijgsbaan 120—both addresses were in the same neighborhood that she had been living. At this latter address, I remember visiting her regularly with my parents in our light blue, VW, Beetle car. One walked through a corridor between the old houses, for Moemoe lived along the back in two rooms at the first floor that she rented from another old woman (Mrs. Martha Colleman) who lived in the house with her brown dachshund, whom my parents called "stoofpijp" (chimney-pipe). An old-fashioned toilet was downstairs, which was accessed via an outside door at the *koer* (that is, a relatively small paved area along the back of the house). Often, Moemoe was found outside, maintaining the garden, tending the flowers. She was very generous to me; for despite her tiny pension, usually she had bought the latest comics from the local paper shop: she bought me the well-known quality series, such as *Suske en Wiske* (the adventures of two middle-class youngsters, their friend professor, their aunt Sidonia, Lambik, and Jerome), and all issues from *Robert en Bertrand* as they appeared (about two vagabonds who are minders of a child-prince and act as undercover agents yet always have to flee from the law enforcers). Her rooms always carried a smell that I cannot properly describe but that I came to associate with old people; perhaps the smell of poorly-ventilated living quarters and perhaps of the chamber pot near the bed. Ma was always a bit wary of Moemoe, for she knew well enough that her *moe* could still bang her fist on the table so that all cups jumped up. Ma needed Frans to be with her, for then Moemoe kept her peace.

Now and then we collected her for spending a day with us in Manebruggestraat. Moreover, her flat in Krijgsbaan was near the newly-built campus of the University of Antwerp, so that Sonja, Walter's girlfriend, who was studying Biochemistry there around 1973–74, would regularly visit Moemoe during lunch break.

Moemoe would live in her old flat until November 1976; what happened to her from that date onwards, I will tell more about in a later chapter. Let us presently return for a few moments to Isidoor Emiel, my biological grandfather: What did happen with him after Moemoe left him? The house at Ternesselei in Kandonk Laar, they apparently sold very much under its value, given that it was the time of German occupation. Emiel moved a few months later than her, namely, in August 1942, to Hove, where his older brother Isidoor was farming at a farm (at Lintsesteenweg 241) that he rented from Count Moretus from Boechout. Emiel went to live with his brother and family (that is, his wife Sophia Flebus and seven of their nine children; the two eldest daughters had already moved out and were living in Boechout) at the farm. Emiel registered himself in Hove at this address and helped as a farmhand. He stayed for about half a year; then, in April 1943, he moved to Zwijndrecht (Jan Van Severenstraat 31: the street was given this name during WWII by the Germans; after the war it was given the name Dorp-Oost). How long he lived there, I could not find out. Eventually, he would have lost about everything. As Denise De Weerdt heard it, twice he looked up his wife Maria Petronella; and once he arrived at his sister's (perhaps Carolina Hortensia, who had become a widow in 1952) as a total down-and-outer with only one shoe on his feet. Apparently, he died in prison in Antwerp (Begijnenstraat). The date of his death, I have not been able to find, but it is prior to 1963 because Maria Petronella's remembrance card on the occasion of her death in 1963 states that she was his widow.

# 8

# Grandparents and ancestors (2)

I N THIS CHAPTER I will explore and share some information about the family Govaerts.

In light of Walter's baptism, I already mentioned the name of Alfons's father as Joannes Constantinus Govaerts (known as "Constant") since he acted as godfather. He was born in Ranst on September 28, 1887. His parents were Petrus Gommarus Govaerts (known as "Gommair") (1861–1936; born in Lier), a farmer, and Maria Elisabeth De Ridder (1862–90; born in Ranst). Joannes Constantinus was the second child in this marriage; after him a little brother was born in 1889, namely, Franciscus Pancratius, who died two months later. After this one, Maria Ludovica was born in Broechem on May 7, 1890. A few months later, on August 5, 1890, the mother, Maria Elisabeth, died at the age of twenty-seven. The three surviving children remained under the guardianship of their father, while their uncle, the deceased mother's brother Franciscus De Ridder, a farmer in Ranst, was legally assigned as surveyant-guardian. Subsequently, on April 26, 1892, Petrus Gommarus remarried in Broechem with Joanna Catharina Van Mechelen (1858–1926; born in Herentals). In this marriage, another four children were born, all in Broechem, who all lived till a good old age. I further note that Maria Ludovica, daughter of the first marriage, died herself at a rather young age, namely two days short of her forty-third birthday, on May 5, 1933, leaving behind a husband and five children. The surveyant-guardianship was assigned to her eldest brother, Josephus Franciscus Govaerts (1885–1971; born in Ranst), who was married (to Maria Cornelia Van Mechelen) and at the time was farming in Hove.

Petrus Gommarus was the son of Petrus Joannes Govaerts (1820–90; born in Ranst) and Elisabeth Van Winkel. I have no dates for the latter, but she would have died young since Petrus Joannes remarried with Maria Theresia Van Winkel, of which union a daughter (Maria Ludovica Govaerts) was born in 1866. As such, Petrus Gommarus, as the third and youngest child of the first marriage, would have lost his mother at a very tender age, and was thus brought up by his mother's sister, who became his stepmother.

Petrus Joannes was the son of Joannes Baptista Govaerts (1783–1870; born in Ranst) and Maria Elisabetha De Vos (1784–1824; born in Boechout). There were nine children in this marriage and Petrus Joannes was the eighth. A few weeks after the ninth and youngest child was born, namely, Anna Elisabeth Govaerts on January 25, 1824, the mother, Maria Elisabetha, died (on February 18), aged thirty-nine (ten days short of her fortieth birthday). The two eldest children, Joanna Maria, born on March 5, 1807, and Anna Maria, born on October 16, 1808, were at the time of their mother's death sixteen and fifteen years old respectively, and would no doubt have helped taking care of their younger siblings. Joannes Baptista, their father, lived till the age of eighty-seven.

Joannes Baptista was the only child of Cornelius Govaerts (ca. 1749–84; born in Lier) and Joanna Maria De Raet (ca. 1745–

1829; born in Vremde). It was not the mother who died young but the father, namely, when Joannes Baptista was but a year old; and the mother remarried (with Cornelius Roelans) and lived well into her eighties.

What I note then is that the Govaerts family, which constitutes one lineage of my ancestry, was for generations established in the area east to south-east of Antwerp: stretching from Ranst to Broechem, and still further south to Lier. It is a rural area where they would have been farming for several generations. I have also noted that my great-great-grandfather, Petrus Joannes; my great-

At the wedding of my aunt Jeanne Govaerts with Josephus Gummarus Thielemans on April 15, 1950, in Ranst. Besides the groom, at the left, the bride's parents, Constant Govaerts and Maria Wouters (my grandparents) are pictured; besides the bride, at the right, the groom's mother, Anna Maria Van Deuren is pictured. Behind them, we see two brothers of the bride, namely, Jos on the right and Urbain on the left. The bride's youngest brother, Alfons (my father) and his fiancée (my mother) feature not in this picture, though they were both present. I never met any of those pictured. Some years into the marriage, Jeanne would leave her husband for a Moroccan man.

grandfather, Petrus Gommarus; and my grandfather, Joannes Constantinus, lost their mothers at a very young age.

Constantinus and his elder brother, Josephus Franciscus, lived and worked at their father's farm in Ranst, Profeetstraat 10, till their late thirties. Josephus married in 1923 and subsequently moved to Borsbeek. Constant married Maria Catharina Margaretha Wouters on June 10, 1925, in Broechem, and a few days later they moved to Kontich, where Constant got himself a job as farmhand. A few months later, namely, in November 1925, they moved to Ranst, to Profeetstraat 1, near the farm of Petrus Gommarus. More than two years before they married, they already had a child, namely, Jozef Govaerts (known as "Jos"), born in January 1923 in Antwerp; they had another three children while they lived at Profeetstraat, where they were all three born: Joanna Maria (known as "Jeanne"), born in August 1926; Urbanus Gummarus Josephus (known as "Urbain"), born in May 1928; and Alphonsus Joseph Ludovicus (known as "Alfons"), born in February 1930. Some subsequent events are, first of all, that in 1936 Constant's father, Gommair, died. In 1941, Constant and Maria bought a farm at Vaartstraat 40 (later renumbered to 48), Ranst, to which they moved. Next, as I have related in chapter three, Urbain died at the age of twenty-eight, on May 14, 1957. Then, as I have mentioned in chapter six, my grandmother Maria died on March 17, 1968. In 1972, Constant moved to a nursing home in Nijlen, where he died on February 20, 1974.

Walter, my brother, born in 1952, knew his grandparents well and regularly visited them at their farm in Ranst. As I have said, I never met them, nor Uncle Jos, nor Aunt Jeanne. The farm, which I never visited, was sold after Constant moved to the nursing home; and it has since become part of a residential neighborhood.

# 9

## My parents' reminiscences

ALREADY MUCH DETAIL has been provided of the circumstances of my mother's youth during the 1940s and, in particular, the war years. Nevertheless, more is to be said about it; even though it concerns a time-period that long predates my own life. I wish to pass on her personal experiences that she told about and that completes the picture that I have been drawing of her life, her close family, and her times. If I do not tell her story then no one will hear it. I will also try including something of the war experience of my father, but I do not know many details about it so that it is very limited what I have to say. The bulk of this chapter is about my mother's reminiscences.

It was perhaps especially during mealtimes that I heard my parents, Frans and Carolina, speak about their past. This used to come about, among others, when I did not quite finish eating my plate or when I cut away too generously from the surroundings of a slice of Gouda cheese. It would prompt the comment from Pa that if it would become war again, it would teach me. Then Ma would react that we should not call for another war, that it was terrible enough: the rationings, the bombs . . .

For our meals, we used to sit for about half the year in the long living room. At the front of the room, that is, at the street-side, a television was installed in a corner and opposite it, a settee, a matching easy chair, a coffee table, and Pa's black-leather reclining chair; in the centre of the room stood a heavy-wooden sideboard filled with china, which covered the wall, and in the middle, a matching, large dining table and six leather-upholstered wooden chairs; on the wall hung a few fairly-large paintings, which mother had received from an architect (Mr. and Mrs. Cels) whom she went cleaning for. At the garden-side of the room, next to the large dining table, there was an Ikea piece of furniture consisting of a low table on an aluminum footing, an aluminum chair with a black seat, and an L-shaped bench, which had storage space under its seating that could be lifted. It was at this Ikea-set that most family life took place; the large, good table only being used when visitors came. Near the Ikea-set, a doorway gave access to the small kitchen. It is at this small table that I listened to all that came up about their distant past; mother sitting on the chair and often moving between the table and the kitchen. The other half of the year, on summery days, we used to sit on large, wooden chairs in the veranda and eat at an old, wooden, kitchen table—sometimes, when it was really warm, the table and chairs were even put outside on the patio at the back of the house. So, these were the places that I remember the three of us—Pa, Ma, and I—having our meals. Most of the time, we sat down together at table for meals. In the morning, however, Pa did not have breakfast but drunk a cup of Roki instead and rolled a cigarette before going into the garden to feed the birds in the aviary. Roki is a drink consisting of grounded chicory that, as such, does not contain caffeine and that all of us drank most of the time with bread meals. Sitting down to eat, I picked up the following from the conversation:

To begin with, an anecdote that is to be situated at the time that Ma lived at Kandonk Laar and her parents ran a dairy round in Antwerp is about butter and Moemoe's pragmatism in dealing with her customers. Some of these customers were bourgeois women. As Ma related, those that were not very friendly or rather arrogant they tended among themselves to call "kakmadammen" (shit ladies). Most likely, these ladies received this unflattering designation for the fact that they pulled up their nose and made a long face when they had to deal with the "peasantry," as if they smelled the stable and the dung. Despite that some of these were difficult customers, they did not wish to lose them. Now it happened that at least one of these customers, when handed a packet of butter, opened it and took some of the butter with the upper side of the fingernail so as to taste it. One day, having tasted the butter, the madam reproached Emma for having mixed in some margarine. In response, Moemoe firmly denied that her butter was in any way adulterated: she only sold the purest products. Nevertheless, the madam insisted on her opinion and adjoined that if Emma could not offer her better and purer butter, she would no longer buy from her. In her consternation, Moemoe spoke with her daughter about what was to be done, for it was to them an important customer. She knew that if she would offer the same kind of butter a couple of days later, she would undoubtedly lose this customer. What was to be done? A few days later, before setting out on their regular round, Carolina saw that her moe was putting a good deal of margarine in the butter that she was going to offer this same customer. Moemoe explained that she had to do something; it was all or nothing. Next, during the dairy round, they offered the madam the butter. Having handed it over, the packet went open and madam took from it; she tasted and said,

"Now you are selling me pure butter alright; this is beautiful butter!"

Another story that is probably to be situated at the same time period is about Moemoe's handbag. In a previous chapter, namely chapter four, I made clear that Carolina did not have much free time in these childhood years of hers. She did though have friends, both boys and girls, with whom she played outside. But even during this rare free time, her moe had a task for her: looking after the brown *net* (handbag). This brown net was a large, leather handbag with two handles such as women at the time used to carry with them. My own generation would see it as something that is part of the stereotype of an old woman. I have still seen Moemoe with this brown handbag or its successor. It would have contained a large purse, a hairnet, a spectacle case, and so on. Moreover, it had on the inside a solid, removable base; under this, Emma used to hide several banknotes: all the money she possessed. She, therefore, did not wish to leave her handbag at home unattended. But when she went to work at the field of one or other nearby farm, it was obviously not possible to take this bag along. Upon leaving the house, she entrusted it to Carlintje, even when she was playing outside with her friends; and she enjoined her to look carefully after it. How was it possible, though, for the child to be running around or throw a ball with the brown net of her moe in hand? Ma explained that as a solution she then hung the handbag at the entrance gate of the yard in front of the house. As it occurred, she would soon forget all about the bag. It thus happened that Emma came home finding her handbag with all her capital hanging at the gate, while her little daughter was playing elsewhere. I can very well envisage that in her frustration it let escape from her half-shut lips, "verdoeme he!" (damned heh!). Such then was "de Moemoe."

One most unpleasant story appears again to refer to her child-hood at Kandonk Laar. At the time, toilets tended not to be in nice bathrooms but in a small place usually at the back of the house at a yard (*de koer*). The toilet itself was a plank with a hole in it right above the cesspit, which was covered by wooden flooring. No white bleached toilet paper was used but old newspapers would be at hand. Carlintje, dressed in her school outfit, went to the toilet and, horror upon horror, the old planks happened to give way. She fell into the cesspit and was sinking away in the mire. Desperately she cried out for help; fortunately, one of the men—I do not remember for sure whether she ever specified who it was—was at work nearby, who ran to her help and managed to pull her out. It was a horrible experience of which she was lucky to get unscathed away. Without help she would most probably have drowned.

Since I am giving a more or less chronological overview of my parents' memories that they talked about, I should turn at this point to some memories of Pa. Born in 1914, he would have been recalled for military service when the German invasion of Belgium loomed, that is, from a date between September 1939 and May 1940 onwards. The invasion took place on May 10, 1940. At the time, Frans would have been married to Joanna. He would have been participant at the Belgian Campaign, which lasted only eighteen days; on May 28, the Belgian army capitulated. The Belgian army was part of a coalition of forces consisting of the Dutch, Belgian, and French armies, and the British Expedition Corps. I do not know whether Frans was part of a combat unit or provided logistic support. I have never heard him talk about the various places he was positioned in those days. It is likely, how-ever, that Frans would have been part of a division that was initially to defend positions formed by various canals in the northeast of Belgium close to the Dutch border. On May 10 the German troops managed to cross the river Meuse and thus were able to attack the Belgian positions at various places. The Belgians managed to blow up various bridges and to pull back towards the Albert Canal. Yet they were totally surprised by the German employment of parachutists. On the tenth, the Fort of Eben-Emael, along the Albert Canal, ten kilometer south of Maastricht (at the time, the largest fort in the world and considered unconquerable) was taken by surprise by about eighty German paratroopers landing on the fort with nearly-silent gliders. Next, the Belgians had to pull back to another defense position. On May 13 and 14, aided by dive-bombers, German armored divisions were able to cross the Meuse near Sedan and Montherme in France and at Dinant in South-Belgium, so that the way to the coastal regions and the north lay open for them. In the meantime, the Luftwaffe bombarded Rotterdam; the next day, May 15, under threat of further bombardments, the Dutch army capitulated. Eventually, the Belgians ended up being closed in on a small stretch of land near the coast, where they managed to withstand the Germans till the British Expedition Forces had been able to go aboard ship at Dunkirk and return to England. On May 28, the Belgian King Leopold III capitulated. A large part of the Belgian army, Pa included, would have been taken prisoner-of-war and transported to Germany.

At some point, perhaps already in the early days of their being recalled for military service, Pa seemed to have teamed up with Maurice Dillen, a small fellow from the region of Antwerp. I remember him telling that they were put on a train destined for Germany but that both he and Maurice managed to escape from the train. Stealthily, walking by night, they made their way back to the north. Frans did not return to his wife but to his relatives in

Arendonk, near the Dutch border. He lived in hiding, moving between a few addresses. (At the time, Moemoe's youngest brother, Uncle Gust, was in hiding behind the hay at the farm of the family Fret in Wilrijk, since young men were being round up and sent to work in Germany, while his wife Jeanne and their two-year old daughter José stayed with her parents and Jeanne's two sisters and their children at a farm away from the city; she did not know where Gust was until he presented himself to her after the war; she hardly recognized him.) One of Frans's older sisters ran a bakery, and he helped at night with the baking. He never talked very much about the entire period; and so, I do not know what contact he was able to maintain during this period with his wife Joanna. I do not know, moreover, how long he had to hide. Of the 600,000 Belgian soldiers, about 225,000 were taken to prisoner-of-war camps in Germany; most of the Flemish soldiers were set free after a few months. Does this mean that Frans would have felt safe to come out of hiding after this period of a few months? He probably did; he would have gone home and would have resumed his work as policeman. I assume that this gave him also a reasonable chance of not being claimed for obligatory employment in a German factory. On November 21, 1943, Joanna gave birth to their first child, Gerard.

Returning to Ma in roughly that same period: She often re-called that one summer Emma ordered her to keep watch in a field by a single cow for the entire summer holiday. As such, she spent much time alone in a hut at the back of a meadow. She said that she often cried there and felt abandoned. As far as I recall, Ma did not provide details about the when and where of her experiences—and if she did, it would have meant little to me at the time—but in ordering her stories, a fairly detailed picture emerges. It is certain that her lonesome stay in the meadow took place after their move to Wilrijk in May 1942 and in the period while she was still a schoolgirl; hence, in the summer of 1942, 1943, or 1944.

As Ma explained, at times, the illustrious cow decided that she had seen enough of the meadow and ran away. When the cow had made up her mind, nothing could be done by a girl. In Ma's words, "Wanneer ze hare steert ophief, kont ge er in loeren en haar achterna lopen; er was geen stoppen aan." ("When she lifted her tail, you could look into it and run after her; it was of no avail trying to stop the beast.") Furthermore, as Ma remarked, once on the run, a cow can develop a good speed. Eventually, the cow and a girl crying out behind her, sometimes accompanied by more children, would be spotted by the adults. The beast would be captured and returned to its meadow until, a few days later, the cow repeated the escapade and the same scene occurred.

Whilst feeling abandoned, Carlintje found much solace in the occasional visits of Madame van Dijck, who went round with booklets for the promotion of devotion to Saint Rita. Both Maria Fret and Carlintje bought every month the latest booklet; and among themselves, they called the lady (that is, Madame Van Dijck) "de Heilige Rita" (Saint Rita). The lady apparently had some time to talk with Carlintje. All these years later, while we were having our meals at the Ikea table, Ma said that the attentiveness shown by this lady saved her. I have in my mind the vague recollection that she spoke of a schoolmaster who talked with her and who saved her; but later conversations with Maria Fret corrected what I thought to have heard and showed that it was this lady that she was talking about. Perhaps that my semblance of a recollection was not entirely wrong though; perhaps the lady was indeed a retired teacher. As regards the veneration of Saint Rita: I related in chapter four that a new church was dedicated to Saint Rita in Kontich in 1937, to which the two friends would cycle after they received a bicycle (around 1946). The salutary visits of Madame Van Dijck must have continued for a good while, for she gave Carlintje a beautiful, small book entitled *Dit is een Tuiltje Rozen* (This is a Bouquet of Roses), in which she wrote "Hartelijk aandenken – 8 mei 1947 – Mad. C. Van Dijck," ("Warm remembrance – 8 May 1947 – Madame C. Van Dijck"). This book by Pater Aloisius Op 't Eynde of the Order of Eremites of Saint Augustine was brought out by the Augustinians of the Saint-Rita Church at Kontich in 1946. Its 460 pages provide an account of the life and spiritual journey of Saint Rita and a large collection of prayers and instructions. It presents itself as a complete guide for the spiritual life. Together with her missal, it would have been most valuable to Carlintje.

Moreover, some children that lived nearby regularly came to keep her accompany in the meadow. These would have included

Roza Torfs and Carlintje in 1944. Possibly, Maria Fret was taking the picture.

her close friend Maria Fret, and Roza Torfs with her two smaller siblings. As such then, God did not abandon his child in her rather involuntary retreat.

It appears to have been not always holiness that occupied them; playfulness appears to have had its turn too. One evening, Carlintje and Maria Fret squatted down in the middle of the Boomsesteenweg, lifted their skirts, and made it stream in a gully run from the middle to the side of the road; and they had a good laugh at it. Imagine! This was not a little road: the Boomsesteenweg is a major road leading straight into Antwerp from the south; at present, it is a major A-road busy with traffic. One other thing these naughty friends were up to was that on Friday evening they stood among the young folk that were some-what older than them and that were waiting to catch the tram that ran along the Boomsesteenweg for going out to the city. Some of the young men were dressed up in their Sunday-best so as to meet their girlfriends, and they were busy combing their hair. When the carriage arrived and the young men were getting on, the two girls would suddenly, violently rustle their hands through the gelled and carefully combed hair and then run away while swearwords followed them. What stories I heard while eating my food with my two elderly parents.

A war was going on all around them; Ma recalled that in the meadows behind them a few airplanes came down. This may well be situated at the time of the American bombardments upon various German targets in April and September 1943, or during the bombardments from March 1944 onwards in preparation of the Normandy landings on June 6, 1944 (D-Day), so as to disrupt German transport possibilities. Carlintje saw a crashed-down airplane in flames with the pilot, still recognizable, burning inside it. On another occasion, a plane had crashed down and when she and some neighbors ran towards it, they saw various body parts on the ground round about. I have unfortunately no information on the airplanes involved; if Ma mentioned it, I cannot remember it. The only information I have is that one American bomber was shot down above Wilrijk by German fighter planes during the April 5, 1943, air raid aimed at the Erla factory in Mortsel.

Once, when Carlintje went from the house into the garden behind the house towards the wooden huts or barns at the end of it, airplanes were flying over, relatively high in the sky. Just before she went round the corner of these wooden outbuildings, she heard a man who was standing there, smoking, and murmuring to himself, "There are the bastards." Carlintje had, however, identified the airplanes as those of allied forces, either American or British. She stopped in her tracks; the man had not heard her coming. Carlintje had recognized the voice of the man; she knew who it was; it was a man who was considered a member of the resistance movement, the White Brigade. She now found that the man was a collaborator, a Black one, a spy. Quietly, she withdrew her steps. She immediately went to inform some members of the White Brigade with whom she was acquainted about what she had heard. They listened and told her that they would take care of it, and she never saw the man again. Ma seemed certain in her opinion about the man. Looking at a distance at it without having more facts, I would not find entirely implausible that it could have been a momentarily expression of frustration if it was shortly after the disastrous bombardments at Mortsel. That said, assumedly, mother was right and the White Brigade dealt rightly with it.

Though she was but an innocent schoolgirl, Carlintje must have been noted by the men of the White Brigade; perhaps the fact that she was not always surrounded by parents or siblings would have created a space in which they could approach her. They entrusted her with a shopping bag full of vegetables in which, however, they hid a brown envelope. They asked her to take the tram into Antwerp and go to a certain street. If anyone asked something, she had to tell that she was delivering vegetables to her aunt in the city. But she was informed that if she went to the given address, a man would approach her and take the handbag with its envelope from her. She did this a number of times. One day, she had gotten from the tram in Antwerp and was walking to the designated address, when a patrol of two SS soldiers who were checking various passersby stopped her at a street corner. Seeing that they had in front of them a rather tense, adolescent girl, they took on a somewhat lighthearted mood with her; she had to hand them the bag and they asked her where she was going. She said she was visiting her aunt. They looked into the bag which had the vegetables at the top and quickly rumbled through it. Carlintje kept quiet. They returned her bag and she was allowed to walk on. With heart thumping, she continued on her missive. They had not found the envelope.

I asked Maria Fret, whether she had any recollection of her friend being a message girl for the White Brigade, but she did not. It seems then that it was something Carolina shared not even with her closest friends.

Another story of hers, which she told several times at table, I have been pondering upon as how to interpret it. Once, when she was in a nearby field with some of her young friends, undoubtedly including the three children of the family Torfs, a German fighter jet swooped down and started shooting at them. A few of the children jumped in a ditch and Ma jumped in an old, metal water-butt. She said it was like hell when several of the bullets impacted on the metal butt and made a terrific noise. But why would a fighter jet attack a few children in a meadow? How to make sense of it? When I recently related the event to Maria Fret and Louisa Luyckx, who both lived nearby at the time, they were not surprised by it and informed me that the Germans, in the days prior to the liberation, that is, when they realized they had to give up the occupation, could be very spiteful, indeed, even to the extent of attacking a few playing children with a fighter jet. It is, therefore, most likely that her vivid memory of the event is to be situated in this period.

My mother's next story that chronologically follows upon it is about the evacuation of Fort 7 of Wilrijk by its German occupants at the time of the liberation at the beginning of September 1944. She did not provide details of names; yet central to this episode is the German officer, Major Wilhelm Metzger (1894–1969). Most of what follows here, I found in a thematic booklet entitled *Wilhelm Metzger: Een Reddende Vriendschap in Oorlogstijd; Wilrijk 1940–1944* (Wilhelm Metzger: A Saving Friendship in Time of War; Wilrijk 1940–44) presented by Wilrica, the local-history group of Wilrijk, on September 5, 2009, that is, sixty-five years after the liberation of Wilrijk.

During the occupation of 1940–44, Metzger was installed as commander of the fort with the task of managing it as a munitions depot for the German Luftwaffe. The major was a deeply-Christian man and a convinced anti-Nazi. He had survived several battles of the First World War, including the battlefield at Verdun in 1916—known as the hell of Verdun— at which over 700,000 young men were killed. After his experiences at the battlefield, he chose to become a school teacher; and in 1936 he became principal of the primary school in the place where he lived with his wife and son. In August 1939 Metzger, then reservist-lieutenant, was recalled for military service. He would become known as

Wilrijk's hero. What happened then in Wilrijk? When they entered Belgium, the Germans brought the various Brialmont forts (eight forts built around Antwerp in 1859 and following years) back into use. So as to make Fort 7 suited for its new purpose as ammunition depot, the Germans recruited Belgian workers. Several rooms in the fort and fourteen new, concrete bunkers that were being built within the fort were used for storing hundreds of tons of anti-aircraft ammunition and airplane bombs. As officer in charge, Wilhelm Metzger did what he could to help the local population. He increased the number of workers in the fort to nearly two hundred so that they could stay with their families instead of being called up by the Gestapo to work in German factories. Several times Metzger sent false reports to the *Werbestelle* (Employment department) to state that all these workers could not be missed by him. In the meantime, Metzger integrated himself in the local community and regularly visited the local church, Saint Jan Vianney. He became good friends with the parish priest, Jozef Pauwels. Metzger had his office in a wooden building behind the church. Pauwels became his confidant and with his help he helped wherever he could. He told Pauwels that he is pretty certain that his friendly relations with the local population are being spied upon and reported to the German authorities by some of his men who are active members of the Nazi-party. Nevertheless, in 1942, because of his irreproachable management, Metzger is promoted from *Hauptmann* to major. Among themselves, his superiors only reproach him his all too Catholic inclinations.

During his stay in Wilrijk, the major was assigned as living quarters an empty house that belonged to a Jewish family who had fled the Nazis. Unexpectedly, this family returns. Metzger, presented with the problem, sent for a German army-truck in which he hid the family. He helped them escape to France, from where they managed to get to Spain and later to England. Years later this family would testify at his denazification process.

When the allied forces made more and more advances, it was clear that the German domination would not last much longer. End August 1944, instead of simply withdrawing themselves, the German leadership ordered Metzger to make preparations for blowing up the fort. By then the major had decided that he would

The main entrance gate to Fort 7 as I found it during my visit in 2010

not obey the order. The explosion would cause colossal damage to the village and many casualties among its population. He did not wish to cause unnecessary bloodshed. The major gave his men orders to stack as much ammunition as possible by the side of the fortress's moat. Begin September, with the help of the Belgian workers, they threw thousands of kilograms of bombs in the water. Meanwhile, his German superiors had gotten suspicious and sent another major from Brussels to investigate the matter. Metzger was informed of his coming; he ordered the

Belgian workers that they were not to throw ammunition in the water "when the fat major from Brussels passes by." At his arrival, Metzger orders one of his under officers to carry the fat major off in a sidecar. Neither of them was ever seen again. On Sunday morning September 3, at 10.30 a.m., he gave the actual order to throw everything in the water. The amount of ammunition was so colossal that Metzger realized that he needed more men. Via the local police and the council of Antwerp, he asked the local population to get involved. Several bombs weighed over half a ton, which were stored in wooden boxes of two and a half meters long, so that they required several men to move them. Upon Metzger's proposal, the Antwerp alderman Albert Vallaeys commissioned the Chief of Police in Wilrijk to get together as many volunteers of the local population as possible to throw the hundreds of tons of explosives in the moat. It was not an easy task for the Chief Constable to get sufficient men because many had been claimed by the German occupiers. During the night, police were cycling along the neighboring streets ringing bells and asking urgently for all able-bodied men to go and help at the fort. All other inhabitants were asked to immediately leave their houses, for there was a real risk that in moving the bombs an explosion could involuntarily happen. At the central ground of the fort large flames were burning throughout the night, since the gunpowder was being taken out of the bombs and being lighted before throwing the bombs in the moat. Hundreds of people were working against the clock. Emma, Eugène, and Carolina were not living right beside the fort but close enough. Where were they at the time? My inclusion of this entire story has been prompted by my mother's mention that during the night they were woken up and that they helped with throwing all ammunition in the moat. Yet I do not recall her mentioning details about their own whereabouts. Eugène was coming up to his eighteenth birthday, so that I suspect that he would have helped in the works at the fort. Emma, then forty-seven, was used to heavy work among men. Would she perhaps have helped with the many boxes of ammunition? What about Ma? I asked her friend Maria Fret whether she had herself helped at the fort; and she said that she did not. Possibly, Carlintje stayed with her mother, Emma, wherever she was; possibly, either or both of them would have grouped in- or outside with their neighbors. For example, in the same little row of houses that Ma lived, along the other side of the pub De Groene Jager, lived the family Torfs, that is, Stinne, and her three children with whom Carlintje was friends. In any case, I do not think they left the area for a place at a safer distance from the fort.

Works in the fort went on till Monday morning 4 September, until the British were already passing by along the Boomsesteenweg. Much sooner than expected, the liberating forces, coming that day from Aalst via the Fort of Breendonk, had been able to cross the river Rupel where the Germans lay in ambush—Robert Vekemans, a military engineer who had been set free as a prisoner of war so that he would help rebuild the Belgian road- and bridges, had managed to stop the approaching tanks just in time, warning them that the main bridge at Boom was undermined, and he guided the column of tanks via an alternative route along an older bridge at Willebroek that was unguarded so that they totally surprised the Germans, coming from behind their positions—and had progressed along Antwerpsestraat and the Boomsesteenweg in the direction of Antwerp. Before midday, at around 11.30 a.m., a column of Sherman tanks of the 3rd Royal Tank Regiment drove at high speed through Wilrijk; their purpose was taking control of the harbor of Antwerp; and here also, Vekemans was instrumental for guiding them and taking the harbor intact. Later in the day, British troops in Sherman tanks and in lighter vehicles of the type Bren Gun Carrier returned from the direction of Antwerp and, aided by local resistance fighters, cleared Wilrijk of armed German opposition. When the liberating forces drove through Wilrijk, many of the local population came outside and lined the pavements. Some of the German soldiers that were fleeing still fired at the population, and a few were killed.

At 11.30 a.m. that day, when he had received a message by field telephone that the British tanks were not far off, Major Metzger and his driver stepped in his car and left the fort. Nearby Café De Valck, situated along the Boomsesteenweg, Metzger gave himself over to the British. Eventually, he would be brought to an American prisoners-of-war camp in France. After the liberation, the former workers at the fort wrote immediately a letter requesting the major's privileged treatment and eventual release. After the war, Pastoor Pauwels and interim-mayor Frans Van Dun travelled to Germany to testify at the de-nazification process. Metzger is officially denazified on June 20, 1947. Again, more than a year later, and after several further interventions of his friend Pauwels, he is allowed to resume his task as principal of the primary school.

Returning to my mother and family; as appeared from the foregoing, the allied, liberating forces were passing by their house. Another story that stems from the days following liberation was told me by Uncle Eugène. He related that he was working in a field not far from their house, and that Carolina also was in the field at some distance from him. As he looked up, he saw that a jeep with black American soldiers in it turned from the road into the field. They had spotted Carolina—probably not Eugène—and were looking for some entertainment. As soon as her brother

Memorial erected sixty-five years after the liberation of Wilrijk. It is located opposite the main entrance of the fort. The engraved text of the memorial reads, in translation: "On 4 September 1944, Wilrijk was liberated by a section of the British Regiment RA–107 HAA–BLA (Royal Artillery–107 Heavy Anti-Aircraft–British Liberation Army) under command of Colonel Frederic Slater, aided by the Resistance in Wilrijk ~ a bold action of the German major Wilhelm Metzger, commander of the munitions depot put up within Fort 7, preserved Wilrijk of a terrible disaster – Wilrijk, 5 September 2009."

noticed what was happening, he ran towards her and placed himself in front of her with his hayfork at the ready. Whether in Flemish or English, I do not know, he advised them friendly but firmly that they better leave his sister alone and continue on their journey. In good humor, they took his advice and left them alone.

It was as yet not the end of the war. For the next half year the Belgian, British, and French towns were bombarded by the V1- and V2-Bombs. The great majority of these were sent to Antwerp and London. Ma related that she regularly saw these bombs approaching. The engine of the V1 was clearly audible—it is known as the Buzz Bomb—and so it could be heard approaching. When the engine went silent, one knew it had reached its destination and was going to fall. The V2 was silent and could not be heard approaching. Anxiously, therefore, people would be scanning the sky, so as to know whether any of these was approaching.

Carolina around 1946/47/48, standing upon the Boomse-steenweg near the little row of houses where she lived (known as *Het Geleeg*). In June 1949 she moved with Moemoe and with Eugène to Neerland 15, a little further along in a side street with a dead end.

These then are the war-memories of my parents that were often brought up, that I have tried to place in their context for a better appreciation of them, and that complement and complete my picturing of these years in their lives. During our mealtimes, my mother sometimes spoke about other events of later years, and I like to include a few of them here as well; some have already been given in the previous chapters.

One day during these post-war years, she went with a friend to a fortune-teller. The woman told Carolina that a man wearing a jacket with shining buttons (that is, a uniform) will one day enter into her life; furthermore, she will win a large prize. We all agreed that the man with the shining buttons was Frans. Ma told that one day, when the divorce with Alfons was in process, the doorbell went and Frans stood in front of her in full uniform. Ma took a fright; because although she recognized him from across the road, she had never felt at ease in the presence of those wearing uniforms: perhaps it was a relic from the war years. Frans noticed that when she opened the door, she took a fright; but he tried put her at ease. I think he came to inform her that he was aware of her difficult situation and that if he could be of any help she should not hesitate to contact him. So, Frans was the man in uniform. But as regards the large prize, opinions varied. Ma kept buying lottery tickets but never won anything more than the cost prize of a new ticket. She kept trying, assured that one day she would win. Pa said that she had already won the big prize: that it was him. They never came to an agreement about it. Well, she never won that large sum of money; he must have been right.

Sometime after that visit to the fortune-teller, she was suffering from problems with her throat, which she found to be swollen. Several visits to the general practitioner did not result in a satisfactory diagnosis. She then read in a paper that there was a re-

*Geachte heer,*

*Zoo u de goedheid zouden hebben, eenige aanduidingen te geven, voor een onderzoek dezer persoon.*

*Van Kesbeeck Carolina Neerland 15 Wilrijk*

Carolina's request to the healer

nowned medium/healer in Mechlin (*Flem.* Mechelen; *Fr.* Malines), who had many years experience. Wanting to be helped, she wrote to him: "Dear Sir, would you be so kind to please give some indication for an investigation of this person." Signed: "Van Kesbeeck Carolina – Neerland 15, Wilrijk" She enclosed a passport picture. The healer wrote his reply on the back of her small piece of paper and returned it to her: "Mechlin, February 4, 1950. Dear Miss, You suffer from irregular working of the glands, in particular, the thyroid gland. Some advice: If you agree with this finding and you wish the treatment, please ask for bottles 6 and 106, enclosing the sum of 100 Belgian francs for expenses. The packet will then be sent with the postage paid. Yours faithfully . . ." In receipt of this reply, Carolina made again an appointment with her family doctor and asked him whether her complaint could be caused by the thyroid gland. The doctor found this was indeed the case. He then pressed her to tell how she found this out. Did she contact a healer? She confessed, and her doctor

The healer's reply

confirmed that the man was right. He proposed to her that she would try to get healing with the medication he could prescribe her. She agreed, and found betterment without having to acquire the healer's proposed substances. I find this story interesting because it showed me that people with paranormal gifts are indeed around. I note also that her complaint may well have been stress related; it was probably around the time that her brother smashed her little cupboard to pieces, a few months before her wedding to Alfons.

At this point, moving on from the 1940s, I wish to return to the reminiscences of Pa. These were more often about his time policing. Throughout his career, he had been a much-appreciated policeman. The locals of his beat knew him and he knew them. At times, he had been called to intervene between man and wife, when the man had been drinking and after coming home had been aggressive towards his wife. Frans was the right man to try calm things down and give an admonition, or perform an arrest if needed.

One of his more memorable interventions took place at the house of a retired circus-man. Neighbors had complained at the police station that a man had come to live at an address in Frans's beat who kept a lion, which had been seen outside the house. Frans was sent to the scene. He often told us this story at table. Though he was not fainthearted, on that occasion, Frans was rather apprehensive about what he would encounter on this call-out. He parked his bicycle at the front of the house and called out. No reaction. He walked up to the house and rang the bell. He kept looking well around him as he stood waiting. No reaction. And then the lion appeared, walking around the corner of the house and towards him. Frans drew his pistol. He aimed at the beast with shaking hand. He wanted to shoot, but he recalled the advice given by his old superior. The advice was, "Turn your tongue ten times around in your mouth before you use your weapon." The advice may seem laughable, and nowadays armed policemen are trained that sometimes they have to act at an instant's notice. But Frans followed the advice given him: duly, while the lion approached him, he quickly started turning his tongue and counted. He was at eight, ready to shoot. Then, a voice coming from along the side of the house called the lion back and assured Frans that there was no danger. A conversation would have followed, in which Frans listened to the man's story and had to tell him that another solution had to be found. He told other stories of his experiences over the many years as a policeman.

Before leaving this chapter, I wish to mention a trip about which Carolina told a number of times. It is about a trip to Marche-les-Dames in South-Belgium that she made with some-one. She never wanted to say whom she made this trip with and neither did she specify when exactly it took place. Nonetheless, it is worth mentioning it, since she obviously never forgot about it. Marche-les-Dames is a beautiful place situated at about ten kilometres from Namur along the Meuse. There is a twelfth century abbey, Notre-Dame du Vivier, and it contains some spectacular rock cliffs overlooking the river. It is famous for being the site where the former King Albert lost his life on February 17, 1934, during rock climbing. There has been some speculation whether he fell accidentally, or whether he was murdered there. During their visit, Carolina and the person with her stood on top of the rocks there. She spoke of being threatened, as the person said to her: "Who would know that I pushed you? It could easily be interpreted as an accidental slip. No one would ever know." Perhaps the speaker was having in mind the circumstances in which the former king died, though Carolina was adamant that it was not said in jest. She spoke of a coldness being thrown on her and of her feeling of being trapped in a very vulnerable position. After this incident she never trusted anyone near her at a height, and she said that she would never trust anyone anymore to be alone with in such a vulnerable situation.

Let me include a final anecdote on a lighter note. Once, when we were at table for lunch, Ma said that she had just gotten herself almost in serious trouble with one of the garbage collectors. Our dustbin at the time was a grey metal bin with a lid and a handle. It was probably around early 1980s, not long before the transition to black, plastic rubbish bags and not long before the wretched, wasteful, plastic era started. Household rubbish was often wrapped in a piece of old newspaper and put in the bin. Now some of the garbage collectors, when emptying the bin, had the habit to give it an extra bang at the back of the lorry, so as to ensure the bin was empty. The result was, however, that the metal bin got pretty dented. One of these men that had this mannerism with our bin had rather long, blondish hair sticking out to all sides. Mother had been watching the approaching bin lorry from the window. Sure enough, the fellow took the bin, emptied it out, and gave it an extra bang. In pure frustration, Ma jumped outside and yelled at him, "You, ugly ape! I see you doing this every week!" As Ma related, the man came up to her and said, "What did you say there!" She backed somewhat down with the fellow in front of her, and she explained to him that he was damaging the bin. Well, at least, he knew it now.

# 10

## School, sport, and life among family (1)

THE FAMILY I lived with during my early childhood consisted of Ma (Carolina), Pa (Frans), and my brother (Walter), who was fourteen years older than me. Having given a lot of background to my family in the foregoing chapters, let me in the here following chapters speak more about our life lived together in Manebruggestraat.

As a young child, I often followed behind Walter. Once during the summer, an event took place in the domain of Tyrolerhof: what event exactly it was, I cannot remember; it involved various stalls for fundraising. As we were leaving, Walter walked fast ahead to the car, an old, second-hand, light-blue, VW Beetle, which was parked not on the large parking space of the domain, as it was full-up because of the many visitors, but in a street nearby. As usual, when I saw Walter in front of us, I ran towards him; also, I was glad we were going home after all the business and fuss. In the process, I sprinted across the street adjacent to the domain. Ma yelled; and behold a car was very near me. I stopped in my tracks in the middle of the street and stood right in front of the car's bonnet; the driver had managed to screech to a halt. Accidents often happen when people are caught off-guard, when we are a little tired or relaxed. My guardian angel, however, must have kept on guard and made sure that the driver did too, and I was unharmed. Walter got a reproach from Ma; she told him that he should have known that I would run behind him.

Fortunately, at that time, life for a child was still relatively simple. I played with wooden blocks, with Lego blocks, with cars, and with an old, wooden castle with knights that had belonged to Walter. I played alone or, as was often the case, Walter played with me.

At home, we had a large, wooden-framed radio on a high shelf. I vaguely remember that my parents bought their first television not long afterwards during my early childhood.

I have mentioned in an earlier chapter about the wedding of Frans and Carolina, which took place on July 20, 1971. At the time, Frans still worked as a policeman on the beat. He did his patrols on the bicycle. Not so long afterwards, however, in 1972, when I was six, Frans had an embolism (that is, an obstruction of a vein or artery by a clot of blood) in his eye, while he was cycling. The symptom of such retinal artery occlusion (RAO), or ocular stroke, is loss of vision. The damage to his eye proved to be permanent. Though, eventually, he was not totally blind in that eye, it only gave him a very narrow beam of vision through it. Besides the concern of his diminished vision, from that time onwards, issues with his heart were also investigated, and he had to take medication for this. He was some time on sick leave and then tried to resume his policing duties. It did not work out; a few times he nearly collided with a car when cycling. After he was requested to undergo medical investigation, physicians of the Administrative Health Service gave the advice that he was more than 66 percent permanently unfit for work from August 1972 onwards.

So as to have something to do and earn some extra money, he found a job as security guard at an old car dump. I remember that Ma and I looked him up there on a Sunday. It was not a good job. Often he was sitting totally isolated in the little office by the barrier. He was, in fact, very vulnerable there, on a deserted site. We saw that a car full of men drove up to the barrier and wanted access without having any official permission to do so. They wanted him to take a banknote, which he, the man of the law, would of course not know about. They turned around, swearing at him. Sometimes, being denied access, they threatened him. He was left at his post unarmed, and he realized himself that the conditions of this job were not good. Why put his life at risk for a job where the owners did not take precautions for his safety and would not have cared much about him? He left the job and did not look for another one. After about a year being on sick leave, he took early retirement from the police force.

From then onwards, he often sat beside the front window, looking aimlessly at the movements in the street. When she was not doing housework, Ma often sat knitting on a chair opposite him by the window.

In earlier years (and I mean here as a married woman), Ma did a few part-time cleaning jobs at private addresses—hence my early memory of being taking along to one of these places—until about 1970. She worked, among others, in the villa of an architect, namely, for Mr. and Mr. Cels. They thought that "Carolina" was too long a name for their cleaner, and so she proposed to be called "Lily," by which name she became henceforth known in Borsbeek. I once asked her about her change of name, and she said that *Lily* suited her; that in fact she had always disliked *Carolina* and the diminutive *Carlintje*, because that is how she was called at home: it reminded her too much of her unhappy upbringing.

A few years onwards, when she had become married to Frans, she applied for a job in the Grand Bazaar supermarket that had opened one or two years before, right across from Tyrolerhof. Since she did not hear from them whether she had been successful in her application, she enquired after a month or so what had happened with her candidature. The management informed her that they had actually sent her a letter soon after she had put in her application and that they had wanted to take her on but that she never replied to the offer. It appeared that since she applied under her married name of Mrs. Peeters, the letter had been delivered to Frans's house across the street, at Manebruggestraat 285, instead of at number 290. Because Frans lived in our house, my parents were letting his own house out; and at the time, a French couple was occupying it. It transpired that when the letter of the supermarket offering the job to Carolina, or Lily, was delivered, the tenants did not hand it to her. The culprit seemed to have been the woman who knew that Ma was awaiting a reply from the supermarket and, apparently being jealous, had opened and destroyed it. Ma was rather devastated that the job, which she had really wanted, had been denied her in this manner. As for the couple: in fact, not long afterwards, they broke up, so that first the woman and then some months later her husband left the house.

Some time afterwards, someone advised her that when Frans would die, his pension would be discontinued. Given that he was a good deal older than her, she decided it best to look again for employment. In case she would come to be on her own, she would then not be left without financial means in her old age. She chose to register for a one- or two-year course that would allow her to be employed to provide homecare, especially to old-age pensioners. She attended all lessons, which were mainly attended by younger women; and after putting much work into it, she succeeded in her exams. To obtain her diploma, she was still to pass through a set period of apprenticeship. At this point, however, Pa put a stop to it. She was going to be much out of the house, and he did not like it. He wanted his wife to be around. He went with her to speak to the course directors: in tears, she explained to them that he did not want her to continue. They subsequently went to enquire what effectively would happen financially if he would die. It appeared that she would continue to receive his pension. Nevertheless, for a long time, she was sorry that she could not pursue this call to work as a caregiver.

So as to have sufficient interaction with people, Carolina became a member of KAV, that is, the organization of the *Katholieke Arbeidersvrouwen* (Catholic Workers' Women). Every fortnight or so, a meeting took place in the parish, and a monthly journal was produced at the national level of the organization. Ma took on responsibility to deliver about twenty of these magazines to local members living in the neighborhood (thus covering a few streets of the parish's territory); in total the organization had over two hundred members in our parish. After a couple of years, she became a member of the local steering committee. Her role was to help organize evening events, which took place every two months or thereabouts: sometimes a speaker came to give a conference; sometimes it was a cooking demonstration. The KAV also got an instructor for gymnastic sessions. Ma joined it; but after some sessions, several women found that it was above their level. Besides this, daytrips were organized by the one responsible for outings, which Ma tended to participate in.

religious education. Unlike Walter, I always followed the two hours religion (as did about one third of pupils in my class), even though I do not remember very much about it. It is a pity, but I certainly never saw a Bible throughout my primary education. I think we only went once into the nearby church, just for an instant, because some were doing their First Communion through school. It was, all together, very much a humanistic education that I received in school. Throughout the years of my schooling, I did not read any religious text or learn a religious song. I never saw a chaplain. This has certainly been a loss.

But in the positive, neither was I subjected to having to go to confessions to a priest in a confessional. It is probably also the reason that I have not been overly occupied with introspection and sin. And in fact, there would not have been much to confess. Two further considerations: First, the perceived need for regular confessions would seem almost to turn baptism into a lie; for baptism is intended to be the ritual regeneration of the human being, the being washed clean in the blood of the lamb, the putting on of white robes, the new birth in Christ and in the Spirit. Albeit, unfortunately, many baptized, even those in Catholic schools, seem not to have profited too much from it for their humanity. Secondly, it has instilled in many who were pushed into the confessional at a young age a provincial idea of God that they have failed to outgrow in later life. The Lord God is not a petty bookkeeper but sees what is in the heart (see Ps. 44:21). In the final chapter, I will elaborate somewhat more about all this, but let us for the moment return to my primary-school age.

In my primary school, I had for the general classes for two years Mr. Bastiaensen as teacher; then for two years Mrs. Geerts; and then for two years Miss Van Hemelrijck. I duly did my homework and, besides this, liked to copy my children's books by writing them out by hand.

For a fortnight once a year, my parents and I went on holiday. The first holiday was to Ostend. My parents rented a beautiful flat at the eighth floor of a high-rise near the beach. All I remember about it is that one night, stormy weather was upon us and that Ma, not being used to living high above the ground, did not like the slight rocking movements of the building that it caused. In years following, they rented a caravan in a large caravan park near Bredene instead.

In 1973 my parents, Uncle Eugène, Aunt Irma, and Herman went by coach with a group for a week to Lourdes. I was deemed too small for the journey and so Moemoe came to look after me. One detail that I remember about this week is that one day Moemoe had prepared a warm meal of homemade soup, followed by mashed potatoes with spinach and sausage. Just after she had put the plate in front of me and sat down, a tiny fruit fly landed on my mashed potatoes and spinach. For sure, I did not want to eat it since a dirty fly had touched my food. The kind moemoe was exasperated: "Mor enfin!" (Would you believe it!?) I guess that if I had been one of her own, she would have turned that plate upside down over my head; and I was probably not far from it. What a spoiled child I could be. I cannot remember whether I eventually ate at least a little of the plate; in any case, vanilla custard pudding followed.

After the example of Walter, Ma wanted me to join the scouts. Likely, the reason for this was that I would do some outdoor activity and, in the process, keep in touch with the youth of our parish. Moreover, I was at school in a socialist environment, and at the scouts I would be in a more Catholic setting. As such, I joined the scouts and was with them perhaps for a year or so. I liked the outdoor walking events, taking some provisions along; I liked playing some football on the open space in front of the clubhouse; and I liked the companionship of some of my former friends of the Tyrolerhof kindergarten. Yet I did not really enjoy the various other features of the movement: though I appreciated some proper walking and physical-endurance training, any macho behavior did not attract me whatsoever. Instead, I preferred gentleness. Once, we went swimming in the Arena swimming pool. I could not swim, but I went along reluctantly with the group; they would teach me to swim. A large swimming pool was a new experience, and I was rather afraid of deep water. As such, I was standing at the edge of the smaller pool. I moved a little about and did a few little exercises to accustom myself. After they had done some swimming and splashing about in the large pool, before leaving, the leadership turned their attention to me. Though I could stand everywhere in the pool and the water was less than waist deep where I was at the time—for we were more or less leaving, and I was wading towards the shallow part of the pool—they got a few boys to push me a couple of times under water by force. I gasped for breath and coughed. It profoundly upset me. They were to teach me to swim and not to attack me, so I considered it treason. I came home and said that I would not go again. Ma agreed that they dealt wrongly with me and respected my decision. After I had not turned up for the following meetings, a few of the leadership came in the evening to our house to apologize. I was upstairs in my room, and Ma came to ask me if I wanted to come down since they were very sorry and wanted to ask me to give them another chance. I refused to see them and never went back. How could I wish to be part of a group that had betrayed and thoroughly upset me at the swimming pool? The scouts were a closed chapter as far as I was concerned.

I was, however, well integrated at school. In Belgian schools, at least as far as I have known them, no lessons take place on Wednesday afternoons. Other activities were then organized, which a good number of pupils attended because the parents of several would have been at work. I usually stayed on these Wednesday afternoons, even though my parents were at home. In the refectory, the curtains were drawn closed and a film was projected on a screen. One had to contribute five Belgian francs to watch the movie. I still remember scenes of two movies that I watched there: one of a Mongol tribe of warriors, the other of Lassie. But outside, on the paved school ground, Mr. Bastiaensen oversaw a game of football or basketball, and this is where I was most often. Somewhat later onwards perhaps, in addition, I spend time at the home of a school friend called Luc (Brouwers). We cycled about; sometimes I joined him getting our meal from the nearby fish-and-chips shop, which we ate at his home; we played football close to his house; or we played at my home. I received a ping-pong set, and initially we played the game on a kitchen table. Looking back, I remember Luc as a very kind and gentle friend.

No pressure was put on me to perform in school. I think that my parents just wanted me to be happy. Initially, apparently, they would have expected me to be rather simple, and they hoped that I would do well enough to get a secure job working for the council as a clerk or the like. But they soon found that I was actually doing pretty well at school.

Luc went to the evening gymnastic lessons in the school. I could never be as supple as Luc; but when I was about 8, he convinced me that it would be good to join him. I thus became a member of the *Deurnese Turners* (Club of the Gymnasts of Deurne). Lessons were given by a young adult man, who was himself an excellent gymnast. As far as I remember, we paid for an outfit of the club, which had a badge at the chest. I never made it to any exercises too advanced, but it certainly helped me to manage the gymnastic classes during regular school hours. The club had its own proper gymnastics hall with surroundings, and a few times Luc and I went there to obtain one or other certificate in basic gymnastic exercises. Though I was but a very moderate gymnast, the leadership was always encouraging. On May 1, the Feast of Saint Joseph the Worker, and thus of the socialists, we participated as members of the Deurnese Turners in parades through the streets of Deurne and in collective exercises.

On Sunday morning I usually went with my parents to Mass. In the afternoon, they often drove around in their Beetle. In the early years I went with them. Often, they followed a part of one of the sign-posted routes, such as the Pallieterland route or the Taxandria route. These auto routes of around one hundred kilometers in total meandered through the Antwerp Campine, a region situated to the east and northeast of Antwerp, right up to the Dutch border, and that covers three quarters of the Belgian Province of Antwerp. The first mentioned route passes, among others, through Herentals and Lier; the other route passes through Turnhout and Geel and leads even into the Netherlands. The routes tend to follow smaller roads through rural areas, and we got out here and there to watch something. I think that Pa particularly liked these routes because they passed close to places that his close relatives lived, namely, Arendonk (where he was born), Oud-Turnhout, and Herentals. As such, these outings often led to a spontaneous family visit.

Other destinations were chosen as well. I joined them touring along the Antwerp harbor. On perhaps two occasions, we came to the *Kerkschip* (Church Ship) *Saint Joseph*. This ship remains stationed in one of the docks (at the time, it was docked at the Canal Dock). Aboard the ship, one can visit the chapel, and some refreshments can be obtained. The ship came into the hands of the Archdiocese of Mechlin in 1950, and it serves as a church- and social center for sailors and their families.

To the southeast of Antwerp, we visited the smaller city of Lier. In Lier is found, among others, the large Saint-Gummarius Collegiate Church; the beguinage with its streets of medieval houses in which the beguines lived—devout religious women who, unlike nuns, possessed their own house with an enclosed little garden and often had a poorer girl as servant—centered around a chapel and enclosed by a wall within the city, and which is now a UNESCO World Heritage Site; the Zimmer Clock Tower and Museum, which is another UNESCO World Heritage Site; and the Felix Timmermans Museum, the former dwelling of the well-known Flemish writer, poet, and illustrator Felix Timmermans (1886–1946). We walked along the tree-lined *stadsvest*, a path or earthen rampart that circles the old city and runs largely parallel with the river Nete and with other waters.

South of Antwerp, I remember visiting with them the Fort of Breendonk. Earlier, I spoke about the girdle of Brialmont forts that were built around Antwerp in 1859 and following years, of which the forts of Borsbeek, Wommelgem, and Wilrijk are part. Because newer weapons that were developed after that time had a greater reach, it was decided by law in 1906 that a new girdle of forts and entrenchments was to be built at a greater distance from the city and its harbor. The Fort of Breendonk was part of this fortified line of defense; it is situated about halfway between Mechlin and Dendermonde. Information about this fort, which was made into a national memorial, can be found on its website. During World War I, heavy fighting took place in defending the fort, but it could not withstand the more powerful German guns that were aimed at the fort while staying out of reach. When the fort was taken, the surrender of Antwerp was complete. During World War II, this fort came again into the hands of the Germans, and they made it into a concentration camp. It became, officially, a transit camp and a major center for the German political police. Between 1940 and 1942, many Jews passed through there on their way to the extermination camps. From 1942 onwards, it gradually became a camp for political prisoners and members of the Resistance. In total, around 3,500 persons were subjected to what has been called the "Hell of Breendonk."

Besides these outings by car, we also cycled along what seemed endless routes, visiting on our way places such as the Grotto of Lourdes in Edegem. The grotto, the Way of the Cross, and the adjacent Our-Lady-of-Lourdes Basilica are a popular place of pilgrimage for the peoples round about. Though the church has long been called the *basiliek* by the people, the title *basilica* was officially attributed by Pope Benedict XVI in November 2008 on the occasion of the seventy-five years of existence of the domed church and of the one-hundred-and-fiftieth anniversary of the apparitions of Our Lady to Bernadette in Lourdes.

Another Lourdes Grotto that we visited on the bicycle is situated just outside the center of Ranst, in the domain Zevenbergen. It was built by the last lord of the castle of Zevenbergen in 1952 and is situated across the main gate of the castle, at the border of the wood. The castle burned down completely in 1989 but has since been restored by the present owners, the Religious Sisters of the Convent of Bethlehem, who have made it into a retreat house.

At times, of course, we visited Eugène and family. We drove up with our blue VW Beetle to the front of the land house that stood alone across the farm amidst fields. Sometimes, when we rang on, no one answered; but getting back into the car, we saw the curtains move slightly at the corner of the front window. It meant that Uncle Eugène was not at home but that Aunt Irma was and was spying on us. We were always very welcome with my uncle but obviously less so with Irma. My mother wanted, however, to keep in touch with her brother and visited for his sake.

The Lourdes Grotto in the domain Zevenbergen as found during a visit in 2019

When Eugène was at home and we were let in, usually, Irma kept some of the time pottering in the kitchen. My cousin, Herman, who was a few years older than me, sometimes asked me to play with him outside. I did so reluctantly. He wanted me, for example, to jump over a deep pit that I knew I could just not make and so did not, and then he scolded me for being a coward. I thought Herman was somewhat right and that I really was not a brave heart as he was and that I lacked courage. But why did I need to jump over this pit anyway? It was too wide. Why would I risk injury for the sake of it? On another occasion, Herman wanted me to eat a large chocolate bar in his tent; I only wanted a piece of it. Herman scolded me again. When we went back into the house, I usually looked unhappy or had had a few tears. When my uncle saw this, without further ado, he gave Herman a good beating on his bottom, which I did not want to happen. Herman ended up crying. It was annoying, for I felt that it was because of me that he every time received it. This is how we usually left. Getting back into the car, Ma said that she feared Eugène was beating the love out of that boy and would come to regret it.

Around the years of these visits, Uncle Eugène got a dog, an Alsatian, whom he called Cor. The animal was not yet fully grown and was not allowed in the house but was, at the time, kept in a shed at the back of the garden. Ma disapprovingly remarked that by keeping the dog a lot of the time in isolation in a dark shed with just a little food and drink, it was being made aggressive. Also in this regard, she remarked that the animal would be lacking loving care.

In the weekends, Walter was usually at home or, at least, around. For most of the time, during the week, he was staying in a military school or barracks. So, what was he doing there? A few words of explanation: At the time that he had been finishing his secondary schooling at the Royal Athenaeum of Deurne, Walter and Sonja were planning to attend a fancy-dress party. Walter was looking for something special, something that would stand out. Now, he remembered that Frans had a niece (Flora Wouters, the daughter of his oldest sister Marie) who lived in the neighboring street and who was married to Yves Verhillen, a gendarme who happened to be about the same height as Walter. And yes, Walter went to ring at their door and asked to borrow Yves' uniform. One would not believe it, but the latter, not being shy of a little prank himself, gave Walter his entire outfit, including his long baton. Standing in front of a mirror, Walter liked it. On the evening, he walked in to the full gathering of the party and, of course, stole the show. He looked the piece and everyone told him how he looked like a real gendarme and gave them a fright. Up till then, he was not sure what he would be doing as a profession, but this was something. In the aftermath, Walter attempted the entry-procedure for the Royal Military Academy so as to become an officer with the gendarmes, but he was not selected. Yet he did not abandon the idea and joined the gendarmes at a lower level. As such, he did three year formation given to noncommissioned officers (one year basic formation and two more years training for picked-noncommissioned officers) at the School for Gendarmes at Ixelles (or *Elsene* in Dutch), one of the nineteen municipalities of the Belgian capital, Brussels. After that, still wanting to become a gendarme-(commissioned) officer, he did two years formation at the School for Military Cadets in Lier; that is in the time period that I was about seven to nine years old. Then, he once more partook in the qualification tests for the Royal Military Academy. This time, he came out top of the list of the eight hundred or so candidates. At long last then, he was admitted to attend the Royal Military Academy in the center of Brussels; this he did for two years. After that, his position as officer was ensured and his career progressed.

When he was home, Walter and I slept in the same room. I liked him being at home, for as I explained in an earlier chapter, it was an ordeal for me to be left alone in the bedroom. Often though, he would have gone out at the weekends and come home quite late. During the day, we often played with a ball on the patio, throwing it in turns across it in a bucket positioned in the opposite corner with a brick in it so as to keep it stable. We did this often for a number of years; Walter had for a long time been playing korfball and was, of course, pretty good in throwing the ball in the bucket.

On Thursday afternoons, my parents went card playing with another retired policeman (Jan van den Eynde), his wife, and some other old couple living near them. During holidays, I sometimes joined them for a little time. Eventually the old policeman gradually lost all his capacities and died. When this had fallen away, Pa was still more at home. After much insistence of Ma and Pater Jef Berghmans (1930–2004; an Assumptionist who had come from the Congo in 1976 to our parish and who assisted Pater Pastoor), they persuaded him to have a look in the meeting center of the parish when the pensioners played cards there. Among them he found another retired policeman, Jan Van Dijck. He subsequently went to play cards there every Tuesday and Thursday afternoon. Sometimes Ma went along as well to socialize or play cards with them when only a

Pater Jef Berchmans, Assumptionist, was a missionary in Congo from 1959 to 1976; parish priest in Borsbeek from 1976 to 2004; and Provincial Superior from 1996 to 1999. While he was priest in Borsbeek, he married Walter and Sonja. He was an ascetic man; would cycle from Borsbeek to Leuven for a meeting; and was much involved with the youth. His older brother, Pater Lieven, who had been a missionary in Congo as well, joined the parish a few years later. Pater Jef died on July 12, 2004, aged seventy-three.

few were there; and she joined him whenever something was organized by the KBG, that is, the *Katholieke Bond der Gepensioneerden* (Catholic Guild of Pensioners). On Wednesday afternoon they usually visited Moemoe. The chair near the window disappeared.

At some point, when exactly I do not recall, they kept a few chickens in the aviary at the back of the garden with the intention to eat them. Now then! The time arrived that the first chicken was to be killed and put into the pot. Frans and I went into the aviary and after some effort managed to get hold of the chicken. My task was to keep it tight with its head above a square pavement stone, while Pa would chop its head off with an axe. He gave it a terrific blow and hit his target perfectly, nearly splitting the slab in the process. I had to let go of the chicken. To our amazement, it ran around the aviary without a head. It surprised me that it did not run into the wire but still knew perfectly how far it could run before turning round. After perhaps a few minutes, it eventually collapsed. My task was ended but Ma's started: after draining the blood, it was to be plucked and cleaned and cooked. They did it once but not twice.

I was most of the time a well-behaved boy and very seldom got punished, but once I received the same lesson that was taught to one of our cats. For we had over several years a succession of cats and one of these had the habit, instead of going outside in the garden for doing its business, to come inside and do its toilet on the carpet in the corner of the living room under the Ikea-set. Pa got hold of the cat and rubbed its nose through the mess it had made. As far as I remember, the cat did it again sometime later, and my parents having had enough got rid of the animal and replaced it with another one. As regards myself, once I was for some reason, that I do not recall, in a bad mood while we were having a bread meal; I pushed things away from me and a cup or a jug with milk happened to turn over and spilled on the carpet and some sugar ended up on the carpet on top of it. Pa grabbed me in my neck and, pushing me down, put my face into it. Well, I have not forgotten it; but, unlike the cat, it did not happen again.

A final recollection with which I end this chapter: One thing I particularly disliked was that Pa sometimes asked me to sit on his knee but then started tickling me, while keeping me in a firm grip. He was counting my ribs, he said. I hated it, for though it was but play, it amounted to a very mild form of torture. This practice would eventually come to an end when I became stronger with age.

# 11

## School, sport, and life among family (2)

A FTER OUR FIRST holiday in Ostend, my parents and I spent subsequent holidays in a caravan park near Bredene-aan-Zee. We walked along the long beach. Once, we took the coastal tram to De Haan, where my parents bought a great amount of

At the caravan park near Bredene-aan-Zee

towels and sheets at a very good price in a shop. In the afternoons they often lay down in the sand dunes, while I dug a pit in the sand or explored the nearby dunes.

One day, while we visited the local market, an egg-incident took place. I had been given a blue, plastic ball in one of the seaside shops and was bouncing it a lot of the time, even when we stood in front of a market stall that sold fresh produce. In front of the stall, a large hamper stood with a great quantity of eggs. Suddenly, I lost control of the ball and it went straight into the egg basket. Horrified, I took it out and saw that I had broken at least a dozen or so eggs. In the meantime, the seller was dealing with other customers and with Ma who was buying some fruit or vegetables, and he did not notice it. Ma said to me, "Keep quiet for I am not paying for all these eggs." We walked on. Undoubtedly, Pa would have said something like, "Snot ape!"

Quite a few things took place in the years following, and I have been struggling to remember the order in which it exactly went. To begin with, I must have been about ten, when coming home one afternoon with my school friend Luc, Ma came to the door crying, and said, "Your sister is here." I am not quite sure that I had ever been told that I even had a sister, yet it was not a total surprise because of these very first memories with which I started this book. It was still enough of a surprise though. Jenny was sitting in the living room with her fiancé, Paul. It was apparently under his influence that she had found the courage to visit her mother. At the time, she was fifteen, he was twenty-four. How correct that lawyer had been who had advised Carolina some eight years earlier about the course to take. Having said hello and going towards the back, towards the workplace at the back of the garden, Luc said: "I did not know you have a sister; you always talk to me about your brother. You never even mentioned you had a sister." What could I say, except play the question back to him? "Did I not?"

A week or so later, Jenny returned. This time she arrived carrying a small suitcase, and she asked to come and live with us. That same evening, Alfons came to the door and demanded his daughter back. I remember on the occasion that when Alfons was at the door, Ma was obviously accompanied by Pa at the door, and she immediately ordered Walter, who was at home, to keep me inside and not to let me come to the door. She was still afraid—and probably not without reason—that he might grab me and take me away. I was, however, not too interested to go to the door, for Alfons had no place in my life and I knew Ma did not want me to meet him. Alfons was made to leave without Jenny. So, this time round, Carolina initiated a court case to obtain full custodial rights over Jenny, who now wanted to live with us. The case was successful: my parents obtained full custody over Jenny, who thus was legally assigned to henceforth live with us. When she arrived, besides the clothes she was wearing—a blue jeans and a white tee-shirt with a car depicted on the front—Jenny brought very little with her. It was apparently all she had. My parents immediately took her along to buy a set of dresses and essential clothing; they further bought a bed and a second-hand bicycle.

What transpired is that Jenny had been living with an older woman, probably the mother of Alfons's second woman. When some years ago I asked Maria Fret whether she knew any details that Carolina might have told her about the other woman, she said to have heard that the woman worked for MIVA and had two disabled children. If this is correct, then these two children were perhaps a reason that Alfons could not keep Jenny with him in the same dwelling. As Jenny related to us, she had been virtually

my mother to stay away from Emma. Nevertheless, we kept visiting.

Moemoe's stay in Immaculata was intended to be temporary; but when this came to its ending, she was not well enough to go and live independently as before. My parents and Uncle Eugène then took contact with the social services about the possibility of moving her to a more permanent nursing home and of having this stay subsidized. A new nursing home had just been built in Wilrijk and they envisaged the chance that she might obtain a place there. The letter they sent was typed by Uncle Eugène and was sent from our address in Borsbeek. Uncle Eugène, though being the eldest of the two children, was always very anxious that the social services would come to his address—a large land house at that—for financial contributions; as such, by using our address, he kept things at arm's length. I still possess a copy of the letter that they sent and I reproduce it here in translation:

Borsbeek, 23–10–76

To the Social Services Department (*Commissie Openbare Onderstand*), Wilrijk, with a copy to the Christian Insurance Services (*Kristelijke Mutualiteit*), Wilrijk, and to Immaculata, Edegem.

About the case of Van Kesbeeck, Emma, inhabitant of Wilrijk, with address Krijgslaan 120, where she inhabits two rooms at the first floor above ground level. At the moment, she stays at the rehabilitation-institute Immaculata, Edegem.

About a fortnight ago, we took contact with the Christian Insurance Services, Wilrijk, concerning [the possibility of] her residing in a nursing home once she would be sufficiently recovered. We have understood that they would take contact with your department, *C. O. O.*, and that a meeting with us would likely occur.

It was planned that the patient would have stayed in Immaculata until the end of this month; yet, to our surprise, it is suddenly announced that she is allowed to return home right now.

By our observation: by simply being awake during the day, she is totally exhausted at evening time. Every day her blood pressure is taken, and this remains very irregular.

A week ago, she complained having chest pain and tightness at the chest. She told us that she felt her condition was deteriorating. It was emphasized to her that she should speak to a doctor about this.

The question to be kept in mind is this: Is she able to go up and down a stairs without the risk of her dying in doing so? She does not have a toilet in her living quarters on the first floor. She cannot tend to her stove because her left arm is paralyzed. A fire risk is real enough. And what about her gas cooker?

In the institute we are being informed that, probably because of her illness, she is very much unmanageable.

Our impression is that the nursing staff is very surprised that she is allowed to go home, given that she lives on her own.

Under no circumstance do we take her home; she needs surveillance day and night. We ourselves cannot provide this, and therefore, we do not wish to take this responsibility.

With highest esteem,

Van Kesbeeck, E.                    Peeters, F., husband of
                                     Van Kesbeeck, C.

Their application was successful and she was permitted to move to the new nursing home *Bloemenveld* (Field of flowers). It was the responsibility of her family to vacate the rooms she rented at her former address. It was left to Carolina to ask Moemoe for the keys of her flat, so that they could start what needed to be done. When Ma asked her for the keys, Moemoe was furious and threw them to her head. Thankfully, she missed her target, and they slammed into the door beside Carolina's face. At the time of this happening, Pa and I were not in the room. Why they did not ask her at a moment they were together in the room, I do not know; for Moemoe would not have risked it with Frans around. Reluctantly, Emma took up her new residence in the nursing home, where she occupied a new, spacious, single room at the second floor, with toilet en suite, overlooking the garden. Nonetheless, her typical expression would be that she was being treated as a dog.

I still vividly remember my parents emptying a storage space under the staircase of her old flat; not much else than a few very old tins of foodstuff.

Looking back upon it, given that Moemoe had mental capacity, it would, in my view, have been better if they could have had her more involved by having a discussion with her about her alternatives, instead of working it out without her involvement and against her will. Perhaps this took place, but I am unaware of such having been the case. If Moemoe wanted absolutely to keep living independently, they could perhaps have helped her find a more suited, simple dwelling at ground-floor level. Again though, as appears from the letter, her health situation prohibited such alternative; and given that she had to leave Immaculata quicker than expected, they had to move her to somewhere at short notice. Moreover, would it have been possible to hold a meaningful discussion with Emma, with Eugène, about her future?

I guess that Moemoe knew well enough that living on her own was not possible, but perhaps she had hoped to come and live with us. In truth, our little house did not have enough space to provide her with her own room. The more so, given that Jenny had not long arrived and had just come to live with us. Perhaps, very perhaps, if the relationship between Emma and Carolina had been a warm and tender one, my parents would have tried to work something out, but such was not the case; and despite her age, Emma would not be an easy-going character to take aboard: it would not have worked.

As it was, my parents kept visiting her every Wednesday in the nursing home, sometimes even on Sundays; Ma did her washing of clothes, even though the home would have done it. Sometimes, I accompanied them. Often, Moemoe and Pa played cards, while Ma looked into a magazine and went down to the cafeteria for a hot drink.

The months passed, and when the time came of our two weeks

Primary 5 of 1976–77 and Miss Van Hemelrijck. I am standing fifth from the left; Luc is pictured fourth from the right; Bart is sitting second from the left. Though I was not particularly religious, I am wearing, nonetheless, the Lourdes medal my parents had given me. In the follow-ing year, Primary 6, we would be joined with the parallel class so that our number greatly increased for the last year.

parents, Willy and Yvonne; our stepfather and mother, Frans and Carolina; Sonja's brother, Patrick; our sister and her fiancé, Jenny and Paul; I; and our stepsister Eugena and her family all had a place in the limousines that took us to the venue in Antwerp where the meal was provided during the day and where the evening feast was held for the larger group of guests.

Uncle Eugène and Aunt Irma somehow were invited to the wedding by Walter and Sonja at only a relatively late date. I remember Ma being apprehensive about it, for she knew it would not be appreciated by Eugène if he was invited almost as an afterthought. Uncle Eugène and Aunt Irma attended the wedding, but they felt insulted—I recall seeing them at the church after Mass; beyond that, I do not remember. They blamed Ma for it, even though she had no involvement in the invitations to the wedding. After the wedding, Uncle Eugène broke off contact with his sister, so that we did not see him any more for several years.

Striking another and lighter note of that memorable day: Prior to the wedding, my parents bought a small, new camera. It had a lever at the top and a number that went up each time one took a picture. The camera was not to be opened before the film was ended and well turned through. I was entrusted the camera at the wedding so as to take some pictures at various times throughout the day. For sure a great job to be entrusted with, and it kept me occupied throughout the long day. Now and then, I drew the attention of some family or of the pair themselves and took a picture. After each picture, I turned the lever at the top so as to set the film ready for the next picture. Now and then, Ma enquired about my progress and suggested I take this or that picture. The number indicated at the top went up one by one. After the wedding, the film seemed not finished yet, for I could still turn the spool of the film and take some more pictures. When the number reached the maximum of thirty-eight or so, we thought that that was it for sure. We thought it great because some films would have allowed for fewer shots. I turned the level a few extra times to completely wind up the film and carefully opened the camera, and behold!, it was empty. I was dismayed; all my effort for nothing. Ma and Pa were surprised as well. It was treason; a scandal! In our naivety we thought they would sell a new camera with a first film inserted. Walter and Sonja never set too much store by our endeavors because a professional photographer was present at the day, and he supplied them with a nice album.

A few weeks later, in September, Jenny started lessons in a nearby secondary school to which she could easily cycle. Given the move to her new home, she had not finished the previous school year in her former school and so had to retake the third year in the new school. The upshot of her new circumstances was that she had the chance of a proper education for as long as it would take her. It quickly was apparent that Jenny had a gift for languages, and Frans and Carolina envisaged that, provided she would work at it, she could become a well-educated lady with a promising future ahead of her. Jenny's heart was, however, not in it, and her mind was set on other matters. In the meantime, at home, soon after her arrival, tensions had arisen between her and me; daily we had squabbles. The change had been sudden for all of us, and Jenny did not settle in too easily. I could be a pest to her, and she was a volatile teenager who often had a bad temper. She was not happy. It was a pity because we loved each other as brother and sister.

I remember two instances of being a pest to Jenny. One occasion took place at bedtime during weekdays, when Walter was not around. The doors between our bedrooms were usually open. After some reading in bed, when I turned the light off, I called out

"Goodnight" to Jenny and to Ma who were reading in their beds. Soon afterwards, Jenny called out "Goodnight." But it had developed for me over the years in a kind of ritual that my Goodnight was the last word. So, perhaps as a kind of obsessive compulsive behavior, I called out again, "Goodnight"; and as usual, Ma duly returned the word. But this annoyed Jenny: for what was the reason of my repeating the greeting except of not wanting to give her her place. So she as well called out once more, "Goodnight." With this, my mental program required me to call out once more, "Goodnight." The result was that Jenny got in a fury, jumped out her bed, and said, "If you open your mouth again, I box your teeth out." As soon as she retreated to her bed, of course, I called out again. Eventually, Ma had to calm things down. This happened for a number of evenings. I think too much psychology was going on for us to cope with in a smooth manner.

Another occasion of being a pest to Jenny took place on a sunny afternoon when we were all outside. Ma and Pa were sitting outside, and I was watering the plants and trees with a hose, when Jenny appeared. She had put on hair spray and wore a new dress, and she was showing herself to our parents. In a mischievous mood, I turned the water hose onto her. Jenny was red with fury. She filled a bucket with water from the pump in the veranda. As she ran after me intending to turn the bucket over my head, she splashed the water all over herself, while the few small fruit trees in the garden prevented her from catching me.

Finally, I remember one incident at breakfast before school. Early mornings were in those days, generally, not Jenny's favored time of the day. We were both at table with Ma and we both had a cup of hot milk in front of us; we used to have Ovaltine, a kind of nutritious chocolate drink, so perhaps that is what it was. I must have said something as part of a conversation, to my mind rather insignificant and it probably was; but the next moment, Jenny threw the contents of her cup in my face.

Perhaps these things just needed to take place. It showed that some character was present. I have recalled here these confrontational moments, but we also had better moments together, and the little time that we lived under one roof was valuable for becoming brother and sister to each other. Undeniably though, we had been thrown together after a long absence, whereas we should have grown up together. I had virtually been for years an only child; for Walter was a young adult by then. It was also the case that, in addition to being a teenage girl, Jenny had grown up in abnormal circumstances and needed to get things out of her system. As it happened, it would take many years yet before she would find peace and stability in her life.

But let me continue with some more details of life around that time. In the chapter entitled *My parents' reminiscences*, I mentioned Maurice Dillen, with whom Pa teamed up during the war and kept in touch for the rest of his life. Sometimes, Maurice visited with his wife, Gilberte, and some of their several children, and we visited them at their house in Wijnegem. Maurice and Gilberte were present also at the evening feast of Walter's wedding and later at Jenny's. They were, nevertheless, a family out with the ordinary. To begin with, Gilberte was quite a large woman, while Maurice was a small, thin man. Their eldest son had become someone who was considered rather unstable and violent: as far as I remember, he was most of the time serving a prison sentence; when at home, he even had threatened his father, Maurice, and we could see the large holes he kicked in the doors inside their house. Their youngest son was somewhat younger than me, and he usually accompanied his parents on their visits. Now and then, Frans called in to the house of his friend, accom-

school for the coming six years. I cycled to school, which was situated about 4.5 kilometers from our house in Manebruggestraat. Only a few fellow pupils of my primary school joined me, including Yves, Frank, and Danny. Some others of my former class went to the technical institute in Deurne (at Ruggeveldlaan), while the majority went to the nearest secondary school (at Waterbaan), which Jenny also attended for a little while when she came to live with us. Luc and some others I associated with went to this latter school. Luc still came to look me up once at home, but I was quite occupied with school and sport. To my regret, I did not make efforts to keep in touch with him or with others of my primary school; and after some time, I would not have dared to look them up unexpectedly at their homes.

The first school year at the Athenaeum in the teaching system that was operated at the time—namely, V.S.O., that is *Vernieuwd Secundair Onderwijs*, or translated, Renewed Secondary Education—was the same for all parallel classes and was called an observation year. I was allotted the same class as Yves and we often sat beside each other; but because we laughed too much during some lessons and were too distracted, we were separated. He put less effort in his schoolwork than I did, and gradually, we lost sight of each other. For the second observation year, some differentiation was made between classes and I chose what was called classics, which included Latin, and which already put me with the better performing students. Of the fifteen different courses that were involved in that second year, I ended up with the top grade "excellent" for eleven of them.

In the meantime, I spend a lot of time running. Every Tuesday and Thursday evening, I cycled to the training sessions of Antwerp AC, who moved premises in these years, so as to have better changing rooms and a better track. It was about ten kilometers cycling; and on my way back home, I was often quite exhausted and hung low upon my bicycle. I participated in running competitions at various locations in the Flemish part of Belgium. An important race for me was the yearly country-running competition for the pupils of all schools of Deurne: I ended up third for my age category in 1978, in 1979, and in 1980. Another highlight of the year was the Belgian championships. For our age category, the competition was a relay race between all running clubs: six times six hundred meters. It took place in Waregem, on the track used for the horse races: It was perhaps why I went so fast. My parents were among the supporters. In 1979, I was the fifth runner in our team and received the baton in third position, well behind the one in front of me. But I gave it everything, managed to catch up with him and overtake him; and then I got the one running at the lead in my vision, and I closed the gap between us and overtook him. I handed the baton over for the final relays and we won the competition. I had run myself more or less to smithereens. As such, we won the race.

At home, I built a large train table in the room that Jenny had slept in during her year with us. For this hobby, at first I bought building kits for putting together, such as a train station. I bought a few boxes with little plastic figures that I carefully painted with an eye for detail. It was a hobby to be done largely alone in quietness. At times, loneliness crept in. I crawled under the train table connecting wires for electric lightning, and other features. In the large workplace, Pa helped me to make some rudimentary buildings myself from three-ply board that we glued together and then painted. Subsequently, using a catalogue, I made little buildings myself of a more developed design. From a book, I learned to make a mountain landscape with tunnels from iron wire covered with newspapers soaked in wall-paper adhesive, which were then painted and covered with self-made trees (from metal wire and pieces of sponge) and green flakes for grass. At a later date, this hobby became gradually replaced with the collecting of stamps; a hobby that Walter had earlier taken up.

Apart from the collective training sessions, I often also went running on my own in one of the local parks.

In the meantime, besides being a member of KAV, that is, the Catholic Workers' Women, and of the Christian Guild of Pensioners, together with Frans, Ma joined a third movement in the parish, namely, *Ziekenzorg*, a nationwide Catholic organization dedicated to the care of the sick. Pa joined, since he qualified as a sick person, while Ma became a volunteer visiting people in their homes. Since through the other organizations she had come to know a good number of people in our parish, she was asked to take some streets under her care and visit the sick living there. In association with this, the following anecdote is worth relating:

At about a hundred meters from our house in Manebruggestraat, a dirt track joined the road on our side. Along the sides of this track, grass grew. In earlier years, when I was a primary school child, it had been for me the best place for learning to cycle, for it was free from motorized vehicles and in case I fell in the verge of the road, it was not so bad. Now, at the corner, where the track joined our street, a large land house stood, surrounded by a substantial lawn. Unfortunately, the couple that lived there could not have that children cycled along the track near their house, even though the house stood well away from it. They were not parishioners but were known as fervent socialists; which is all I ever knew about them. A few times, Ma had seen that these people had chased me and my new bicycle away. As a result, it came to a vigorous exchange of words between them.

Moemoe, Pa, Paul, and I playing cards at the back of the house; looking on is Jenny. Moemoe was not one for having others peek into her cards. Ma must be the one taking the picture.

After that, they did not talk to each other and had become enemies. Several years later, when Ma had been a member of Ziekenzorg for some time, the man living in the house became gravely ill. On account of this, one evening at dinner, Ma said, "You never guess in whose house I have been this afternoon." Having heard that the man was ill, she had rung at their door. "Ach, I thought, the worst they can do is slam the door in my face." When the woman of the house had opened the door, she had obviously been quite surprised; nevertheless, she let my mother enter. She even offered a cup of tea and expressed her regret of having been so intolerant in years past. In the aftermath of this visit, Ma returned a number of times to them. And when I met that same woman in the street, she would greet me in a friendly manner.

On another occasion, her assistance was called upon by Pater Pastoor. He had brought a couple of emergency home-visits to a woman in her thirties who had a well-paid employment in infor-

Pa (wiping the sweat of his forehead), Walter (measuring), and I (watching) determining who is closest to the little ball in a game of *pétanque* (or French *boules* game); in the set that we had, each has two plastic balls for throwing. This picture shows well the garden, the workplace at the back, and the aviary in front of it. Right behind the workplace stands Gartner's chocolate-praline factory.

*188*

mation technology but whose marriage had collapsed and who was in a state of depression. She had taken to drugs and her well-furnished flat was in a state of complete chaos. She was much of the time lying in her bed without wanting to get up. She undoubtedly had been in touch with professional psychologists for some time, since she was unable to work, but without too much effect. Somehow Pater Pastoor must have been called upon for assistance. Since he himself did not know to whom else he could turn for help with this, he asked Carolina (whom he and all local people knew as Lily) whether she would be willing to help and try restoring some hygiene to the flat. "Just see what you can do." No one else knew about it and the lady was not known in the parish since she had come to live in a new block of flats. Ma took up the challenge; she may even have been given the keys to gain access to the flat. She cleaned the place, she listened, and she helped the lady regain her self-respect. She aired to me a few words about what she found there. After perhaps a month of hard work, a turn for the better was at hand. The flat had become a clean home once more, and the lady was grappling with her situation. After two months, she drove up to our house and came to hand Carolina a bouquet of flowers; from now on, she would do her best to get her life back and had returned to work. No one locally would have known about it, except that Pater Pastoor knew, Frans knew, and I have not forgotten either.

For our yearly summer holiday, Frans and Carolina rented for two weeks a bungalow on the outskirts of Bihain, a small farmers' village near Baraque Fraiture (the highest point of the Province Luxembourg) within the Municipality of Vielsalm. Bihain offered us a landscape of fields and large forests. It was perhaps our most remote holiday, for the bungalow was standing on its own amidst fields near a forest. Paul and Jenny joined us there for a couple of days.

At the Athenaeum, from third year onwards, classes were further branched into various study-options or directions. At the conclusion of my second year the board of teachers had written in my report the advice that I should choose Sciences as overall study-option. I chose Latin-Sciences for my third and fourth years, which were called the Orientation Years.

Having lived a couple of years in Wilrijk, Jenny and Paul bought a new-built house in Manebruggestraat, at number 274; thus, only a hundred meters from our house at number 290. Jenny then started work as a check-out operator at the Grand Bazaar supermarket in Borsbeek. Not so long afterwards, in November 1980, when she was nineteen, she had her first child, Sven.

It was perhaps around that time that Jenny won some money with the National Lottery; part of her gains she used to buy me a real ping-pong table from the supermarket; until then we had been playing on a large board that we painted green. It was very kind of her.

On April 1, 1981, I participated once more in the yearly country running competition for the pupils of all schools of Deurne organized by the Municipal Sport and Youth Council: I obtained second place in my youth category. All other years that I participated during my six year at the Athenaeum, I obtained third place. So, the second place's silver for that race was the best I ever managed; I never won it. That year also, I competed with Antwerp AC in the 25th International Wellington Relays Competition at the horse-racing course in Ostend. The race was quite late in the afternoon and for a good while we had been playing football on the beach, which had come about spontaneously between our team and those of other teams. Mon, our coach, looked at it rather apprehensively but did not object; because, as he said afterwards, even though he knew it meant less chance of a successful race, at least we had a good sunny day at the beach. We won the race; and as we were heading home, Mon told me, having had quite a few, "You ran as if you had a piece of dynamite in your behind."

That summer, Antwerp AC organized a week sports holiday in Saint Moritz, Switzerland. They had been asking my parents to let me join them on this event, and so I went. I actually do not have a single picture of that week. It was all pretty professional; rather beyond my level of sport involvement: the idea was to do a lot of running at high altitude so as to increase the number of white blood cells and thus the capacity of the blood to distribute oxygen throughout the body. We even took a cable car up the mountain to run at greater height still.

Not long afterwards, I went with my parents for the yearly two weeks holiday to Ave-et-Auffe, where they rented a caravan on a caravan site. As at previous holidays in the Walloon region of Belgium, they had chosen a beautiful rural site where they could make quiet walks amidst the fields and forests. Ave-et-Auffe is a village that is part of the Municipality of Rochefort in the Famenne region within the Province Namur. Mon, the running coach, was somewhat concerned that I did not make the most of the aftermath of the altitude training in Saint Moritz by participating in various competitions; but at least, I took the training schedule with me that he gave along, and I tried to keep to some extent to it. I was, of course, not doing any training on the track but ran up and down along lonely roads.

Besides the local walks and my runs, that holiday we brought visits to various interesting places that are situated in the neighborhood of Ave-et-Auffe. At the neighboring village of Han-sur-Lesse, we visited the caves of Han. These caves were formed as the result of underground erosion of a limestone hill by the river Lesse. It gave an awareness of the dwellings of its prehistoric occupants and of the wonders of nature. The last part of the visit took place in a boat. It was not the first time that I visited a prehistoric cave with my parents: as far as I remember, we once visited on a daytrip with Uncle Eugène, Aunt Irma, and Herman the Goyet Caves formed through erosion by the Sambre at Gesves near Namur; a visit that impressed me with the re-creations of gigantic saber-toothed tigers, wolves, and bears that lived at the time the caves were inhabited. During this holiday, we visited in another neighboring village the impressive castle of Lavaux-Sainte-Anne. I remember it featured a natural-history exposition of the Famenne region, as well as an exposition of various torture instruments that were used in medieval times. In yet another neighboring village, namely, at Lessive, we visited a terrestrial station for spatial telecommunications built by Bell Telephone. At the time it had just one large parabolic antenna for capturing signals of satellites (since then, several others have been added) and a museum. The visit was undoubtedly made mainly for me.

Finally, I think it was on the way home that we visited the Marian domain at Beauraing, where the Virgin Mary appeared several times between November 1932 and January 1933 to five schoolchildren under a hawthorn bush that is situated in the corner of the garden of a convent nearby a railway bridge.

Back home, not long afterwards, I won with our team of Antwerp AC for the second time the Belgian championships relays. For our age category, the race we won was the 4 x 800 meters on the Tartan track at the Heysel Stadium in Brussels. (It is in this stadium that the disaster occurred before the start of the 1985 European Cup Final between Juventus of Italy and Liverpool of England, during which escaping fans were pressed against a wall that then collapsed: thirty-nine people were killed, mostly Italians, and another six hundred were injured.) At these 1981 championships at the Heysel, my parents were still present.

I continued my schooling and spent many weekends in Ranst with a school friend, Paul, and his family. They lived at the time in an apartment about one and a half kilometer from our house

but had bought some land in Ranst where they went in the weekends. It included some woodland and one or two meadows in which they kept sheep. There was an overgrown drive at the front leading to a large cabin, to which they were building an extension for a ping-pong table. As it happened, I helped provide Paul's father wooden planks that he used for the roof. These planks actually came from Gerard, Frans' eldest son, who was a Heavy-Goods-Vehicle driver for the tobacco transport company based at the Antwerp docks. Tobacco was being transported in large wooden crates that were used only once. As such, Gerard sometimes dropped off a load of them and built a wooden hut on our vege-table patch and stocked it with fire wood. Some of it found its

Our Lady of Beauraing

way. The race itself was not a success, for I was ill with flu-like condition and was pale. It was rather in vain that I participated and I did not perform at my best; I did not get into the finals.

In the following winter months I joined in a very few competitions and that was more or less it. Study became evermore demanding while the amount of training required for competitions in the juniors age category—that is, for those who are eighteen and nineteen years old—was beyond what I could give to it. And the same undoubtedly applied for some others of our team. Perhaps I could have done better if I had spent less time with my school friend Paul and his family during weekends. In any case, I stopped being in touch with the team.

Looking back, would I still do all this running? I suppose winning some competitions became something I could be proud off, something that has helped define me.

Yet has it been worth it? If I could relive these years, I very much doubt whether I would again run myself to smithereens. No, I would not do it again. Moreover, well considered, who still remembers these few Belgian-Championship contests in some of the youth series of the late seventies and early eighties? It is unlikely one still finds a trace of it. With hindsight, I would only participate in such competitions with much more time spent in training sessions or not at all. One needs to make the commitment to stay close in touch with the team and the coach and follow schedules correctly; otherwise there may be nothing to protect oneself from just digging too deep at competitions.

That being said, competitions aside, I would definitely still go running—as I have kept doing—but for the sheer pleasure of it and for physical and mental well-being. Running allows one to exercise the entire body and be in touch with one's body; it is the most natural sport. I have found running rounds in a park helpful for steadying the mind, for taking some distance from study or work; perhaps it helped me to adopt a right mind frame for openness to a relationship with God.

But much has changed since I left Antwerp AC and probably for the better: running has become more than a mere competition sport. Over the last thirty-five years, jogging and social running events have become widespread. Antwerp AC itself has changed and has been continued in Brabo Atletiekclub, which has come about by the fusion of the old Antwerp AC with other local teams, and which now has both male and female members; and besides this, interestingly, at the same premises (right besides Rivierenhof Park), another club, Antwerp Athletics, has arisen, which profiles itself on its website as "a club that in a pleasant and recreational manner wants to guide and motivate people to run. . . . Everyone trains at his/her level and receives for this the required guidance of an experienced coach." I well remember Peter Fischer, a former runner of Antwerp AC, who is chair and overall responsible coach of the new Antwerp Athletics. If I would be a teenager again, I would join once more and, given these more reachable premises, aim to devote more time than I managed in my former days. As it happened, however, I moved away and continued on my very own journey.

In the meantime, at the family front, Steven was born at the beginning of 1984 as the first child of Walter and Sonja.

My brother-in-law, Paul, gave me driving lessons soon after my eighteenth birthday and I obtained my driving license.

My sixth and final school year at the Athenaeum came to its conclusion and my results were quite satisfactory. I decided to go study physics at the University of Antwerp. The physics teacher supported the idea; the math teacher thought I was not quite strong enough in mathematics. I went ahead anyway. Perhaps it is still worth mentioning that during my last school year, I heard from other students that the lady teacher of religion who made us buy a Bible had been arrested in the school. Apparently, she was teaching those of the first year and had told them that we have a good angel besides us on one side and a bad angel on the other side. It is a teaching that most likely can be encountered in rather folkloristic spirituality and that stems from a second-century Christian book called *The Shepherd of Hermas*; what it wants to make vivid is the idea that in one's conscience one can be drawn by good and bad intentions. It is more common to encounter the idea of a guardian angel accompanying an individual without the notion of a demon at the side of each one individually. In any case, her lessons apparently made some of the small pupils scared, and they complained to their parents. She was eventually prohibited from teaching. When she still turned up at the school in defiance, police were called and she was carried off in handcuffs. I thought it to be a sad turn of events. One extra-curriculum event that I recall of that last school year is that we went kayaking: the descent of the river Lesse over a distance of perhaps twenty kilometers. We each boarded a two-person canoe; and I teamed up with Paul. That same canoe journey I did some years earlier with family (excluding my parents) as well as on a day outing with Antwerp AC.

At the end of the school year, a party was held in the school and I ended up drinking too much and being sick the next morning. Ma and Pa were away for a few days, probably with one of the organizations of the parish; but I was to participate in a street run in the center of Antwerp, which had been advertised through school; it was an event in which Walter also participated. Being sick till almost right up to the moment of the start, I still ran the sixteen kilometers (ten miles) in a little over an hour, which was madness. It would have been better had I simply run along with Walter at a somewhat more steady pace. Better still, I should have stayed home from the party, which I did not really enjoy anyway, so that I could have enjoyed my first street run.

Shortly afterwards, I undertook a cycle tour in the south of England with my school friend Paul. Starting off in Portsmouth, we made a circular circuit, passing through Winchester, Stonehenge, and Salisbury. At one point, we took a smaller road, not of

At Salisbury during a bicycle trip with a school friend to the southern counties of the UK at the conclusion of my secondary school years (1984)

proper asphalt but rather of grit, that made a steep descent. We went probably too fast and my front wheel buckled and then totally collapsed at the uneven surface. I flew into the nettles along the side of the road. As I groaned somewhat, my friend straightaway said that I could groan as much as I liked but that it did not affect him. Anyway, I was unscathed but needed another wheel. Paul was helpful in cycling on to the local village and there they took him with a car to a shop in the city where a wheel of the right size was found. I did not forget the incident though; after our return home, I hardly visited anymore and we lost contact: partly also because we entered upon different university courses.

That same holiday, I cycled with Patrick, Sonja's brother, to Barvaux-sur-Ourthe, a village situated on the river Ourthe in the municipality of Durbuy. We were staying a few days with Walter and Sonja, who had booked a chalet in a holiday park nearby the village. It was a cycle of about 150 kilometers to get there.

As regards Jenny, she was often in a bad mood. In a way, her childhood had been stolen from her; and now at early adulthood, she rebelled. She liked to socialize and going out; Paul, her husband, liked to have a nap on the sofa. She would have liked to join a sports club, but Paul was not in favor of it either; and when she stayed away from home ten minutes longer than usual, he already went looking for her. In short, her marriage with Paul was not going too well, and she started to look for escapes. After some upheavals, the situation stabilized somewhat and a second child, Karen, was born to them in August 1985.

Yet for my narrative, I need to return to the autumn of 1984, when Ma's illness manifested itself. It would mark the beginning of the last chapters of life on earth together with my parents: a period spanning five years that I will turn to in the coming chapters. It is roughly the period also that I studied physics at university.

# 13

## "Five more years" (1)

B EGIN OCTOBER 1984, I enrolled for a science degree in physics at the University of Antwerp, at the RUCA campus (Rijksuniversitair Centrum Antwerpen) in Wilrijk. Officially, the name of this campus has been changed in 1991 from Royal University Center Antwerp to University Center Antwerp since education has become a responsibility of the federal Flemish Government, but the abbreviation RUCA has remained in usage. The program for the physics degree consisted of mathematics, physics, chemistry, and computer science. For a large proportion of these classes, we were joined by those studying for a math degree, though we had considerably more laboratory classes than did the math's students. One girl, Sabine, from my classmates in the Royal Athenaeum did the math's degree and one boy of my former class, Leslie, started the physics degree with me.

Considered from a pedagogical standpoint, overall, the math lectures were given in an appalling manner. Basically, the lecturer would be writing on the blackboard and stop now and then to say something about it to the few at the front who were the bright ones. Only a proportion of students could grasp what it was all about while they were copying. For the classes in analysis, a branch in math, these written notes were all that was available; no printed notes were available, and no books were being recommended to us. I had difficulty keeping up with copying the blackboard, but I did not intend throwing in the towel so quickly. Leslie made perhaps a more realistic decision than I did; he had enough after a few weeks and decided to go for a pilot-formation instead.

During the first weeks an initiation took place for freshmen. The student union for math and physics' students was called Winak (coined from the Dutch terms *wiskunde*, "math," and *natuurkunde*, "physics") to which all students in those faculties belonged (and nowadays, also computing-science students). At the end of the last lecture of the day, a group of students from the other years would burst into the auditorium, all dressed in white laboratory coats with an orange and black scarf diagonally hanging from the body over one shoulder; the coats being covered with various drawings. All members had such a coat, and I would later do the same with the one I had acquired for chemistry classes at the Athenaeum. A few of the seniors took to the platform and addressed us. One or two of the bright students at the front would have none of it and wanted to leave. But this did not do for the seniors, who asked them to participate a little, for one had to become a member of the group. One bright fellow took his bag and did not want to be part of it. After an attempt from the seniors to have him change his mind and him being obstinate, they tore his shirt and pushed and threw him out; he did not return to the course—From Winak's website it appears that nowadays apparently the voluntary aspect of membership is better upheld. After a lot of silliness, we were jostled out of the room and had to walk through some fields to another building. At some point we came at a pond; we were not to go around it, oh no. The boys had to take their shoes off and carry a girl-student on their back over it. I and the girl on my back managed to get to the other side unscathed. These playful initiations would take place during a few days and then with all other student unions a march was organized through the streets in the center of Antwerp. Each student union had an open trailer on which a few of the seniors stood; and we, freshmen, and other seniors walked behind it: there was a lot of noise, silliness, and beer being part of it. In any case, I quickly seem to have made friends with some other physics students.

Especially for the classes in analysis and algebra I felt quite inadequate, but I kept copying. Often though, it was simply quite ridiculous. Perhaps about a hundred students were in the auditorium for these classes, and I remember on one occasion sitting in the middle of the room beside Carl, whose eyesight was not very good, for a class analysis. The lecturer was rapidly filling the large blackboards with analytic definitions and equations. Indeed, one needed rather good eyesight to carefully read and copy. The one board having been filled up, he pushed it upward and started the empty board that came down. Afterwards, he did the same with the two boards besides these. And then he started back at the first board which he wiped clean, and so on. I was well behind and was trying to copy before it was being wiped off; Carl copying from me. At some point I failed to notice that the lecturer had moved the boards up and down and, as a monkey, copied the same board twice entirely; Carl still copying from me and not noticing either. In the meantime, we had of course gotten further behind and struggled to get everything copied before it was gone. What a desperate situation it was. Back at home, I eventually studied the sheaves of paper and tried to make sense of them at my own pace. But the physics program consisted of many hours a week of lectures and laboratory work; for the latter reports had to be handed in within time limits, so that I would generally lag far behind in time before I would get to look at the notes gathered in the lectures and at the printed courses that were available for some subjects. A number of students decided it was not for them and dropped out. Even Carl would drop out after the exams at the end of the first year, though he had been a very good student at the Saint-Xaverius Institute; he decided to change to an engineering course as quite a few others did. I would come to realize in that first year that my only chance of success was by attending the classes that I absolutely needed to attend and to not attend quite a few others of which course notes were available and work at the papers in my own time and pace. I had to do it my own way. As time went on, I became the student who missed the most classes, even though attendance to all classes was expected.

Since the university campus was at a distance of between ten and fifteen kilometers, that is, less than ten miles, I was able to cycle to it; though some days I took the VW, Beetle car of my parents. I was still living at home.

My parents and I still went regularly to church. They usually went to the ten o'clock Mass on Sundays, while I often attended the eight o'clock Mass: it was a Mass without a choir and without hymn singing; overall, a more meditative event which I preferred; and it was more time efficient for me.

Mother was still a member of KAV but was not so much interested in it any more: women of a younger generation increasingly had taken over responsibilities from those she associated herself with—a few years later two separate groups would be formed: KAV and Young KAV. In the meantime, she had become a member of the Legion of Mary. She would have attended prayer meetings. I am not aware of this local group having been involved in missionary outreach among the populace, but I may be wrong. About this membership, to my knowledge, probably not ten words were spoken at home. Another involvement with the parish was that she partook once a year in the great spring cleaning of the church and would keep doing this till her last years.

I still went running fairly regularly but now always on my own; I was no longer involved with competitions. As I did for a large part of my youth, I ran towards a local park, Boekenbergpark (Beeches-Hill Park), where I ran a few times round a beautiful circuit. Over the years, I often halted at the same spot between the trees at the foot of a slope not far from the main entrance (but not visible from it), where I did a few stretching exercises. The place became so familiar that it was as a little homecoming to stop at the spot and perform my exercises. I often thought, "Here I am again." Earlier, one of the disciplines I sometimes performed was to sprint up the slope, run slowly down again, and repeat the same a number of times. During the years that I stopped there, a standing board had been put up explaining about the creatures that made up the community surrounding the ivy-covered tree nearby. Gradually the board deteriorated as wetness got to the paper behind the glass.

One evening in the late autumn of 1984, as I came home with my bicycle from the university, I found my parents sitting at the Ikea table, heavily upset. I knew Ma had some days earlier visited the general practitioner with a concern about something in her breast. The doctor, however, had reassured her after brief examination that it would almost certainly not be something to be worried about but had sent her for a biopsy, which was a painful affair. The result of the biopsy: she had breast cancer. It was a great disappointment, especially after the reassurance of the doctor. They were both crying.

enough though, as I look back upon it, despite all that vehemence, he gave very little importance to prayer or a personal relationship with God. He said that he did not need to pray, for God the Creator knew all. He read the Bible regularly; but I have never known him to consult commentaries on scripture or any theological publication that might inform or challenge his own outlook: his own literal reading was and had to be the only true one.

Several times a day, Pa walked up and down to the aviary at the back of the garden; the workplace behind it had a sizeable window that allowed for looking into the aviary.

I was about twenty. Often, in the weekends, I was alone at home with Bingo for quite a bit of the time: Carolina and Frans regularly went for a drive and at times ended up visiting his relatives or Moemoe or went cycling. Sometimes I just sat in the dark living room in front of the window with Bingo beside me. Though I liked quietude, I did not like to be alone in a house by myself. A large cross hung above the door in the living room and at these times, I would be driven to pray to the cross asking a safe return for my parents; I knew Pa's driving skills were not anymore quite what they had been. Bingo knew what was going on and had an uncanny instinct that told him five minutes in advance that my parents were going to come home. At other instances of such times, when I heard the slightest noise somewhere in the house, my old demons were in sway again. It happened that I took one of the crosses and went around the dark house holding it in front of me to chase away all demons. Was there someone in the dark corridor? What if someone was hiding in the cellar? I needed to reassure myself by going everywhere with that cross or by continuously making a sign of the cross in front of me. I also went outside in the garden in the darkness to the workplace at the back so as to close it, or just in attempts to confront and overcome my demons. Bingo just made the most of it and raced around, stopped to have a pee against the flowers, and did not worry too much about any demons. To be honest, I was pretty mad or at least pretty disturbed mentally at times. It was an awful and long mental battle with ups and downs: Is it entirely over? Probably not. So, has faith, that divine gift, come about by a heavy commotion in the Ur-sentiments including fear and worry, those lowly creaturely sentiments which were already shared-in by people millions of years ago? Yes, it seems to me: certainly in my case with my turbulent mind. Though inquisitiveness and lucid reasoning have a role as well in the reception of faith and in preventing it being suppressed. Dwelling upon this a little further: It may be proposed that it is when being driven beyond what is tangible (that is, that which presents itself immediately to the senses and with which capitalist consumer society expects us to be preoccupied with most of the time) into the realm of original sentiments and powers—perhaps accessed only in more or less disturbed states of mind—that the lowly (as nearly opposite to divine) creature may come in touch with its own elementals and hither by the most elevated divinity be bestowed with the most precious gift of faith and new, authentic insight and life that come with it.

Perhaps around that time, I decided for my bedtime reading to read in the Bible. I had my small student-Bible that the lady-teacher of religion in the Athenaeum had made us buy. I probably started at the beginning. Having arrived at the book Wisdom, I read how Solomon asked God for wisdom. Inspired by this, I prayed God regularly for the gift of wisdom. I read through the Gospel of Matthew, a few chapters at an evening. I was familiar with the stories and the portrayal of the life of Jesus, for I had heard the gospels being read over the years in church. But now that I read the entire gospel myself in sizeable chunks at a time, it affected me deeply. I was greatly touched by the story of Jesus' life; and I believed that, in essence, the story gave a truthful picture of him. I cried when I read the Passion for the first time with full attention. The affirmations regarding the efficacy of prayer equally made an impression on me. Such as in Mark's Gospel, "Truly, I [Jesus] say to you, whoever says to this mountain, 'Be taken up and cast into the sea,' and does not doubt in his heart, but believes that what he says will come to pass, it will be done for him. Therefore, I tell you, whatever you ask in prayer, believe that you have received it, and it will be yours" (Mark 11:23–24). I had in mind at the time that a war was going on—I cannot even be sure what conflict I was thinking of: perhaps the Iran-Iraq war or the Israel-Palestinian conflict—and thought, "What if someone empowered by faith in God should stand in the middle of the fighting factions and cry out, 'Stop!'" The gospel text is so adamant that I found it to confront me directly with a challenge. My parents were already both asleep in the next room. I got up and sat at the side of my bed deliberating whether I should just go away and leave everything behind right there and then. Would they hear if I passed through their bedroom, opened the door, walked down the stairs, and opened the front door and closed it behind me? I first would have to leave a little note for them. What was God asking of me? I deliberated. Luke 14: 28–30 came into my mind: "For which of you, desiring to build a tower, does not first sit down and count the cost, whether he has enough to complete it? Otherwise, when he has laid a foundation, and is not able to finish, all who see it begin to mock him, saying, 'This man began to build, and was not able to finish.' I went back into bed and thought that I should prepare myself better. Was it a failure or was it wisdom to be prudent and more pragmatic? I guess the latter.

Up to that time, in the season of Lent of the foregoing years, a communal penitential service had been organized in which no private confessions took place, but that year—or thereabouts—in the Lenten, communal, penitential service, the faithful were encouraged to go for private confession. Pater Pastoor (Pater Johannes), Pater Jef, and his older brother Pater Lieven (Berghmans) took up position in a different place where people could meet them individually for confession. After the communal introduction, probably to my parents' surprise, I went out and went to Pater Lieven who was to be found in the weekday chapel. I had never been to confession and had not received any prior instruction about it. Pater Lieven—the old, saintly missionary with his long, grey beard—was sitting in the chapel and it was clear that one had to go sit next to him. I did not know any of the conventional formulas but would simply have expressed that I am very sorry for my sins. He gave the absolution, a small penitence, and said, "Congratulations." So, I was glad I had gone to see him. When I left and closed the door behind me and looked up, I saw Ma waiting in the hall, and she went in to see Pater Lieven after me.

Now, returning to Uncle Eugène: Besides reading his Bible, he was a fervent practitioner of consulting a swinging pendulum above various charts or above trays of remedies; that is, the ancient art of divining (which can be by means of a divining rod—especially for underground water or minerals—or of a pendulum). Several decades earlier, he had gone to learn this art from an elderly woman. Since I had quite a bit of trouble with hay fever, he proposed to consult his pendulum about it. I was open to the idea. I read some of his old, French books about it, and I acknowledged the accounts of his about the instances he had been able to help others with his pendulum. Later, I would even buy two pendulums and some books and charts. Though I spent some time trying to initiate myself into this art, it has not come to anything: mainly because eventually I decided that I needed to spend my time and efforts elsewhere. From what I read, I am still convinced that some practitioners are very gifted in this and are really able to divine on various subjects and able to help people with illnesses.

My uncle's opinion was that my hay fever was mainly due to malignant nutrition. In particular, he was convinced that chlorine had built up in my sinuses and in my head so that my vitality and memory were being affected as well. He proposed some adaptations in what we ate. My parents already grew much of their own vegetables, which for the winter period were cooked and preserved in glass cans, and fruit, which also was being preserved in cans or made into jam. They also grew potatoes, which were kept in the cellar in a large wooden crate and sprayed with a product (made by Bayer chemicals) that prevented too much sprouting. According to Uncle Eugène, that product was chlorine based and was also used as a poison. He proposed we threw all the potatoes out and stock up with his own potatoes. The following years, my parents still grew their own but no longer sprayed anything on to them but now and then went through them and took off the shoots that grew from them. Uncle Eugène proposed that they bake their own bread, which from then onwards they did. Pa had worked in a bakery in bygone days, and Eugène came to show how it was done as a refreshment initiation so as to start us up. Uncle Eugène proposed, in addition, that we open up the old ground-water pit that lay unused at the back of the house just beyond the paved area that lay behind the veranda. A new hand pump was installed and we kept the water, at first in a large bin with a lid and some years later in a large milk can bought from the farmer. In fact, much of this is a back-to-nature approach that does not particularly require the insight gained by a pendulum.

In addition to the change in nutrition, he proposed I take some products and I trusted him with this. In particular, I was to take some black graphite tablets, because these would absorb chlorine, and Aldrox in liquid form, which is an Aluminum-based medicine. The effect of all this was that my hay fever temporarily got worse just at a time that I was preparing for exams of my second year physics. In addition, he advised me to take Epsom salts so as to supplement magnesium, of which he claimed that there is a deficiency in overall present-day nutrition. I followed his advice and took Epsom salt for several years. It appears indeed that magnesium is a good supplement for the mind and hence for students; however, no longer would I take it in Epsom salt but only in a proper supplement in tablet form. Presently, I would be much more careful before taking anything such as Aldrox or

Epsom salts, which can have adverse effects if not taken for which they are not intended.

Uncle Eugène also voiced that in his opinion Ma never had cancer. He denied that the operation had at all been necessary and believed that the doctors had been utterly wrong in their assessment.

We surmised that his advice was in certain aspects excessive, but we still gave him considerable credit. Looking back upon it, some advice was sound: such as moving away from drinking lemonade and drink water instead, and the baking of homemade bread. These things I do to this day. But Uncle Eugène, as well as Aunt Irma—who, by the way, believed in the art of divining but did not think much of her husband's adeptness in it—would say that tomatoes are bad since the pits give you cancer, bananas are bad for the liver, apples are bad because they are acid; in fact, nearly everything was bad. I, as well as my parents, most likely went too far along with him; but he was in his own manner very imposing and kept insisting.

A few chapters ago, I noted that several years earlier, before the years that we were out of touch, Uncle Eugène got an Alsatian, whom he called Cor. At the time, Cor was kept in a dark shed in the back of the garden. After we got back in touch, almost ten years later, Cor was no longer around. We saw that in the middle of the garden along the side, a large, iron cage had formerly been erected that was standing empty. It had been for the purpose of Cor. The dog had always stayed outside, except during the bitterest nights when it was allowed in the garage. We learned that the dog had died after only four or five years; that his fur coat had shown large bald patches towards the end. Uncle Eugène claimed that the reason for this had been the chlorine in the tap water and that this eventually made the dog die prematurely. But later I learned also that the dog had been mainly fed white bread and water. I should have been alerted by this but was not at the time. I now perceive clearly that Cor would not have died from tap water but from malnutrition; the animal had not been properly taken care off. One does not sustain an Alsatian with white bread soaked in water; it is a very cheap way of feeding but is tantamount to neglect. It illustrates to me, moreover, how self-deceived Uncle Eugène was in certain aspects.

My parents admired the garden of Uncle Eugene for the fact that it did not have a single weed and that he was able to grow strong vegetables. At least once we went home with a number of leeks. He admitted though that he sprayed his garden with DDT, which is illegal but which he still managed to get somewhere. The fact is that DDT causes cancer and that what we ate from his garden would not have been the healthy, home-grown vegetables that my mother and father took them to be.

I realize that I have gone on for some length about my uncle, but his influence and the effects thereof have been pretty significant both for me and for my parents as I will give further details of.

During that summer when I was adopting the various changes and products proposed by Uncle Eugène, my hay fever was quite severe and my ability to concentrate was nil. I would sit down in the morning to study but daydream instead, and while still at it in the evening, I did not manage to turn a single page all day. I should not blame my uncle for this entirely, but his proposed measures certainly did not help me at the time. Inevitably, I failed the second year of the degree; my frustration was augmented by the fact that I knew I had the capacity to have done much better. So, I had to retake some courses of the second year, as in fact did several of my fellow students.

After I finally passed the second year, I contacted Christianne. She had been in my class at the Athenaeum of Deurne for several years and she had been one of the students who, as me, followed the Catholic-religious-education classes. She went afterwards to study biology at the same university campus, that is, the RUCA campus. She lived in Merksem and I once had briefly met her at the sports centre there while I was competing with Antwerp Athletics. Later, at one of the large-scale parties organized by the various student unions at a location in Antwerp, while I was among the physics- students, I had once gone up to her while she was standing among the biology students and invited her for a slow dance. Sometime afterwards, at the beginning of summer, the academic year having finished, I wanted to telephone her and ask her for a date. The problem was that I did not have her address or telephone number. But I had some clues: I knew she lived in Merksem not too far from the sports center De Rode Loop; I knew also that she took the bus to school and hence, assumedly, was living in a side street of Bredabaan where the bus passed along. I found in the telephone book four entries for her surname that had an address in Merksem. I mapped them out and found that two were in a side street of Bredabaan not far from the sport centre. I guessed both might be family of each other and took my chance by telephoning the house that was further down in the street. I got an answer of a mature man and asked to speak to Christianne. He asked who it was and I gave my name. He knew who I was and went to get Christianne. I had phoned the right number at my first attempt. I spoke with her on the telephone and asked whether she wanted to meet. She did but only at the end of the summer after her exams, for she had to prepare for the second sitting of the first licentiate at the UIA. (It is the same course that Sonja did years earlier.)

In the meantime, though, my mind was being pulled in diverse directions. Just before this, I had gone to a physics party at the end of the academic year, and I remember thinking while sitting there that I might take an unconventional path based upon faith in God. If Christianne had agreed to meet shortly after my call, things would probably have developed from there. But that is not the way events unfolded.

Before the academic year had ended, I already had enquired, together with a few other students, about studying for the licentiate degree (roughly equivalent to a master degree) at the Catholic University of Leuven. Eventually all other students went to UIA in Antwerp; but I had heard that the quality of lecturing was not too great there, and I went instead to Leuven (which has a larger physics department) as the only one of my year. As it is, I never telephoned Christianne later in the summer, and I did not go to the UIA campus. Admittedly, I have felt guilty about this. But it just did not happen.

# 14

## "Five more years" (2)

MY GOING TO Leuven brought many new experiences. I no longer could study from home but had to rent a room. Albeit, looking back upon it, the distance from Borsbeek to Leuven is not so enormous; if I would do it again, I had better commute by car from home. But at the time, I needed to be away from home. My room at home was above the living room, where the television was often on quite loud. I was also getting annoyed that most conversations turned around the marriage problems of Jenny.

At Leuven, I went to evenings of Bible study organized by the University Parish. It was guided by a Jesuit. Each time, I got into discussion with him since I interpreted the narrated experiences of the apostle Paul in a literal or descriptive manner, whereas he took them in a more figurative way. After a few times, I dropped out.

The year before I went to Leuven, Ma had mentioned a girl who wanted to be in touch with me. It was the daughter of the physiotherapist in Wommelgem whom my parents had been visiting twice a week for several years for treatment of the arthritis of Pa. The girl studied chemistry at RUCA. Eventually, as Ma informed me, she went to Leuven the same year I did, since she was disappointed with the teaching at RUCA. Unfortunately, she did apparently not cope well in Leuven either. After perhaps two months in Leuven, I decided I was ready to look her up and asked Ma to enquire about the address of her lodgings. But by that time she had given up the course and, moreover, her cousin having just died, she was in a mournful state at home. It was then not the moment to make contact. Looking back, I wonder why I did not take the initiative to look her up later at her parents' home in Wommelgem, for the family knew me well enough; I even helped her brother with a little mathematics tuition a year or so later. Again, I have felt guilty about this. But it just did not happen; I never met or spoke with her. Apart from what went or did not go through my mind, I would have been struggling with adapting to the physics program at Leuven University, with the time-consuming commuting by train and bus, and with all what happened at home. But perhaps these are just excuses.

What I can report from that period at home is that my parents delighted in seeing their grandchildren. What was unfortunate was that it occurred that as a way of punishment of his children, Paul forbade Sven and Karen to visit their grandparents. My parents—Ma particularly—took that very hard. It is here to be considered, of course, that for a long time she had been separated from her own daughter, Jenny; it was therefore just too much to take.

Now it was the yearly custom of KAV, of which Ma was still a member, to pay for a trip to Lourdes for a sick person. The choice was made by a few core members and for 1987 they selected my mother, known to them as Lily. Hence, the next summer my parents went for a week to Lourdes together with another couple, Jan and Bertha Van Dijck, whom they regularly met to play cards: Jan was a former colleague of Frans in the police force and Bertha and Carolina got on well. It was my parents' second visit to Lourdes, since they had visited it about fourteen years earlier with Uncle Eugène, Aunt Irma, and Herman. This time, they went by night coach and they found it much harder than they had expected to travel that way. Jan travelled along to Lourdes, even though he did not take the faith that seriously. At everything he would make demeaning comments. But he was Frans's friend, and Frans was always a loyal friend who would follow along with Jan, who thus exerted a certain influence upon Frans. The fact was that to large extent Jan spoiled what should have been a holy and beautiful pilgrimage.

In the meantime, Jenny's marriage had become untenable. During the week Carolina and Frans were in Lourdes, Jenny telephoned and asked whether I could help her to move out and remove furniture while Paul would be at his work. The circumstances were such that it was best I refused; she had some other men to help her to move out. As I took Bingo for a little walk during the day, I passed Paul and Jenny's house, since it was but about one hundred meters away from our house, and saw the removal van. Unfortunately, I failed to notice Sven and Karen in the car parked along the curb. Sven was a little boy and he would have been desperately banging at the window to draw my attention: his home was being broken up before his eyes as his parents were splitting up; and would he still see his grandparents and me and Bingo? Twice I passed and twice I failed to see him and Karen, as I looked the other way or looked down.

Later in the day, I was working outside at the back of the house on my bicycle. I knew it was about the time Paul was going to come home. I knew well enough that a great uproar was pending; and indeed soon after, while I was at the back of the house, I heard a loud roar as Paul came home further down in the street.

One minute later, he was ringing at our door as I had expected. When I opened the door, the entire neighborhood was standing at their doors, looking on. Paul shouted out, "Bob, come and see, come and see, everything is gone. Oh no! Oh no!" It was a big shock to him; and indeed, it was a pity that things had evolved this way. I trotted along with him to his house, all people looking on. I was grateful that Ma and Pa were not at home; for I knew— as probably Jenny knew—it would have been terrible for Mother particularly. Paul asked, "Had I seen it, when they moved things?" Yes, I did. "Why did I not telephone his work?" I did not. "Did I help?" No, I did not. Later onwards, Paul's father, Achiel, came also to see me. He was sorry for Paul's family and also for Carolina, who was held in great esteem by him. Walter as well came around at some point that evening.

When Mother and Father returned home from the Lourdes trip the next day, Paul stood already awaiting them at the corner of the street; instead of allowing them to come home first. I was sorry my parents had to be subjected to this. Ma came home crying from her Lourdes week.

For a period of more than a year, Jenny and Paul fought each other for guardianship rights over their children. It was a painful affair into which Ma and Pa were being drawn by Paul.

During this period, on the family front, a second child was born to Walter and Sonja early in 1988: a girl who was given the name Liesbeth.

As regards Moemoe; my parents kept visiting her every Wednesday and often on another day as well. They would have brought with them some washed clothes, a newspaper or magazine, and some fruit. On one occasion in that year, 1988, Moemoe asked Ma to take her wedding picture (of Ma and Pa) and that of Eugène and Irma away with them. She did not want them back.

These photographs had been hanging on the wall in her room suspended from a bar at the top of the wall with thin cords and attached with hooks. The glass of both framed pictures and the attachment hooks were broken. To all appearances, she had hit them from the wall with her stick in a rage. Yet my mother kept visiting her, and Uncle Eugène did as well.

According to personal notes that I would have started to collect a couple of years later, it is only in the course of 1988 that I began to pray the Our Father regularly on my own. Once I started it, it became a custom for me to kneel beside my bed, just before I went to sleep, and pray the Our Father.

In my parents' bedroom, on the chimney, was a sizeable statue of Our Lady of Banneux,

Our Lady of Banneux

and right above it, a large crucifix hung on the wall. Given the layout of the top floor of our house, I had to pass through their bedroom to get to my room. It happened that I prayed also there the Our Father when I passed through and addressed a few words to Our Lady. I knew of the existence of the Hail Mary, but I did not know the words. Now in front of the chimney with the statue stood the dressing table of my mother; and I knew that she kept some devotional booklets in it. So, I found the prayer right there and learned it. It became a very precious thing to me that I was now able to pray secretly the Our Father, the Hail Mary, and a few sentences that I added. I could pray in front of the statue and lift up my arms to heaven.

During a Sunday Mass at which Pater Jef preached, I heard him emphasize that it is proper not only to ask God but also to thank him and, at times, being able as well to listen to God. Heeding this advice, I began my private prayer with thanking God for my parents, followed by an Our Father and a Hail Mary, then I asked God for the gift of faith, and concluded with a moment of non-activity, of stillness.

As regards my study: I did not do well at my exams, despite that I still prayed for wisdom and despite all the effort put into care for healthy nutrition. Undoubtedly, it did not help that the room I rented proved to be in a terribly-noisy building full of students and that my neighbor liked to have parties in his room throughout much of the night. It made life impossible. For the following academic year, I found accommodation elsewhere. Nonetheless, I passed at the end of the summer; probably thanks to the candles Ma burned, in addition to my own prayers.

During that summer of 1988, my parents participated at a two-day trip with the Catholic Guild of Pensioners. They were supposed to spend the night in a hotel but insufficient rooms were available, with the result that a few people were transferred to another place; Frans and Carolina were among them. By the time they arrived back home, Ma had developed a heavy cough. She attributed this to having spent the night in a damp and drafty room. Only after a lengthy period did she overcome this cough.

A few weeks later, she started to suffer again from her lungs. She was often out of breath so that the doctor sent her for a few days to the university hospital for observation. The outcome of this was that she was found to have fluid on her lungs. Once this was removed, they sent her back home. But a fortnight afterwards, her condition required her to return to hospital and have once more fluid removed from the lungs. At that point, chemotherapy was proposed that would consist of an intravenous drip with medicines administered every second Thursday for four times, thus the entire treatment was to take two months. It did not seem that there was much clarity provided to them by the medical profession as to her overall health situation. Since they were in the dark as to her true condition, Eugène drove Ma to hospital for a conversation with the consultant who provided the treatment. She was assured that she would be healed. Prior to the proposed therapy, Uncle Eugène said a prayer for healing with imposition of his hands on her head. Ma complained to me afterwards that she did not have sufficient time to concentrate on the prayer because he had done the prayer and ritual too fast. After this, Uncle Eugène did not think that she should proceed having the therapy; but Mother, not quite sure, went along with the course of action proposed by the doctors. When she went to hospital for the first part of the therapy, which was to begin with draining the fluid from her lungs, it was found that there was none. Nevertheless, she received the first drip and was sent home. The days following she was very nauseous, could not eat, and had to lie down most of the time.

A little prior to this, at the beginning of the second and last year at Leuven, in October 1988, I joined one of the basis or core groups of the university parish. It was a group of eight friends. We went each Wednesday evening to the Mass in the church of the university parish, which is located in the Beguinage of Leuven; we went for meals together; and every fortnight we met for discussing a theme. Around the time that Ma was struggling with her lungs and was unwell, I went for a weekend with this group to a youth house in Scherpenheuvel run by the Salvatorians, or Society of the Divine Savior, which is a religious institute. I remember that during the night I prayed there for Mother, for I did not like to see her suffer. I prayed that her trials would come to an end and that she would be happy.

I was not much at home, for during the week I was in Leuven; and even during that weekend in Scherpenheuvel, I was away from home. It was, moreover, dreadful travelling with trains and buses during the weekends and very time-demanding. On Sundays I had to leave home shortly after lunch.

One day during these weeks, Frans had brought carrots from the vegetable patch; but without giving it too much thought, he had washed the dirt from them in a tub that was full of rather dirty rainwater. As it happened, after the meal, Ma, who was already much weakened, got even more ill. I heard the story when I came home. I was told that Bingo, who tended to be mad for carrots, did not want to touch them. Pa did his best; but to their mutual grievance, it did not always work out. Ma reproached him in her misery. It was all sad.

In mid December her family doctor was called for, since she had pain in her legs due to the fact that she was lying down much of the time. The doctor prescribed her medication.

Just after New Year, as it had been planned for some time, I would go with my physics class for a week to Moscow and Leningrad. The trip included visits to physics departments, including the famous Landau Institute for Theoretical Physics, located in a small town near Moscow, and some touristic outings.

The evening prior to my departure was that of the Thursday that Ma received the third drip. I was to collect her at eight o'clock in the evening from hospital with the car; she had been in hospital from around midday. When I entered the room that she was lying in, I found her awake. She recognized me and was trying to communicate something but was unable to do so. She formed the words with her lips but could not make them audible. I saw that she was still under the influence of an anesthetic and, therefore, considered that she seemingly had received the drip not long before. Obviously, she was not ready to go home. I went to see the nurse, who told me that Ma had had an unexpected reaction to the drip and advised me to wait in the waiting room. They appeared busy and not forthcoming with more information, so that I did not ask further. At ten o'clock, I went to see Ma again and found her asleep. Again, I went to the nurse and asked her if Mother would go home that evening. In a rather indifferent manner, I was told that she would spend the night in hospital and that she could be collected the next morning. It was the end of the conversation; she did not wish to give further information. That morning, however, I was to leave by plane for the trip to Moscow and Leningrad. With some doubts in my heart, I went ahead as planned. I knew my parents wanted me to go on this trip, which they had paid for. They themselves had never travelled by air and over such distance to a country such as Russia, and they would not have wanted that I would have stayed behind because the therapy did not quite go to schedule that evening.

While I was on the trip, I realized what Ma had wanted to communicate to me in hospital: she had prepared a list for me of a few names and addresses that I was to send postcards to. With all that went on, I had unfortunately forgotten it. It filled me with humility to realize that my parents loved me in so many little ways and that at the time that she was in such a pitiful state, Ma only thought of reminding me to take with me the list she had prepared.

When I arrived back home, things did not appear well with her. Her thick, brown hair was all falling out, and I heard what had happened when the third drip had been administered and also when the fourth had been given.

When the third drip had been given, an additional drug had been included for preventing the nausea it brought about. However, this added drug caused a violent reaction. Upon its administration, Ma would have been beset with madness: she started to abuse the two other patients in her room and threw everything she could lay hands on. The nurses managed to restrain her and inject an anesthetic. Not long afterwards, I would have entered the room. The doctors feared that her brain got damaged and did some investigation. They declared that no damage had been done and sent her home.

A week later, when I was still in Russia, already a fourth drip had been administered; this time without the added drug. She was immediately sent home. Pa helped her to the ground floor of the hospital and sat her on a chair while he went to fetch the car. In that space of time that he was away, she would have fallen from the chair. Though she was pitifully unwell, she was sent home.

The following day was the day that I returned from Russia. She was a little better by then but was still very weak and had to lie down most of the time. She was a sorry sight lying on a blanket on the couch in the living room and with her plentiful hair falling out in clumps. At the end of the weekend that I had been home, I pondered whether I should return to Leuven. However, Ma had been ill for a few months and they said that it would be ok; that Pa would look after her. I was sorry to leave again, but I had plenty of work for my course. When I bade them goodbye,

Ma sat smiling at the side of the bed. Before I went through the front door, I called out that I was leaving; Ma came to the top of the staircase; and I noted that she had already in hand a booklet of Pater Valentinus, o.f.m.—known by the faithful as the saintly father of Hasselt—for the praying of a novena.

My parents put up this plaque on the wall of their bedroom besides the door. It shows Pater Valentinus Paquay (1828–1905; beatified in 2003) and a prayer; translated in English it says: "Jesus! O loving Father – In misfortune and in pain, I have no other will than to be without will. Unto you, O sacred heart, I entrust all my grief, command all my sorrow. + In joy or in pain, always be content."

The following day, I telephoned in the evening from the physics department where I was working late in a laboratory for my thesis, so as to ask how she was doing. It was Walter who answered the phone. He told me she had died. He thought I was phoning back and knew already, since he had tried to get hold of me at my residence and had told my landlady. But I had not returned to my room yet, so I did not know until he picked up the phone. He would come to collect me in Leuven. Mother had died.

When we arrived in Manebruggestraat, Pa was sitting on the bench of the Ikea table; Uncle Eugène was sitting on a chair. Before Walter came to collect me, he had already made arrangements with the funeral director and with the parish priest for a burial and for the letters notifying her death to be printed. It appeared that when she had tried to eat something in the evening and was returning from the table to the sofa, she had sunk to her knees. Father had helped her onto the sofa. She asked that he would ring the doctor. By the time that the doctor arrived, she had died.

The days that followed were extremely hard for Frans. When he came down in the morning, he walked into the kitchen with his hands covering his face, crying. But graciously, the second night after Ma died, he saw her in a dream in the company of Saint Rita while they were taken up into the heights. Uncle Eugène asked him how he knew it was Saint Rita. He answered, "Since she looked like the statue of Saint Rita that stood on top of the side board in the living room." For this little statue, he had years earlier made a wooden surround covered with little plastic roses. The dream gave him comfort. On subsequent days, I saw him sitting at table reading in the Bible or with a small prayer card of Saint Rita held in his both hands, praying intently.

Initially, I considered speaking with the doctors about the exact cause of death; but eventually, I didn't. They would simply have told me what suited them, and it did not interest me that much at the time. I never even knew who they were. As I recall it, the doctors do not seem to have communicated an honest assessment of her health even to my mother. Walter, however, found details of the medications contained in the intravenous drip that had been given her and asked his neighbor, who was a consultant, what he could deduce from it. He answered that it is medication for the treatment of recurring cancer. So, from this would appear that she was not being treated for a severe pneumonia, or not merely for that. Nevertheless, Uncle Eugène kept insisting—to Carolina while she was alive and to us after her death—that she did not have cancer.

Granted that cancer recurred, even that it may have been virulent; it did not seem to me that she died from the terminal stages of cancer. In all appearance, she seemed to have succumbed as a result of the treatment. Her state of illness after each hospital visit made her so weak that, as I see it, her heart failed. Whether she was given the most opportune medication in her condition, I am not certain about. Certainly, the third drip with the added medication was a disaster and most likely accelerated her demise. And the way she was dismissed after the fourth drip was scandalous. I have never forgiven the medical profession for the way my mother was dealt with in her hour of need. But I believe that other reasons existed as well that contributed to her weakness. Earlier, I mentioned that Uncle Eugène advised us to drink water from our own well because it would not contain chlorine such as tap water. The fact is that this well was located at much less than ten meters from our cesspit. At some point after Ma's death, I became aware that cross-infection occurred. The water smelled as being infected.

We boiled it, but still, this may not have killed all bacteria immediately. Well considered, in former times, at the end of the nineteenth and the first half of the twentieth century, many Belgian children died just after they were weaned—as happened to several of Moemoe's siblings and to her elder sister's children. Unclean drinking water would have been a factor. I now believe that it has most likely been a contributing factor in Ma's weakness. These various factors together I assess to have been the cause of her heart failing a few days after she was administered the fourth drip.

The funeral took place in a full church. The professors of the department of molecular physics (where I did my thesis for the licentiate in physics) came from Leuven, together with some doctoral students, and Sandro Usala, a fellow student with whom I was friends and with whom I cooperated for laboratory experiments that required two students working together.

No doctor deigned to send condolences for her bereavement or showed any sign of humanity. More correct is that likely it would not even have entered their minds. In all appearance, to the hospital medics she would merely have been part of a statistic, and they would not have wasted time giving a spoken or written word to her little family either. What we kept receiving from the hospital over the following months, though, were bills for the chemotherapy and the drugs that they had administered.

The funeral being passed, one week or so later, I picked up my study. By then I was well behind and, though it was already February, had still to start measurements that could be used for my thesis, since my promoter had failed to obtain the required liquid crystals in time. What he did greatly help me with though is that he allowed Anita, the department's secretary, to type out my thesis, which was not a little task and which she fulfilled to a very high standard. I worked daily until late after midnight so that I did not have time for anything else. Unfortunately, in the meantime, Pa was alone at home, and he did not cope well. I succeeded at the first sitting of the exams with distinction. My thesis was perceived to be of a high standard; and, of course, it was beautifully presented.

My study for the licentiate was completed, but I did not know what road I would follow from there onwards. What I was fairly clear about was that I did not wanted to work merely for earning money. I wanted to make myself useful and to do something I would enjoy doing. One option that I considered seriously was to direct myself to the field of electronics. I went to enquire at the Industrial College of Don Bosco about the possibility to register as a free student and to follow some courses that would inform me about hands-on insights in electronics and would increase my insight in information science. I envisaged that it would equip me for the repair of supercomputers and for designing them. But my proposal for combining various courses in electronics that were normally spread out over the entire curriculum encompassing a few years was not so practical since these were often given at the same time. I then enquired about the possibility of studying through evening school for adults; but most that was offered in the curriculum, I already knew: only some practical classes would be of use to me. The professor who promoted my thesis discouraged this road and was of the opinion that I should either continue formation at postgraduate university level or as soon as possible go find work. In addition, an industrial engineer in electronics who worked at the department of molecular physics advised that instead of following these courses at a High School I would be better to learn through doing self study.

I had still to fulfill my conscripted military service. I had provisionally asked further postponement that would allow me to continue studying for one or two more years. In view of the idea of self study, I withdrew this request for further postponement and became enlisted with the contingent of 1989. Hence, I was called to present myself for a day of medical and other tests. Since my back is quite bent, the medics were not sure I was fit for military service; but I was registered for service nonetheless. In view of my elderly father who was alone, I requested that after the initial period of formation I would be allocated to a military barracks that would allow me to go home every night. This request was granted. The military service itself would last one year. Eventually, I received a letter informing me that I had to present myself for service at the beginning of March 1990; I was enlisted with the transmission troops, a section of the infantry.

In the meantime, I kept wondering whether I would truly be of use for people's wellbeing as a specialist in electronics or information technology. Was there another way that I might follow more profitably as a Christian?

I did not really have great interest in learning about animals or plants, but I was very much aware that people require good nutrition and air and therefore that it is of crucial importance to take care of the natural world. I decided that environmental protection was of greater interest to me than electronics and that it was somewhat more continuous with my formation in physics. I then enquired at the UIA campus about courses in environmental science and about the possibility to coincide these with my forthcoming military service. An interesting course would indeed be given that was still very new and mainly intended for various professionals that police environmental policies or advise the government on these or work at environmental agencies or associations, at water-purifying stations, at laboratories charged with control of food nutrients, and the like. Combination with military service was difficult since courses were given during two week days, but various pre-course materials were available that I could start with through self study.

I still remember clearly that around this period I saw on television a documentary about the Philippines. Pictures were shown of a gigantic waste place (Smokey Mountain) on the outskirts of Manila. At this place, several thousand people "lived" from what they found among the waste. It showed their cabins amidst which huge trucks hurtled daily. Again the question occupied me whether as a Christian I could be more profitable than as a specialist in environmental matters?

In those days of trying to attain discernment, I visited our parish priest, Pater Pastoor, and we spoke about my plans for the future. Since I had finished my course, I had been more regularly in touch with the Assumptionist priests who ran our parish. He too thought it a good thing to try find work in environmental matters, for example, in a water-purifying station. Smiling, he then added, "Alternatively, perhaps you could take over my place here." I answered that my thoughts had indeed vaguely turned towards the possibility of life as a missionary, but that I could not leave everything behind just like that; I was living with Father. Pater Pastoor was relieved that lately I showed more interest in the church. He said he had been wondering for years what had become of me, since I had never shown an interest in the parish or its activities. He continued that even while I was but a kindergartner Lily had entrusted to him that she did not know what would become of me but that she would not be surprised if I would become a priest. When later onwards, I went through Ma's prayer booklets and cards, I found indeed a prayer for vocations in a small plastic wallet together with a passport picture of me. This appeared to confirm what Pater Pastoor had told me. But I knew that my first task as a Christian was to stay home, and I entrusted myself to God with the thought, "that His will be done."

At the beginning of October, I acquired the pre-course material (five stenciled, preparatory course books in the subjects of math, physics, chemistry, economics, and environmental law) for the environmental course at the UIA and I slowly began work on these. In those weeks, Walter found on teletext—which was a relatively new system that allowed text to be broadcast on the television—a job advert from the Social and Economic Council of Flanders (SERV) for a licentiate in sciences with interest in ecology. I would not have thought to look for jobs and much less to apply prior to my military service, but Walter said that it would not necessarily disqualify me. I applied; and yes, I was enlisted for a comparative exam at the end of November. Again, around that time, I received a call from a school, Saint-Ursula Institute in the town of Onze-Lieve-Vrouw Waver. They had obtained my telephone number from the University of Leuven and asked whether I would be willing to teach physics in their school for a few weeks as a replacement for an ill teacher. I accepted this interim appointment, even though I had not completed a teaching qualification. My very first day, I remember, I had to take seven classes with next to no preparation. But I survived it. My last day in the school was October 17. Shortly afterwards, I was asked to teach math in another school, Sancta-Maria Institute in Zaventem.

The days of All Saints and All Souls, November 1 and 2, when it is the custom in Belgium that people visit the cemetery and put flowers on the graves of their deceased family members, was a particularly hard period for Pa. He went every day to the grave of Ma; but those days, he took particularly hard. As he said to people, Ma had been the second wife he lost through breast cancer. It did not go well with him.

When a fortnight later he got up from bed, he did not feel well. He said that he had pain in his chest. I asked whether he wanted me to ring his family doctor, but he did not want that. He would take it easy that day and stay at home. I should have known that chest pain requires immediate medical attention, but I didn't know it. He went to bed like this. At three o'clock in the night, he came to my bed and asked me to ring the doctor. He could not breathe and thought he was going to die. I got the doctor out of his bed and he came immediately. He gave an injection and I had to call for an ambulance from the local hospital, *Onze Lieve Vrouw van Middelares* (Our Lady Mediatrix). The doctor reproached me for not having called him earlier. On arrival at the hospital, they immediately took an ECG scan (electrocardiogram), and he was admitted in the intensive-care unit. It appeared that he suffered a heart infarct. I asked the nurse whether I should stay and whether I should go teaching the next day. I was told that I would only be allowed five minutes in the day and five in the evening, so that it was best to go to work; if need be, they would phone me. The next two days, the nurse told me that it was not going well with Frans; they could not increase his medication anymore and that he did not have a desire to live. The third day, it went a little better. Pater Pastoor brought him the sacrament of the sick. He asked to pray for him to Saint Rita, the saint of hopeless cases. The fourth day, while I was teaching, the head teacher came to fetch me upon a telephone call from the hospital. He was dying. A lot of time was lost in the school, when they tried to connect me to the hospital; they just could not manage their telephone system. Eventually I just had to run off without having spoken to them. It was an hour's drive with the car. It was in vain, he had died by the time I got there. Pater Pastoor was there and he told me that Pa had wondered where I was. I realized that I should have stayed these days more around than I did. I blamed the medical staff for not having allowed me to visit properly. Both Mother's and Father's death have given me a grudge against the medical profession that has never left me.

Father died on November 17, 1989. The nurses told me that he wanted to die. Before the funeral, Walter went to look in the cemetery at the spot where he would be buried. It was in the same meadow that Ma was buried. He would be buried in the next row of graves from the one Ma was laid in. This next row had nearly reached the spot behind her grave. Walter saw the gravediggers and asked them whether they could leave one space open in the row and open up the place next to it, so that he would be buried just behind her. And so it was done; Father's grave was in the next row at the same height as Mother's grave so that they lay head to head. Gerard had a gravestone placed upon Frans's grave that was identical to that of Carolina. But a few others of Frans's children, who had disowned him many years before, were annoyed that money was spent on this (and on a proper funeral and a coffin) and said that as far as they were concerned they would have put him in the ground just like that.

After the funeral, I taught for a few more weeks. I withdrew my candidature for the SERV job since I had not been able to prepare for the exam; and given my changed situation, I wanted first to think things over. In the remainder of the time prior to my military service, that is, from mid December until end February, I did not accept further interim teaching jobs.

The future now looked quite different to me. I was no longer bound by anything. Though I was mournful that both Ma and Pa had died, and now especially that Pa had died in such a state of sadness, I saw God's hand in it and was of the opinion that I would best enter a religious order.

In the meantime, Uncle Eugène now kept visiting me very regularly. He certainly wanted me to enter upon priesthood and wanted to influence me towards that as much as possible. He was keen to point out that the married state was often not a happy one anyway and that no one was more useful than a priest. Looking back, the fact is that for his own life choice he himself did not think of entering a religious order or the secular priesthood; I do not think that he would have touched it even with a ten-foot pole. Instead, he always hid behind the excuse of his ignoble birth, which he alleged would have disqualified him.

I enquired with a few orders, but the only ones I really had had regular contact with were the Assumptionist priests who served in my home parish in Borsbeek. The Assumptionists, having been founded in the nineteenth century by a French aristrocrat, Père Emmanuel d'Alzon (1810–80), presented them-selves as having a regular prayer life, as being active in various areas of pastoral activity (missions, schools, La Bonne Press in France, parishes), and as having a familial atmosphere among them.

Through his work as gendarme, Walter had become friends with a priest who was a member of the Missionary Oblates of Mary, another order that was founded in nineteenth century France; its founder was Eugene de Mazenod. Walter introduced me to his priest friend with the intention that I might replace my military service with a two-year humanitarian service in one of the missions of the Oblates. The priest proposed to contact a missionary in the Philippines, where I might be of some use and have a firsthand experience of the world's poor. Unfortunately, the answer that returned a fortnight or so later was that at a time of strong nationalism in the Philippines things would not be safe for a Western newcomer; the missionary was not in favor of me coming to join him. I made a similar enquiry at the provincial house of the Assumptionists in Leuven, where I was introduced by the Assumptionists of Borsbeek, but they were not keen on the idea either. They did not know me personally in Leuven and it was too sudden for them.

Instead, I would, after all, start my conscripted military service on March 5, 1990. Looking back, it was a pity that a firsthand missionary experience was deemed not feasible. Instead, a year would be wasted on petty tasks in some military barracks.

But prior to this, I was still some time at home in Manebruggestraat.

I sat alone at Christmas. Thinking about the various struggles of my parents, all they did for me, and their goodwill filled my eyes with tears. They were good people; and I was sorry for my own failures in response to their love. I put up the tree that had been brought out every year and that Mother used to decorate and the little plastic crib. I sat in the dark with Bingo. It was sad, but I was grateful for the great privilege to have known them; for their great love. Bingo understood and was aware that things would not be the same again; Mother and Father had died.

# 15

## Military service

A ROUND THE PERIOD that I began my conscripted military service, I attended a few weekends at the convent of the Assumptionists in Leuven that they organized for getting to know each other. Besides myself, a few other young people were enquiring about a life with the Assumptionists. One other candi-

This picture hung at the upstairs landing of our house in Manebruggestraat: "Praised be / believed be Jesus Christ for all eternity. Amen!"

date was Stijn, who was not even twenty and who had just completed a technical school where he learned about gardening skills. He was to start his military service as well, a few months later than me. At these early meetings, sometimes a young lady called Nadine was present, enquiring about the female order that Père d'Alzon cofounded, namely, the Religious of the Assumption. Another lady of a more mature age, Veronica, was enquiring about joining the Oblates of the Assumption, which were founded by d'Alzon as the female branch of the Augustinians of the Assumption. One other young man, Mark, was a few times at these weekends, but he did not pursue further as he could not bring himself to give up his job in Brussels as a driver of the underground trains. Eventually, it was Stijn and I that were said to be doing a pre-postulancy by regularly attending these weekends during our military service. In addition, through cooperation with the Assumptionists in Borsbeek, it was organized that I was to have somewhat more involvement with the parish as one of the youth leaders. As such then, my days were generally pretty full.

During the first month of my military service, I received the formation of an infantry soldier. I became part of a group of about thirty-six men divided over two dormitories. Of those in my dormitory, one name stands out: Van Bielsen. He was a farmer's son of just eighteen; the youngest of our platoon. A lot of time was spent on drill exercises and, towards the end of the day, on the cleaning of rifles and boots. Sometimes during the drill, when one made a mistake, as happened a few times to Van Bielsen, the commanding officer would shout in your face, but Van Bielsen would be quite unperturbed by it all. After one long day, we arrived tired in the room; instead of cleaning his rifle as the other men, Van Bielsen went exhaustedly to his bed and soon was asleep. I was cleaning my rifle around a table with half a dozen companions and we looked at Van Bielsen. We knew he would likely be picked on in the morning when the rifles would be checked. We decided to quietly take his rifle and clean it up for him. The next morning, at six o'clock, the officers came in and we stood besides our bed. They asked Van Bielsen to dismantle his rifle so as to see whether the various parts were clean. Van Bielsen did so and put the parts on the bed; he did not seem in the least surprised that it was clean. My neighbor and I glanced at each other; and smilingly, we shook our head. The officer looked at the rifle and found it, to his own surprise, in order. Van Bielsen put it back together and that was it.

We were made to camp for a few days in a wood and our small two-men tents were to be set up in a large circle with the officers' tent in the center. In the middle of the night, gunshots! As we had been ordered, we put on our boots and laid in front of the tent with our rifle at the ready. After a while, the officer went round and checked on us. Eventually, the alarm was called off. It

Picture taken at my being called up for conscripted military service, October 3, 1989

was rumored that one soldier never bothered to jump outside with his gear and rifle but instead had turned around in his sleeping bag and went back to sleep: Van Bielsen. The officers somehow never found out. We had a good laugh about it.

On another night, in the same wood, I was ordered with one other soldier to keep guard and walk, silently, around the circle of tents; each one on an opposite side of the circle of tents and keeping some distance from it along a circumferential track among the trees. Of course, it was completely dark in the midst of the wood; I could not see anything. I circled around for a while but then found myself step right onto a tent. Some movement inside; I quickly made myself out of the way. I thought that I had ventured too close to the tents; but as I was aiming to get some distance from the circle of tents, I passed to my surprise more tents. How weird! As it happened, I had stumbled upon the officers' tent right in the middle of the circle.

At some times I did struggle with what was demanded. We carried heavy rucksacks and a rifle. As I am quite bent and lean, the straps bit into my shoulders and tended to cut off the circulation so that my arms went numb after a while. Once, I could not carry on any further and the entire platoon had to pause so as to give me a break. On one sunny day, we were training with the use of gasmasks. We were to complete a circuit one by one with our gasmasks and had to run and dive across a path with our rifle so as to defeat the bullets of an imaginary enemy. The sweat was pouring out of me, and I had to pull off the gasmask for I believed I was close to a heart attack. I needed to breathe freely. An officer was shouting us onwards but then perceived that I was at my limit. Another day that involved a bit of suffering occurred when during a march a strap of my rucksack gave way; I got behind and the same officer stayed behind with me and one other one that straggled behind—possibly Van Bielsen—until, biting my teeth, we caught up with the others.

The commanding officers knew that I had done university studies and that I was perhaps the most educated of the platoon, themselves included. Perhaps it was a reason that at times they liked to pick on me. Once, we had to spread out along a line so as to scan a field for I do not know what. We walked slowly along with our rifles ready. Now, where I was in the line I came upon a large pool of mud and cow shit. I knew the command would be given, and it did: "Govaerts, crawl!" I took it all in my stride; though it is not so easy to crawl forward while all the time resting the rifle upon the forearms preventing it getting dirty.

One last incident of those field exercises of that initial formation that I wish to mention is that it happened that we had to march through a brook. The command was to make sure the rifles did not get wet. One of the commanding officers stood along the bank. But I slipped upon the pebbles in the middle of the stream and automatically brought my arms down to prevent falling. The rifle went right under. I poured the water out of the barrel and . . . gave a big smile to the officer. He stared at me and, instead of trying to shout my head off, turned round and walked away.

In the mornings, I did not waste time to try getting a breakfast in the dining room: there was a lengthy queue to get to it, and I needed the time to get ready as it was. But I made sure I had with me a pack of large, square, student biscuits, and I went round those in the room that did not get to breakfast either. They gladly partook. One had of course to be a little careful that the officers did not find out. In the evening, if we had free time, most went to the canteen. I went instead to the chapel that was found in the barracks. As such, several evenings, I had the opportunity of entering a quiet space and saying the Rosary. The one in the bed next to me asked me where I had been all evening since he had not seen me with the others in the canteen. I said that I was in the chapel. He was surprised but appreciated that I gave the honest answer. Once or twice, I accepted his invitation to join with our companions in the canteen.

The following fortnight, I received an additional formation for transmission troops in another military barracks. During all that time, Bingo was alone during the week—during the weekends, we were allowed to go home. As far as I remember, I left Bingo access to the garden and to the workplace in the back. A neighbor from across the road —the same neighbor who formerly fed the birds in the aviary of Frans during our former holidays—came in to give him food and water and took him for a short walk. However, the neighbor next door told me that throughout all days Bingo was barking. I spoke with Pater Jef about this. He advised that since I was planning to join the Assumptionists, I would not be able to keep him. I was aware that the only viable solution might be to have Bingo euthanized by a vet; Pater Jef agreed.

After the initial period of formation, I was allotted to a local barracks in Schawijk at the outskirts of Wommelgem. It was close to home as I had requested in view of living with Father; even though he died in the month following this request. At the time, this military domain had underground bunkers filled with telex machines and a large broadcasting mast. I was assigned to the logistic department. I set out in the morning before seven o'clock with my bicycle and would be home again at about five o'clock in the evening. Once home, I took Bingo for a walk; I cooked, ate, and did the wash-up. By that time, it was about eight o'clock.

I made great efforts to try eating as healthy as possible. Upon Uncle Eugène's advice, I baked my own bread; just as Pa had done. Every few days, I baked. Yet, at the time, I was still learning to do this properly: it would take me more than half a year before I could produce a presentable loaf of bread. During all that time though, I kept eating my failed attempts that were supposed to be loafs. Yeast for making bread was at the time available in lumps of one kilogram purchased from a bakery and was to be kept in the fridge. A piece was to be cut from it and warmed in tepid water and then added to the flour in a bowl. Presently, things are made easier with dried yeast, commonly sold in supermarkets as sachets of Fast Action Yeast.

At least once a week, I would cycle to the farm at the other end of Borsbeek with a plastic bucket and had it filled with milk, for Uncle Eugène claimed that processed milk had chlorine added to it so as to preserve it longer. I even made jam and had prepared preservation cans with soup vegetables in the cellar so that soup could quickly be made. I realized, though, that I would not be able to continue all this once I would join a religious order. Moreover, it took so much of my time that I did not have time to sit down and read something or do anything intellectual. I was not happy with this but felt I had to make all these efforts for health reasons, such as my hay fever and lack of concentration. I prayed that I would be able to fulfill that what I was destined for; that I would bring forth fruit as a worthy Christian (see, for example, Mark 4:20 and parallels; Matthew 7:17; John 15:2, 16).

In the later part of May, a week of military exercises was taking place at Beverloo Camp, near the municipality Leopoldsburg in the Belgian province of Limburg, east of Antwerp. This camp encompasses a large military terrain and several permanent blocks. Part of its history is that during the Summer Olympics of 1920 in and around Antwerp, it was used for various shooting events; whereas during World War II, it was occupied by the Germans who used part of it as a prisoners-of-war camp and as a transit camp for the Holocaust. In his days of military training, Walter would have taken part there a few times in exercises. Perhaps about ten men of our barracks in Schawijk, encompassing both professional soldiers and conscripts, were selected to partake in the exercises for the week. I was to stand by as reserve in case one of them could not make it. It increased for me the acuteness of the problem what I was to do with Bingo.

Each day when I came home at about five o'clock, I found that Bingo had throughout the day been trying to get inside the house. The dirt on the windows showed that he had been jumping up against the windows, and he had been scratching the door with his paws. It was not good for him to be all days alone. Moreover, I knew I was going to be away for some weekends, possibly the week at Leopoldsburg, and I was intending to go for ten days to France in September. I asked Liliane, a neighbor across the road who always liked Bingo, whether she and her husband, Stan, could take him. But they could not. I asked Jenny; but she also could at the time not provide a home for the animal. I finally contacted Canina, a charitable organization who ran an asylum for cats and dogs. They thought it would be difficult to find a new home for Bingo, given his age; and that even if a new owner could be found, dogs often cannot forget their past and they are not happy. They were willing to take him in but they advised that the most humane solution would indeed be to have him euthanized by a vet with an injection. I decided upon that course; at least, I could then be certain that he would not end up in a laboratory for various inhumane experiments. The next day, after I came home in the evening, I telephoned the vet and, with pain in the heart, immediately walked with Bingo towards his house. I had spoken with the vet about this possibility but a few weeks earlier onwards, and he was sorry to see me that evening. Bingo was only about seven and a half years old. I stroked him while the vet gave him the injections.

One of the conscripts assigned to go to Leopoldsburg presented himself in the morning at the roll-call with his arm bandaged up. He alleged to have incurred a severe wound when working in a garage. No one believed him. In any case, he got out of the week exercises in Leopoldsburg; and I was called upon to go instead of him, since I was the first reserve.

In the bunker of the barracks, we each had a locker with our personal equipment. As I walked down the steps towards the lockers so as to make some preparations for the camp, I stepped on one of the straps of the rucksack that I was carrying in my hand and fell on my back; the middle of my back hitting the sharp steel enforcement edge of one of the steps. I cried it out from the pain in my back; but I managed to get up and crawl to a chair nearby the lockers. No one was about, and I sat on the chair for a little while in misery. Normally I would have called to see a doctor and get some time off for I could not walk upright; but I could not do that, for I would be thought of as having done it on purpose out of fear of the exercises. It would be seen as coward-ice. I just had to keep quiet and see it through.

The next morning I cycled up and crawled in the back of the Bedford truck where I sat with the others on the wooden bench for a bumpy ride; and many more bumpy rides were to follow that week on the rough roads of the military terrain. I struggled through the week in pain, but it was worthwhile to share in the various shooting exercises. The training was organized as a competition between various battalions. One event in it was a running competition through woods with our boots on. My heart was not in it because of the back pain. I set out gently and could not make large steps and lift my legs properly; indeed, I still could not walk properly upright. But I kept running despite the pain; and as I have experienced more than once, running helped me to get some betterment. Gradually, incredibly really, I passed the other participants one by one and moved towards the front of the race. Eventually, I ended in second position and was con-gratulated by the colonel for having gotten some good points for our battalion.

Besides all this, during a few nights we were to play war. The first of these nights, we were to sit in twos in pits and defend the camp from an anticipated attacker, which consisted of a company of Walloons. Unfortunately, it started to pour and our pit quickly became a mud pit. Soaked and muddy, we peered among the trees and bushes ahead of us. My companion thought he could see soldiers among the bushes. We soon started firing blanks in the pouring rain, and there was yelling from the attacking soldiers that ran towards us. The following night, I was part of a little group under the command of a sergeant and we had to move through the darkening forest towards the camp and attack at the agreed hour zero. I was carrying a sizeable field telephone. But our sergeant was not sure how to find our target amidst the woods and proposed we follow another group at some distance. We walked for some time in the darkening wood and jumped in a ditch when a jeep passed us. When we came out of the ditch, off course, the sergeant could no longer see the other group ahead of us. A lot of peering at the map and the decision that we return to the trucks—I did not have the map in hand and did not know where we were in the dark wood. At some point, we seemed to pass through a clearing, and we heard the unmistakable squeaking of tanks around us. I hoped they were equipped with infrared light and had a better idea of where we were than we had ourselves. Anyway, it was not my choice to be walking there: I simply obeyed orders and that was that. I just hoped that we would not be flattened. Sometime later, lying in the back of the truck that brought us, I was awoken by gunshots and a lot of upheaval: the rendezvous of which we were supposed to be part.

One time, we went with the truck to the shower block. There was a queue for each cubicle. When I eventually stepped into the shower cubicle, one or two were still waiting at each cubicle. I did not hang about and proceeded quickly, but when I came out washed and dressed some minutes later, I was rather surprised that I could not see anyone anymore. Even the fellow who was waiting behind me was gone. I think there was still someone in one other cubicle. Sounding from the horn of the truck; and lo and behold, I found all my companions sitting on the benches in the back, so they gave me a hand and heaved me in beside them.

Back at the barracks in Schawijk, sport stood high on the agenda when no other duties were required. Regularly in the afternoon we went running; sometimes, when no one else was available for running, I set out on my own. The regular destination for these runs with others or on my own was the wood of the domain Zevenbergen, which I had in years past visited with my parents on bicycle outings. When I was on my own, I could make a stop at the Lourdes Grotto at the border of the wood. How odd it was being able to stand there at the grotto while doing my conscripted military service.

I ran along the paths in the wood of the domain Zevenbergen. Once, going a good speed, my balding head was scarred by a low branch over the path that I had not spotted. Soon I was bleeding a good deal and held a handkerchief over the wound so as to prevent the blood running all over me while I made my way back to the barracks walking and running. By the time that I got back, it was just past five o'clock, so that I passed the others who were leaving in their cars. My little, blue sports bag was left in the corridor at the door of the logistics office.

Being part of the small logistic team of the barracks involved various tasks. Besides a few professional soldiers, two conscripts were assigned for logistics. One week both of us were sent to some large upper rooms near the military hospital in Antwerp. Our main task: the painting of the handles of about two hundred spades that were set aside for this touching up from among the several hundred that were kept in these rooms. Inevitably, it meant that the two of us spent quite a bit of time together. My companion at the time was Paul Van de Casteele. We got on well and sometimes played chess when we were in the office, but we had a very different outlook upon life. I liked quiet, wore a wooden cross, and—as Paul knew—was preparing to enter religious life. Paul could not understand this, and he thought that I was quite fanatical in my outlook upon life, similar to those American sect leaders who manage to get people behind them and then lead them in a common suicide. He liked me, but I was different from the others. He thought I had the potential to become a guru. "Why did I want to become a monk?" "Why did I not get a girlfriend just like him?" for I was nice enough. It did not make sense to him. He did not believe in God; he did not believe Jesus existed: he would rather believe in Bambi. Though he did not believe in anything; he wanted to discuss these things. As regards the existence of God, I expressed that I could not believe that the infinitesimal, hot plasma at the origin of the universe several billions of years ago worked upon by various physical forces would by a process of blind evolution have given rise to people capable of empathy, compassion, and love. In my view, a personal being had guided the entire process without whom there would be no universe and no higher beings, even people. Paul disagreed; he did not believe love existed. I asked him whether he had ever received love, for example, from his mother; or given love? "No." Did not his girlfriend love him? Did he not love her? "No," it was a matter of convenience; the filling of emptiness; instinct was a factor. Would he not give his own life for her if it was needed? . . . I can, of course, not remember the exact wording of that long ago conversation, but I very well remember it and the overall tenor of it. In addition, Paul could not believe because more than once he had been betrayed by (those whom he thought were) his friends. He said that "the human being is a malicious creature." My impression of him was that he himself was not malicious. Almost daily, the conversation turned to God.

In the meantime, I lived on my own in Manebruggestraat. In foregoing years, when my parents were still alive and when I was a student, I had a hi-fi stacking system and often played popular, modern music, sometimes quite loud. But with my faith outlook having becoming prominent, I moved away from this and some-times played classical music instead. After my parents died, I could not stand listening to the popular, modern music any longer. I found this music left a sense of emptiness. I no longer liked it. Even classical music did not particularly interest me at the time. I wanted and needed to dwell in quietude. I liked the peacefulness of a quiet house. As in former years, I still did not like being alone in a house during the evening and night, and I carefully locked every door and lowered the heavy roller blinds of the window. I was still a little wary on my own, but I was a few years older now and mentally somewhat stronger; and I found support in faith.

One day, as I was dusting the furniture in the living room, which was left unchanged from former years, I found myself in a state of complete serenity. I liked moving about quietly, in silence gently doing the tasks that needed doing. I wished, and do wish, that my entire life could be lived in such a state. That particular day, I found myself enveloped in a great peace, which was none other than the grace of God.

# 16

## A trip to Lourdes

MAY 11, 1990 was the day that I brought Bingo to the vet for ending his life. In the evening, I wrote down some thoughts. Inevitably, the day had given me a renewed awareness of the fragility of life. I considered that while our days are filled with various activities, we all need to die; and that at our dying, all that we—counting myself here among the Christians—are left with is our faith, and that all that counts are the actions we took or failed to take during our life. These actions testify to the love we bear in our hearts and lives.

That same day I finished reading a biography in Dutch entitled *Burgraaf in Habijt* (Viscount in Habit: the Life of Emmanuel d'Alzon, Founder of the Assumptionists; 1962), by Steven Debroey. It was worthwhile reading the book that had been given me in Leuven by Pater Arnold Castro, the superior of the Flemish province of the Assumptionists. Having read the book, I wrote down that the impression it gave me of Père d'Alzon was that of a worthy and great Christian. I showed the book to Walter, and he read it as well.

In July and August, I spent time writing about my parents: notes that have been most helpful for the more elaborate account provided in the foregoing pages of this book.

In mid September I was present as one of the youth leaders at a weekend organized for the youth of the Saint-Johannes-Berchmans Parish in Borsbeek; the name given to this group of youth was the Plussers. As was often the case when I spent some time in a group, I felt downcast at my coming home—though I actually never felt as such in the army. After the weekend with the Plussers, I found myself the least of all. While I knew myself to possess a very sensitive and intense character, I often found myself failing to express what I intended to say or do, so that I seldom was satisfied with myself afterwards. Coming thus home from the weekend, I watched in the evening on television the final episode of the movie *Around the World in Eighty Days* (1956), adapted for television, after the famous adventure novel by Jules Verne of 1873. The main character in the story is the extremely punctual, single gentleman Phineas Fogg, who lives in his London dwelling, where he has just employed a new servant. Having become involved in an argument in his gentlemen's club with all the other members about whether it is possible to travel around the world in eighty days as claimed by an article in The Daily Telegraph, Fogg insists that he will prove its veracity by actually making the journey. He bets with the other members that it is possible and puts in half his fortune, to be lost or doubled. Watching the movie, it entered my mind that, in fact, I could identify pretty well with the private, punctual Phineas Fogg who appreciated regularity in life. Towards the end of the movie, Fogg eventually expresses his great love for the princess whom he saved and helped to escape from India. I thought that I myself should in future perhaps try to express better what is in my heart and mind. It did not change my mind that before all I wished to serve the Lord God, but I hoped that I could serve him better than was the case at the time. I ended my written-down thoughts that day with

the prayer that the Lord would forgive me my multitude of weaknesses and that in future he would guide me along new ways. I
concluded with expressing my desire that God would enable me
to bring his will into effect.

A few days afterwards, I travelled to Lourdes. I was still fulfilling my conscripted military service at the time, which I had
started over half a year earlier. Each month, we had right upon
two days holiday. I had been saving up these days so as to travel
to Lourdes, and I planned to stay about ten days away from home.
The train ticket that I purchased was intended for young people
and allowed me to make four train journeys within Europe. It was
ideal for my purpose, for it meant that I could make a staged
return and visit some places in France on the way back home. But
my first journey was with the night train from Antwerp-Berchem
station all the way to Lourdes. Walter took me to the station in his
car on the Friday evening that I left. The train was to leave at
seven o'clock. Curiously, I found that the berth that was reserved
for me was located in a wagon in which I found no other people
present. The conductor checked my ticket before we left and
confirmed that it was indeed this place that had been reserved for
me, although the wagon was apparently supposed to have been
kept empty. He kindly fetched some bedding for me to put on the
berth nevertheless. So, that night I travelled in quietude to
Lourdes in my private train wagon. I lay down and was woken in
the middle of the night when wagons were rearranged for the
continual of the train's journey; every indication was that we had
reached Paris. In the morning when it was light and I opened the
blind, it was obvious from the mountainous landscape that we
were in the south of the France. It was exciting.

The train arrived on the Saturday morning at ten fifty. During
the entire journey, I was left undisturbed in the otherwise empty

wagon. I stepped out of the train into the sunshine of Lourdes. Twice, my parents had visited this place of pilgrimage; and now, I had reached it myself. As a first task, I searched and found a room in a small guesthouse; in a bakery I bought a few cakes and in a grocery a few bottles of water. These practicalities having been taken care of, I went to the grotto, where I burned a candle. From there, I went to pray in the Rosary Basilica and viewed its interior. Afterwards, I had a quick look in the Upper Basilica—in French,

The Lourdes Grotto

"basilique supérieure." I probably would have sat myself some-where on a bench to eat what I bought in the bakery and drink some water. I visited the places where Saint Bernadette lived in Lourdes with her family: first, the house of the family Soubirous; next, the Boly Mill, where Bernadette was born in 1844; and thirdly, Le Cachot, or the Dungeon, the former prison, a dark and cold room into which the family moved in late 1857 when François Soubirous, Bernadette's father, had become unemployed

and the family lived in dire poverty. It is from there that Bernadette went to the "Massabielle" Cave with one sibling and one
friend so as to gather some wood and bones for burning. On
February 11, 1858, at this unglamorous place, she saw Our Lady
for the first time, and again, regularly, in the weeks following.
The final apparition to her took place at Massabielle on July 16,
1858, at a time when the civic authorities had placed a large fence
in front of the cave. Looking on from a distance over the top of
the high fence, Bernadette saw the smiling, very beautiful lady; a
vision that engulfed her in ecstatic joy. Having seen these places
related to Saint Bernadette and the visions, I visited the castle,
which contains a museum about the history and folk culture of the
Pyrenees. My last visits that first day were a quick look at the
hospital and school that Bernadette attended, before I had a
proper dinner in a restaurant. In the evening, I participated in the
Candlelight Procession. And having returned to my room, I wrote
a few postcards.

On the Sunday morning, at nine o'clock, I attended the international Mass in the Underground Basilica: a large, concrete
construction of modern architectural style with a low ceiling that
can hold up to 25,000 people; its official name is the Basilica of
Saint Pius X, and it was consecrated on March 25, 1958—that is,
in the centenary year of Bernadette's visions— by Angelo Cardinal Roncalli, the then patriarch of Venice, who had earlier been
the Papal Nuncio to France and who later became Pope John
XXIII. After the Mass, I visited the exposition "Bernadette and
the Message of Our Lady" in the Pavillon Notre-Dame. It was
then time to buy something to eat in a bakery and in a grocery. As
I made my custom for most days, I would eat some bread, a few
rolls with cheese, or a pastry somewhere where I could sit undisturbed. That afternoon, I joined a bus journey to Gavarnie, which

is situated near the border with Spain. The route taken by the bus was pretty spectacular along the mountain passes: we came along Saint Luz de Saveur and the Pont Napoleon. At Gavarnie we were given perhaps two hours, which allowed for a walk along the path to the famous Cirque de Gavarnie, a colossal ancient-amphitheatre-shaped rock face formed by glacial erosion over millions of years. Waterfalls come down from the snow-covered top of the cirque. It was a beautiful afternoon amidst the glorious landscape of the High-Pyrenees. Returned in Lourdes, I had my evening meal in a restaurant, as I was wont to do during my journey. Since it was a rainy evening, I stayed in my room afterwards.

On the Monday morning, some light rain fell, but it quickly turned into another beautiful day. It was my third day in Lourdes. First I went to the grotto, where I said a brief prayer and burned a candle. At nine fifteen, I went to the Salle Mgr. Laurence for a presentation on the message of Lourdes that was followed by a guided Stations of the Cross within the domain of the sacred site: along fourteen stations depicting various scenes of Christ's Passion—from his condemnation to death, to his carrying the Cross, his encounters along the way and falls, to his crucifixion and death, as well as his taking down from the Cross and place-ment in the tomb—we slowly progressed along a steep, winding path. At each station, the pilgrims were guided in a brief medita-tion, some silence, an Our Father, and other prayers as we moved towards the next station. After the group disbanded, I still had time left before the half-past-eleven Mass that I planned to attend in the Upper Basilica of which the official name is the Basilica of the Immaculate Conception. In the time left before the Mass, I made a brief visit to the Church of Saint Bernadette, which at the time was newly built on the other side of the Gave; it had opened only a couple of years before, in 1988. It is situated opposite the grotto, at the place where Bernadette stood on July 16, 1858, when she received her final vision. In the afternoon, I visited the parish church. From there onwards, I got a ticket for the funicular towards the summit of the nearby Pic du Jer, which is almost one thousand meters above Lourdes. It offers magnificent views over that entire region of the High-Pyrenees.

Having returned from it, I walked towards the grotto along the outskirts of the town. Arrived there, I washed my face and said a brief prayer. In the evening, after my meal in the restaurant, I participated for the second time in the Candlelight Procession.

Tuesday was another day of good weather, around twenty-five degrees Celsius. It was my fourth day in Lourdes. As on the previous day, my first visit was to the grotto where I burned a candle and said a brief prayer. From there, I made my way to the Crypt where I spend some time in prayer. The Crypt is the sanctuary that was first built within the Domain, from 1863 until 1866; it was officially opened on Pentecost 1866. It is situated above the grotto and underneath the Upper Basilica. After my visit to the Crypt, I spent time climbing the steps at the first station of the Way of the Cross. At ten thirty, I was in the Church of Saint Bernadette for Mass. In the afternoon, I joined another bus journey: this time to the Sanctuaires de Bétharram, the place of an ancient Marian shrine and place of pilgrimage that is situated along the Gave du Pau in the vicinity of Lourdes. The second stopping place of the bus journey was the city of Pau. That evening, the last of my stay in Lourdes, I went once more to the grotto and participated for the third time in the Candlelight Procession.

The next morning, I took the train to Toulouse where I spent two days. They were two very warm days. A thermometer showed it to be thirty-three degrees Celsius on that first day. I visited various sacred places in the city: the Basilica of Saint

The Basilica of Saint Sernin, Toulouse

Sernin, the Church of Notre-Dame du Taur, Les Jacobins, which is the first Dominican monastery, the Museum of the Augustinians, the Basilica of Notre-Dame de la Daurade, which was dedicated in 410 and which was originally a pagan temple dedicated to Apollo. The last evening I went to drink something at the Place Saint George.

My train ticket allowed me to make one more stopping place on my way back to the north. The city I chose to visit was Cahors, and here as well I spent two days. Having arrived there, I left my luggage in a locker in the station and walked towards the center of the city. As I was wont to do, I bought some cakes in a bakery and sat down at the Place Lafayette situated next to the Church of Saint Bartholomew. From where I sat, I had a beautiful view of the surrounding mountains and of the nearby river Lot. A hotel was found adjacent to this place, upon which I went to collect my luggage. That first day at Cahors, I walked around, visited the

Cathedral of Saint Étienne, and read a book at the Place Lafayette. The second day, a Saturday, I crossed the river and took a
walking trail that led up the mountain across from the city. Finding a little bench, I sat all day overlooking the city. As always, I
had a book with me and read a little. Unfortunately, I did not
know any sacred songs and I was not a comfortable singer, but I
felt the need to sing God's praises, so I very poorly sang some
Alleluias. I felt close to God. Although I had climbed up the
mountain along a narrow track, I noticed that, after I had already
sat there a good while (until well in the afternoon), that perhaps
less than fifty
meters from
where I sat was a
cafeteria or the
like, which was
accessible by car
and which quite
a few people
visited. Never-
theless, the little
bench served its

Cahors, the river Lot, and the mountain across
from the city

purpose for me that day; it had been sufficiently secluded. In the
evening, I took the train and travelled back home. This time, I did
not book a berth but sat quietly in a chair.

Certainly these months, I felt a need to deepen my insight into
the Christian faith, for my formation had been very limited in
this; of course, to my advantage had been the fact that I had kept
going to church on Sundays, so that I was not a total stranger to
the life of faith. The desire for greater insight I expressed in a
conversation with Pater Pastoor. As we sat in his study room, he
reached for a catechism that he himself had found very helpful

and profound. It was a Catholic catechism of 1975 by a Swiss parish priest, Anton Schraner, translated into Dutch as *Katholieke Catechismus* (1979). I said to Pater Pastoor that I would look into it, but he was already writing at the front of the book, "Aan mijn vriend Bob, P. P." (To my friend Bob, P. P.) and handed it to me. It is a book that I studied and have indeed found very helpful. I would say that besides the Bible, it has been the most important book for my learning about the faith. Was it the book that I had with me on my pilgrimage to Lourdes and on that bench over-looking Cahors; it may well have been. My personal notes of thoughts that I at times penned down in the evening tell me that I certainly was reading it in the months following that journey. In particular, on October 22, 1990, I noted down that I was reading about the holy sacrament of the altar and that it made me realize more fully what a magnificent wonder it is: that by eating from the consecrated bread we are being united with the Body of Christ. It also made me begin to understand what we say in crossing ourselves: "In name of the Father, and the Son, and the Holy Spirit." I concluded my notes that day with the prayer: "Lord, have mercy on me; for I am not worthy that you come to me."

Just a few things may be worth reporting of the period that en-compasses the last months of my military service. First, towards the end of February, I spent another weekend at the convent of the Assumptionists in Leuven; present as well were Stijn, Peter Helsen (another young man who was enquiring but eventually never joined), Veronica, Nadine, Pater Edmund (an Assumptionist who was member of the community located in the secondary school of Zepperen in the province Limburg of Bel-gium and who was put forward as the prospective novice master) and the members of the community of Leuven. I wrote down

about this weekend the detail that the first reading of the Eucharistic celebration was the story of Genesis that narrated about
Abraham and his son Isaac; God requires Abraham to offer his
son as a burnt offering on one of the mountains in the land of
Moriah. Abraham obeys the word of God. And having arrived at
the mountain, he built an altar and bound Isaac upon it. When
Abraham takes his knife and is about to slay his son, an angel of
God calls out to him not to go ahead; God had seen that Abraham
did not withhold anything from him, not even his only son, and
that was enough: Abraham had passed the test. I read this text as
having a historical basis, a literal truth; but the others that were
present at the weekend considered it to speak about an internal
process that Abraham was going through. I was troubled by their
stance. How did they know that the thing did not happen to
Abraham as told? Of course, one could read this story and many
others in the Bible as just that, as stories, and give them a psychological interpretation; but why do we then still need faith in God
except for deluding ourselves? I was left not understanding. I had
done years of physics study and had developed a well-trained
critical mind, but this did not take away that I had also an openness of mind in faith. Of course, I still had to begin theological
studies—and as if this would provide clear-cut answers to all
things to do with God. The others appeared to be at another
wavelength from myself; they appeared comfortable with their
interpretation that biblical texts as this one are largely couched in
metaphorical language. As said, I was troubled. Insistently, I
begged God that I would not put my mother and father to shame;
that in my stupidity, I would not cause harm to the kingdom of
God. I prayed for mercy.

Another thing that I wish to report of this period took place
one morning just after the eight o'clock Mass on Sunday morn-

ing. I left the church and walked back home; perhaps about one kilometer in total. A girl, or rather young woman, who had been at Mass soon came beside me on the pavement while she sat on her bicycle and peddled along at walking pace. I remembered her to be Ingrid with whom all these years ago I had been in the same class in the Kindergarten at Tyrolerhof. I reminded her of that. I do not think I had ever spoken a word with her and had not really encountered her since, except from a distance. In fact, I had never heard her speak. I walked along and all the way she just stayed beside me, not saying a word. I tried to have some conversation, but my mind was closed to her intentions since it was full with my soon going to join the Assumptionists in Leuven. It is strange how one's mind can be closed off in certain ways and be full of what is in one's head: was it God's doing or just me? Ingrid did not say a word. When I arrived at the house in Manebruggestraat, I invited her to come in but she shook her head and cycled away. As has often been my approach, I wrote a letter to her. I did not know her address but I asked Pater Pastoor. In fact, I asked Pater Pastoor to read my letter. He thought it was a well-intended letter and that there was nothing wrong in it. He was hesitant whether it was a good idea to put it through the letterbox but did not disapprove either; though he added that if ever it would come to a cause of canonization it might add a complication. I said that I was not too worried about that—what a thought anyway!—and did not see why it should be so. He understood that I wanted to leave Ingrid some word. Basically, I wrote, as I said above, that my mind had been totally set upon the Assumptionists and that I thought that word about this was out and that she came to speak me about it; I explained that I thought she was perhaps considering such road, for she was a quiet and, in my impression, a rather withdrawn person. I asked her to pray for me as I would for her.

Begin March 1991, I fulfilled my year of conscripted military service. Within a week from this, I would move to the Peda Sint-Augustinus, the provincial house of the Assumptionists in Leuven. The beautiful dining-room furniture, the Ikea set, the kitchen chairs, the television cupboard, cooking pots, vases, toys were given to the social department (OCMW) of the local authority in Borsbeek; while Pater Jef collected the good tea set, the glasses, and so on. Other items we took to Walter's house, to Jenny's apartment, to Sonja's parents, and some large objects, among which a large fridge (destined for the kitchen), my hi-fi stacking system (for the common room), books (for the library), a small cupboard, and so on, and myself included to the Assumptionists in Leuven. I was leaving Manebruggestraat behind. It was March 6, 1991.

A few days earlier, in the middle of the clearing out, I reminded myself in my personal notes of Mark 10:17—31.

> And as he was setting out on his journey, a man ran up and knelt before him, and asked him, "Good Teacher, what must I do to inherit eternal life?" And Jesus said to him, "Why do you call me good? No one is good but God alone. . . . Go, sell what you have, and give to the poor, and you will have treasure in heaven; and come, follow me." At that saying his countenance fell, and he went away sorrowful; for he had great possessions (Mark 10:17–18, 21b–22).

Though I was reading the text at the time, it was not applicable to my going to the Assumptionists in such starkness. First, I did not have great possessions, though I was materially comfortable enough; secondly, not all I possessed was given to the poor: entering religious life has been made into a long process. This process encompasses the following: a first stage is postulancy, usually for a period of about half a year; then the novitiate, usually for one year, sometimes longer; temporary profession, minimally for three years, sometimes it is extended by the candidate's request; only then can perpetual profession be undertaken. It is only when perpetual or solemn profession is undertaken that a religious takes leave of all his possessions; prior to this, as is often the case in our times, the candidate may leave the institute and have to find rented accommodation; the institute will prefer not having to help or will not help financially. Nevertheless, most of my material things were given away—for I was moving from my parental home into a small room—and all my finances were handed over to the bursar of the Assumptionists for keeping. I gave the instructions that only a portion of the value of all that I possessed was to be kept under my own name; other instructions were appended to the other parts. And these have indeed been executed later in time, several years later, despite all events that went in between.

# 17

## Among the Assumptionists (1)

L EAVING MANEBRUGGESTRAAT IN pursuit of a life founded
on faith, I went to live with the Assumptionists in Leuven.
That major step having been made, one would expect that everything would gradually develop and lead onwards from there
according to consistent choices and this with the guidance offered
within the institute as life marched on. It was not to be;
Halvestraat in Leuven was but a first step. My path would be one
of constant soul searching, various twists and turns, and disap-
pointments; a path not of certainty but of uncertainties; a path of
one becoming more and more irrelevant; disregarded; a path of
feeling betrayed, and of failure; of one despairing in the wilder-
ness, getting nowhere. Even now as I write this in my fifties: yes,
unfortunately, I have not succeeded in getting anywhere. But still
I would wish to make progress towards God, towards living
constantly in his presence. In this chapter and the next, I will
cover in some detail my time spent with the Assumptionists, a
period of more than three years that followed upon my leaving
Manebruggestraat, beginning with my arrival in the
Assumptionist community of Leuven.

At the time of my arrival, the community would have consisted of four or five priests, "Paters," varying in age probably

between early fifties and early seventies. I am not sure whether Pater Edmund, who was to be the novice master, had already transferred from the community of Zepperen. Another Assumptionist priest, who worked as a journalist and who lived in another Assumptionist property in Leuven, often joined us for the midday meal. Attached to the community was one man of around sixty with a learning disability, Mark, who set the tables and helped with the kitchen duties. He had his own room in the convent. Given the smallness of the community and the size of the building, the majority of rooms were rented out to university students, several coming from the two secondary schools run by the Flemish Assumptionists.

The day after I arrived in the Assumptionist community in Leuven, I went to the job center and made myself available for supply teaching. As it happened to be the case, Stijn, the other candidate, would complete his military service only a few months later; the start of the formal year of novitiate would therefore only

Peda Sint-Augustinus, Leuven

be at end September.

Each day, the community prayer moments included Morning Prayer followed by the Eucharist, and Evening Prayer. At about nine o'clock in the evening, I went to the chapel and prayed one or two decades of the Rosary and read a chapter from the Bible. Below the main chapel, at the bottom of the stairs, was located the sacristy where the priests vested for Mass; and beside it, that is, under the main chapel, a smaller chapel was to be found. This was at times used in the evening for adoration by a young lady and, sometimes, a young man who both were associated to the Medjugorje prayer group that met weekly in the convent. The community members used, however, the main chapel for prayer in common and private. Following the example of the mentioned young people, I soon replaced in my prayer moment the reading of the Bible with a short adoration.

On April 12, 1991, I added to my notes, prompted to do so by a little meditation text that had been read during Morning Prayer. According to the Breviary—that is, a book of prayers covering the main liturgical prayer moments outside the Eucharist that is being used by most religious and some pious laypeople—these prayer services include a short scripture reading; but in the community that I joined, it was customary for each member in turn to choose instead an alternative reading. I quickly discovered that often texts were being chosen devoid of any significant spiritual content and that I found not really helpful at all; texts that came from a kind of liberalism that reduced religion largely to social and moral teaching. Now, for a long period I struggled with the question how to interpret the various wonders described in the Bible: as figurative speech or as having truly happened. Reading and hearing about wondrous events in biblical times and about others up to our own times certainly was a factor, at least confirmatory, in my own conversion. I found also that for engaging into conversation with others who are skeptical about faith it is needed to have considered such issues. To some extent, I recognized myself as well as many others in the apostle Thomas who came to believe only after having put his finger in the wounds of the risen Christ. As I found out, many religious, however, do not believe in miracles that transcend the natural level. Even though it is the priests who have completed years of philosophical and theological studies, they will seldom give a straightforward answer when asked about it. As I said earlier, it troubled me. When that day in April I heard a text being read from the periodical "Bezinning op het Woord" (Meditation upon the Word), a publication from the Liturgical Commission of the Diocese of Roermond in the Netherlands that provides an introduction to the liturgy for each day, I found it, for a change, appealing so that I went to photocopy it and glued it in my folder with notes. Though I do not know the name of the author, I include here a translation of the text:

> The story of the miraculous multiplication of bread we encounter at times in the liturgy. Everyone knows it. But at the same time is it one of the most difficult to understand events in the life of Jesus. An event such as a miraculous healing we can still understand in a certain manner; it is a miracle that happens sporadically in our own time as well. Often the miraculous multiplication of bread is being explained as the story of the "sharing together": if all people would but share among themselves, there would be enough for everyone. Of course, this is true: if we would use the resources of the earth justly, there would be sufficient for everyone. But the wonder of Jesus implies first of all that Jesus multiplies the small quantity of bread that is present. Moreover, it has a much deeper dimension as

well. It is a prefigurement of the Eucharist. In the Bread, Jesus gives himself to us as food and we are being filled more than earthly bread would ever be able to fill us. Our spiritual hunger is being satisfied: the hunger for the real life.

The most profound hunger of a human being is his hunger for real meaningfulness. A human being cannot live without perception of the meaning of life. And that meaning is Christ. Through His resurrection, we know that we also will once rise with Him to new and eternal life. Christ says, "Who eats of this bread will live forever." Then our entire life is being placed in a new light: sickness, suffering, and death have no longer the last word; but neither has earthly prosperity or "sharing together." Our life is being placed in the divine Light, in which God's glory is the last Word.

Of this belief, the apostles testify. They cannot keep quiet about the magnificent things of God. Even violence cannot prevent them from proclaiming the faith. May also we be enlightened by this Light and just as the apostles testify with frankness of our faith.

I appended this in my notes with the prayer, more or less the same that I wrote in my notes at other places, in which I asked the Lord God to grant that I would not put my mother and father to shame, that in my stupidity I would not cause harm to the kingdom of God, and that he would grant that I may bring his will to completion.

A few days later, on April 15, that is, after the Easter break, I started teaching in the Miniemen Institute, a Catholic Technical College in Leuven, until June 30, the end of the school year. The building was a former college of the monks of the Order of Minimes; from 1841 the Sisters of the Paridaens Institute, Leuven, a Catholic Institute for girls, took on this building as well as, among others, the Saint-Joseph Institute in Antwerp for offering free education to poorer children. No religious sisters were around when I came to teach at the school. I was to teach ten hours physics and math each week to students of the fourth and fifth years. Discipline in the school was very poor; I was the third teacher for the post after two teachers had resigned from it. The school was officially without a director and the PE teacher had taken over as an interim director (Mr. Kris Florquin, who in fact would stay on as director until his retirement in 2019). Some classes were very large, as pupils had been adopted who had been dismissed from other schools. It was pretty terrible. But I finished the job. I could fill a few more pages of these months in that school but I better not, for this book is becoming too lengthy as it is. Perhaps just a few details: I walked up and down from the Assumptionist monastery; and on one occasion, some of my pupils said they would wait for me after the school hours so as to beat me up. But it did not happen. On another occasion, a fellow (Bart) got out his knife and came and stood in front of me while I was before the blackboard. The others jeered him on, but I told him to go back to his place, which he eventually did. On another occasion, the same had a pot of paint and poured it over my desk and in front of the blackboard. I cleaned it up and continued with what was left of the time. At the end of the year, I failed about a third of the students in one of the classes, who, as a result, had to retake the year. One of the troublemakers, Bernard, came to me when he had received his result and as I happened to pass by: I told him that I had not been making favors at the deliberation when he had been boycotting my lessons and been playing the fool with me; each his turn. He nodded. A few weeks later, I needed to be at the town hall; and behold, just across from the entrance, all of them were sitting outside having a drink at a pub.

I thought that I would get it then; but in fact, they were quite friendly and offered me a drink.

In the meantime, the Assumptionists encouraged me to complete my teaching training, for I still did not have a teaching qualification. I had already followed some lectures on this during my physics study but never completed it. I was required to attend the classes of two courses and pass examination, as well as give one exam lesson in a school: I did not have to first give set hours of practice teaching since I had been or was teaching. The exam lesson I could give in a Catholic school run by nuns who were friends with the Assumptionists. But reading and studying the books in pedagogy appeared at the time extremely boring to me. My experience in the Miniemen Institute did not encourage me either. The result was that I unsubscribed from the course and cancelled the exam lesson. The exam lesson would have been no problem, but I could at the time just not face the boredom of preparing for the exams in pedagogy. I did not feel motivated at all for this. I had, moreover, been pretty busy, as most of the time, and something had to give way.

I mentioned that I had adopted the habit of praying some decades of the Rosary around nine in the evening. From July, when I was on holiday, I placed the Rosary prayer shortly after midday. In the evening around nine, I then placed a prayer consistent of thanking God, followed by an asking God for mercy for my shortcomings, and adoration, which was in process of constant adaptation.

Near the end of July, a few days preached retreat took place for the Assumptionists of the Flemish province in Saint-Gérard, a village in the province of Namur. Stijn and I were participant. The locality Saint-Gérard was originally called Brogne (since a spring of brown water, called Brogniau, was located there). It was renamed after Gérard of Brogne, who founded an abbey here in the tenth century. In this abbey in rural surroundings, monks lived according to the Rule of Benedict, and a village developed around it. Buildings were renovated in the eighteenth century, but the few remaining monks dispersed after the French revolution when French troops passed through and a large part of the buildings was destroyed. It eventually came into the hands of the Assumptionists, who from 1919 to 1969 received their formation in philosophy and theology here: including Paters Johannes Berchmans Borghoms (Pater Pastoor) and Lieven and Jef Bergmans, whom I knew well from Borsbeek. They had mentioned to me earlier that it was a quiet and secluded place for their formation: a place well suited for taking distance from the world and developing greater communion with God. But no longer were these buildings in hands of the Assumptionists; it now belonged to the village of Saint-Gérard and had been made into a meeting place for youth. A community of retired Assumptionists was presently living in another large property in the vicinity of the former abbey, and it was there the retreat took place.

Whoever gave the retreat I cannot remember, but what I do remember is the wash-up moments. Among the Assumptionists it appeared that it was seen as good community spirit that everyone took part in the wash-up and the clearing of the tables. This, however, could take on ridiculous proportions. It meant that almost the entire Flemish province of the Assumptionists descended upon the kitchen. One would be frantically washing-up and several would be around for the drying. Not enough kitchen towels were put out, but they opened some drawers and soon the entire stock of towels was in use. So many priests and brothers were crowded in that kitchen that dripping plates were handed on over the heads to those who could not get near the sink. Everything seemed to have to be done in a frantic manner. At the end of the labor, when we all poured out of the kitchen, I saw more than a dozen soaked towels hanging over a drying rack: the wash-up had been a great success. I was seen not quite to have the community spirit because after the following meal I tried instead with the clearing of the table, but a few others saw to that, so I sat and talked to an older priest or went outside, where one or two smokers were to be found.

I remember as well that one day, at lunch, I sat opposite Pater Johannes. Lettuce was part of the meal and we all put some on our plates. Then Pater Johannes took the vinegar dressing, or whatever it was, and said to the one sitting next to him, "You need to put some of this on it." By the time that his neighbor could answer, Pater Pastoor put a good deal of dressing over that one's lettuce. His neighbor took a deep breath and wanted to start protesting, but again before he could say something, Pater Pastoor had already exchanged their plates and said, "I see you do not really like it; for some people, you cannot do anything good." We laughed.

The next morning, when we were seated at the breakfast table, Pater Castro announced that Pater Johannes (Pater Pastoor) had been found dead in his room. Pater Lieven was sitting beside me and told me that Pater Pastoor had not been well for some time and that the evening before he had been very upset. The background to this was that on that foregoing day another Assumptionist had in the meeting been telling of various things he had been doing: that he had burned his Belgian ID in solidarity with asylum seekers and was arrested for it, and so on. Later onwards, back in the rooms, Pater Pastoor had told Pater Lieven in a state of alarm that he had achieved nothing in all his life. Pater Lieven would have none of it and had told him: "Listen here, let that man brag, no one would have done more for the people under your pastoral care in Borsbeek than you have." And indeed, it was true, for I was well aware of his role in my own story and that of my parents that I have been telling in earlier chapters. Pater Johannes had been born in the Netherlands on November 18, 1914—a few months after my stepfather, Frans Peeters— and died on July 25, 1991. I would have liked him to be my spiritual guide during my formation, but it was not to be.

As it happened, immediately after our stay at Saint-Gérard, an international group of youngish, solemnly-professed Assumptionists was brought together, and the venue that had been chosen was the Peda Sint-Augustinus in Leuven. Stijn and I were, of course, not participant to the official program of various meetings organized for these men from diverse nationalities all over the world, but it was interesting to meet them in the chapel, the refectory, the common room. We even joined one evening in a game of football in a nearby green zone. They stayed for about two or three weeks. As part of their program, they would travel for a few days to the places in the south of France where the founder, Père Emmanuel d'Alzon, had lived. Since it was a unique occasion to see these places at the root of the Congregation of the Augustinians of the Assumption, it was decided somewhat as an afterthought that, even though I was but at the beginning of my religious formation with them, I could join them. We travelled by coach and it was a most interesting week. Pater Edmund joined as well. We visited Vigan, the birthplace of Père d'Alzon; Nîmes, where he was vicar general of the diocese and where he obtained the Collège de l'Assomption, from where he would found his new order with the encouragement of Mother Marie-Eugénie de Jésus. Along the journey, we stayed a few times overnight in the convents of religious sisters that shared in the same root of the Assumption: among others, in the large convent of the Orantes of the Assumption in Cachan, a southern suburb of Paris. In Paris, we visited the motherhouse of the Religious of the Assumption; the Chapel of the convent at Rue du Bac, where in 1830 Catherine Labouré received apparitions of Mary; and we visited the offices of La Bonne Presse (presently, Bayard Presse) and the community of Assumptionists associated with it. We also visited a large community of the Oblates of the Assumption: I do not remember where it was exactly.

When we returned, it was the time of the funeral of Pater Pastoor, which took place in my home parish in Borsbeek, in the church of the Saint-Johannes-Berchmans Parish, where he had lived and served. The entire international group of Assumptionists, about twenty religious, participated in the funeral Mass and I sat among them. It would have been unique in the parish's history to have witnessed such an international gathering.

Later in the summer, I was invited to join Pater Edmund for a visit to the French novitiate community in the outskirts of Paris. It was, once more, an interesting visit in which I met the French novice master, Père Marie-Bernard; three French novices (one of whom was leaving); some Romanian novices who attended the French noviciate; as well as André Sève (1913–2001), an Assumptionist priest and former journalist who wrote a number of books including the well-known *Trente minutes pour Dieu* (1974) and *Ma vie c'est le Christ: Emmanuel d'Alzon* (1980), which I read during my military service; and one or two other young Assumptionists. I got on well with the novices and Père Marie-Bernard. Emphasis in the novitiate community was on the spiritual life; the recitation of the Divine Office was accompanied by a zither. I would not have minded if I had been sent to this community for my year of novitiate. But Stijn, the other Flemish candidate, did not know French and I was to accompany him in Leuven. I had the feeling that Père Marie-Bernard, though strict, was someone I could talk with. Had I been sent there, it is likely that I would not have left. Though the main purpose of the visit was obviously meetings between Pater Edmund and Père Marie-Bernard, it is in a few words with me that the latter more or less expressed his doubts about the suitability of Pater Edmund as novice master.

One day, Pater Edmund proposed that we set out for the center of Paris. All I remember is that Pater Edmund wanted to walk along the Champs-Élysées up to the Arc de Triomphe. Unfortunately, the man could not take time for things. There was no time to stop and look at this or that. He just wanted to walk very fast from one end to the other end of the avenue. I was not really interested in that kind of walking; it was unnatural. We set out together, but after some time I fell five meters behind, then ten, twenty . . . Pater Edmund ran on without looking back. He obviously did not need my company. I decided to stop and wait till he had disappeared among the many pedestrians in front of me. I waited a few moments and yes, he was gone. I was satisfied that he was gone; I could breath and did not have to rush. Instead of walking on, I returned at a more relaxed pace, got into the underground, and found my way back to the community. Père Marie-Bernard queried how it was that I returned back on my own. I said that I could not keep up with Pater Edmund and that I had decided to return. He shook his head; it obviously confirmed his assessment of Edmund.

I was at the start of living a religious life and wanted to live in God's presence: in my praying, in my walking, in my sitting, and in all aspects of life. In fast walking, just as in frantic washing-up and in rushing along in every activity, the idea of walking in

God's presence is simply not there. God is left behind. Practicing the presence of God is essential for the contemplative God-seeker. Pater Edmund was a good man—just as most of the Assumptionists—but he simply did not have it. Not surprisingly, it did not seem possible to enter into profitable conversation either, even though in the novitiate we would go through all the mechanics of lessons, meetings, assessments, and so on. I am sure that Pater Edmund wanted to live a holy life and tried hard; but in my assessment, as he ran along, he ran past God. As a beginner religious, I needed support in my God seeking but would be thrown back more and more upon myself. But let's continue with some detail of the day-to-day events of my time with the Assumptionists.

Back at the Peda Sint-Augustinus in Leuven, the main meals took place at midday and were prepared by Gaby, who had been employed a little while before my arrival in the community. For the evening meal, usually some soup was to be warmed up. Usually, as far as I remember, Gaby prepared something for the main meal on Saturday. For the Sunday, Pater Paul, who was the bursar of the community and the older brother of Edmund, made the preparations. Sometimes though, he had to say the Mass at a nuns' convent. As such, I soon volunteered and became involved to help out with these kitchen duties. The refectory was right above the kitchen and the food dishes were placed in a hatch and then send upwards by pulling a rope. Pater Paul and I soon each took turns for these meal preparations. During the week, I spoke at times with Gaby: she had been a religious sister and missionary but now lived on her own as a consecrated woman. I had put my mother's cookbook of the KAV (Catholic Workers' Women) in a drawer in a kitchen, and Gaby consulted it at times. Sometimes, I did not have my meal with the community but had my weekly fast day and ate some bread with a little syrup at the kitchen table downstairs. Gaby half disapprovingly said that I was just doing it so as to get away from the others and do my own thing; that she saw through me. I protested that that was not the case. She had had a long experience in religious life, and we could talk while she was stirring her pots. She was a spiritual person and had taken the job in the expectation that she would find some spiritual support and be able to attend some masses in the convent; but she was disappointed that this turned out not to be the case and felt rather uncared for.

Wherever I have lived, I liked to tidy things up: I dislike untidiness and disorder. In the corridors some cleaning cupboards were found, and I cleaned the one out near my room so that it could be used properly and so that one could find what one looked for. The large chapel and the little chapel underneath each had their cupboard for sacristy purposes: a sink, vases, spare candles, and so on. I noticed that when people of the Medjugorje prayer group tried to get to the sink in the upstairs cupboard, which was long and narrow, they hardly managed to get near it because of the mess. I spend time tidying it up. Pater Lieven sometimes came from Borsbeek to tidy the library, but he had so far only managed to organize the French books; for the rest it was still in total disarray. I spend a few late evenings up to midnight moving the books about and in a short while managed to get it usable. I always have first tried to put the house where I stayed in order before starting things away from home. I cleaned the high kitchen windows and cleaned this and that.

My notes of September 16, 1991, show that I was at the time preoccupied with attaining a deeper understanding of the Eucharistic sacrament. In earlier reflections I noted down my realization of the symbolism entailed by the sacrament; that, moreover, the bread truly becomes the Body of Christ; and that by receiving Holy Communion we are being united with the Body of Christ. I just finished reading a long French text by Tomislav Vlašić on the Eucharist from the School for Peace in Medjugorje, which had been given me by the young lady who used our chapel for adoration and whom I mentioned earlier. (For further information: Vlašić was at the time a Franciscan friar and a Catholic priest who during the first years of the apparitions, that is, from 1981, had been the spiritual director to the seers. In 2009 he would be laicized after accusations of sexual misconduct, diffusion of dubious doctrine, suspect mysticism, and disobedience towards legitimately issued orders.) I noted further that I had finished reading about the life of Clara Jung of Antwerp (1887–1952), a book written by Reverend J. Nulens, which had been a book of my mother. Clara Jung received the stigmatic wounds of Christ and was buried in the cemetery in Borsbeek. In this book as well I found thoughts about the Eucharistic Sacrament, which took on a great importance in Clara's life.

Ten days later, on Friday September 27, 1991, Stijn and I began the novitiate with a Eucharist in the chapel of the convent. About fifty people were present: several Assumptionists and a number of religious sisters; as well as Uncle Eugène and Aunt Irma. The following day, Pater Edmund, Stijn, and I went to Postel, a Norbertinian (or Premonstratensian) abbey within the Province of Antwerp, very near the border with the Netherlands, in an area known as the Kempen (the Campine). Pater Edmund had chosen the place as tranquil surroundings for making arrangements about the forthcoming year as regards prayer and meals.

Pater Edmund proposed a prayer routine for us somewhat more organized than that for the other community members. Prior to the Morning Prayer and the Eucharist, he placed half an hour meditation to be held in common, that is, we sat at our places in the chapel reading quietly some spiritual text, a prayer, or just sat in silence. We would moreover not only participate with the community in the Evening Prayer, but the novitiate would also practice Midday Prayer. In the course of the day, we were expected to keep another half hour meditation by ourselves. It seemed to me best to write these down so as to remain focused. As a suitable help to begin with, I took each day a little section of a book by Phil Bosmans (1922–2012), a priest of the Missionaries of the Company of Mary, a religious congregation founded by Saint Louis de Montfort (1673–1716). Phil Bosmans wrote numerous books that were very popular. The one I read for my meditation was *God, niet te geloven* (1988; God, Unbelievable). Let me select one of the thoughts that I wrote down during these meditations on that book, namely, on the topic, "I cannot prove God"; at the time, I wrote this in Dutch, but I provide here an English translation:

> In my estimate, a beautiful formulation is: "With your mind you can trace (*op het spoor komen*) the existence of God, but you cannot catch (*grijpen*) and grasp (*begrijpen*) God."
>
> Indeed, our intellect cannot exhaustively prove God; nevertheless, it is valuable to carefully consider some tangible things that God presents to us. It is valuable to reflect upon faith and try to put down a rational foundation for it so that, when faith is not evident, we can be supported by this. And I as well am somewhat as Thomas.
>
> But if one wants to grow in faith and live faith, one needs to involve the heart. It is finding oneself touched by someone like Mother Theresa who takes up one dying, or more close to

home, by the simplicity and goodness of my own mother. It is awareness of our conscience, which discerns good and evil.

Believing is not only a matter of the intellect but of the entire human being.

Believing is a grace that we receive from God.

Lord, I thank you for my mother and father.

Every Monday and Tuesday, all three of us would be taking part in the Inter-Novitiate Cooperation (GNW: Gemeenschappelijke Noviciaatswerking). We did this as part of a group of twenty-four novices and novice masters and mistresses of various active congregations (male and female) and of the Premonstratensian Abbey of Grimbergen. The days would be well filled with various classes: among others, a course on the Gospel of Mark; an introduction to spirituality; an introduction to religious life; on spiritual guidance and prayer; and on the liturgy. These GNW days took place in a large Jesuit convent in Heverlee, just outside of Leuven. It housed a large community of retired Jesuits and, in addition, a great number of university students to whom they provided accommodation, just as the Assumptionists were doing on a somewhat smaller scale in the Peda Sint-Augustinus. On Wednesdays—perhaps it was every fortnight—Stijn and I were to drive to Borsbeek, where Pater Lieven would teach us about Pater d'Alzon and the beginnings of the Assumptionists in nineteenth-century France, and about the missions in Zaire. Pater Lieven prepared several booklets and put a lot of work into it; his lectures on the missions were most entertaining: in the late seventies, as requested by the general superior, he had written an account in French of the Assumptionist mission in Zaire with emphasis on what took place behind what was more officially known, including details about the personalities of various missionaries, and so

In the noviciate of the Assumptionists; les from Pater Lieven with fellow novice Stijn (1992)

on. He had in later years translated some parts of his text for the sake of a lay-brother—that is, a religious who is not ordained to the priesthood—who did not know French. For the meetings with Stijn and me, he took the project once more to hand and translated the entire text in Dutch. The title in English can be rendered as, *Fifty Years Mission Work by the Assumptionist Fathers in North-Kivu, Zaire, 1929–79.* On the remaining days, we had lessons by Pater Edmund and some of the other fathers in the convent in Leuven. All together, it was a well-filled program.

Most classes at the GNW were pretty interesting. Less agreeable to me, I found the exposition by Rev. André Goossens (1939–2020), a professor at the Seminary of Antwerp, on what is *supposedly* the biblical interpretation of the Eucharist. Goossens argued that the Mass did not have a mysterious meaning; that there is no Eucharistic mystery. I have no longer retained my class notes; but in my personal notes (of October 16, 1991) I wrote that Goossens held that when Christ pronounced the words of institution, "This is my body," he was taking himself up in the salvific history of his people. In other words, Jesus was telling his companions that this history had now taken on a new phase with him; that he was the Messiah: he was giving the bread a Messianic perspective. Goossens continued that it is only afterwards that the disciples came to understand that the paschal meal had once more received an additional dimension with Jesus, who thus had become present to them in another manner. This discovery on the part of the disciples would be represented in the apparition narratives at Luke 24 and John 21, which each speak of an unknown man who is only afterwards discerned to be Jesus.

This explanation shook me interiorly as an earthquake. Afterwards I went to the chapel within the building and prayed on my knees. I found that everything was being thrown over, and I wondered, "What am I pursuing; what am I doing?" . . . But in this darkness, I could still continue with what I was left with: "Thank You, Lord; thank you for my mother and father." The most discouraging aspect of it all was to me that the others did not appear to have any problems with such explanations." I kept, notwithstanding, to the vision upon the Eucharist that I had developed with the help of the Catholic catechism of Anton Schraner and the (suspicious) text of Tomislav Vlašić.

That evening, a Monday evening, the program provided for a simple being together in one of the common rooms. Since my mind was preoccupied with the lecture given by Goossens, I entered into conversation about it with Etienne Herrebaut, who was one of the two novices of the Augustinians. He was somewhat older than the others: at the time he was thirty-six, and he

existent. The chapel is a place of pilgrimage, and beside it had been built a house that had over time been extended and renovated. At the time of my visit, two Flemish Assumptionists lived in the house, and the bursar's office was located there. The present chapel was built in the fourteenth century and is known as *Chapelle de Marie-la-Misérable*. This chapel has been thought to have replaced a more primitive chapel—when it was built is unknown—that stood at the same place and that was dedicated to Our Lady of Sorrows. Living nearby this former chapel in a humble dwelling in the village of Woluwe-Saint-Pierre at the end of the thirteenth century was a recluse, named Maria, who had renounced the world and was a mendicant by virtue for the poor. A rich nobleman wanted to seduce her but she refused indignantly. Soon after, he managed to hide a valuable cup among her belongings. He then had her arrested on a charge of theft, vagabondage, and sorcery; and she was condemned to death despite her protests. She was buried alive and a pointed pole was driven through her body. Legend has it that the guilty man became insane for several years but eventually recovered at the grave of his victim. He admitted his crime and became the advocate of the veneration of the one whom he had caused to be tortured to death. Whether this legend is true or not, miracles would have taken place at the place of her execution, and pilgrimages developed in which substantial crowds gathered. As a result, her remains were transferred and buried under the chapel's altar; or alternatively, the chapel was built at the place of her execution. As it is, the present chapel has a cult to Our Lady of Sorrows but more popular is the cult to the said Venerable Marie la Misérable, who died in 1302 as a martyr of chastity. The chapel is already being mentioned in a document of Pope Urban V of 1363, in which he promises indulgences to the faithful who visit the chapel or enrich her with donations. A

Marie la Miserable

Wolnwe St Jambert

The front of a prayer card that I found in a book in the library of the Assumptionists in Leuven

yearly pilgrimage continues to take place; apparently the only one in the Brussels region to date. Presently, a community of five Assumptionists resides there that is associated to the charismatic, Assumptionist, Maranatha community in Brussels.

Given that Stijn and I were the only ones who had entered the Flemish province of the Assumptionists in decades, it occupied my mind how we could reach other potential candidates. I proposed to the Provincial Council the production of a flyer and of posters. I designed the flyer and two posters and these were printed. I subsequently went to put them up in various student hostels around Leuven. It was in vain, for no one ever reacted to it.

In the meantime, Stijn and I stayed in relatively small rooms at the top floor of the convent. These rooms had a sloped ceiling with a large window in it. In the rooms around us several students resided. After half a year or so, we moved to rooms on the first floor, again amidst students. It was not ideal, for these students obviously had a different day rhythm than we who were trying to live a regular religious life. Some had their girlfriend staying at nights, even though it was against the rules of the house. It was not ideal to have all this going on around us. Near the end of a substantial evaluation written down on April 14, 1992, I gave vent to my frustration with some element of dark humor not entirely absent: "I resent that I live here amidst so many students. Soon, I will throw all doors on a heap and burn them; and all radios, on a heap and burn them; and all students who walk about and open their mouth, on a heap and burn them."

Throughout the year we were expected to perform some pastoral activity. I went every second Sunday or so to Pellenberg, a hospital/campus that forms part of the university hospitals of Leuven, so as to assist the chaplains with taking Holy Communion to patients in their rooms prior to Mass and to assist as a Eucharistic minister at the Mass in the hospital chapel as well.

Begin June 1992, when the GNW classes had finished, Pater Edmund, Stijn, and I went as helpers to Hooidonk, a revalidation center of the Christian mutuality. We were part of a group, helping disabled people who came to the center for a week's holiday. It was a total new experience for me to spend a week with disabled people and to help them with various daily matters. We each were assigned a sick person whom we had to help in the morning with washing and dressing, and we had to help them in the evening. During the day we helped various people as the need presented itself. Various entertainments were organized: for example, looking outside in the grounds for some persons dressed up as various characters. It was beautiful weather and so we could go a lot of time outside with the people in wheelchairs. The evenings were spent in the bar, where various things were being organized.

In the meantime, I went to the chapel, until it was about time to collect our charges from the bar. One month later, we returned to the same place and assisted as helpers to a group of religious: nearly all were ill and older nuns, and a few disabled priests, among whom Pater Karel Maurissen, an Assumptionist. This time I was not assigned to a single person for personal care in the morning and evening but was made co-responsible for an entire floor of people who needed some but not total assistance. As during our earlier week, it was again very beautiful weather.

At various times, I wrote long evaluations for myself as regards where I was in my thinking and in my vocation; and I wrote various pages for the novice master. Taking from these many pages, I include here some sections of what I wrote to the novice master on July 20, 1992:

> To begin with, I want for a moment to consider a few passages from Mark's Gospel, namely, the scene in the Garden of Olives, Mark 14:32 vv.; and the Passion narrative, Mark 15. We were asked to prepare these texts for the final classes given by Pater Tyson, s. j., at the GNW. It may be helpful to reproduce here partially my reflections formulated at the time.
>
> My personal comment upon Mark 14:32 vv.: After the meal, they return to Bethany. They pause at a garden called Gethsemane at the foot of the Mount of Olives. Jesus desires to pray and he takes Peter, James, and John along with him. He distances himself a little and prays: "Abba, Father, all things are possible to thee; . . ." In his distress and suffering he looks for support from his disciples, but they are asleep. Up to three times (a construction of Mark) Jesus takes up his prayer and three times he returns and looks for support from his disciples. But they are unable to withstand falling asleep. Subsequently, he is taken prisoner.

This passage brings home to me the great importance of praying with Jesus. By focusing in our prayer upon the accompaniment to his suffering, we can soften his suffering and cooperate in the coming of his kingdom.

My personal comment upon Mark 15: I am touched by the silence in which Jesus wraps himself; as a lamb led to the slaughter. . . . In silence he walks along the way that God leads him. How painful it must have been for him when Pilate asked him the bland question, "Are you the King of the Jews?" given that everywhere he had manifested in word and deed the sensitivity and sublimity of God the Father and of himself. How painful it must have been for him, who treated everyone with love, when the people shouted "Crucify him!" How he must have suffered under the ridiculing and the crucifixion. At the ninth hour, he will cry out [in reciting the first verse of Psalm 22], "My God, my God, why hast thou forsaken me?"

It is in this suffering that Jesus has shown his love to extremis. And it is exactly then that God the Father would have been very close to him. God is not entered upon in skipping through a garden with flowers and singing birds. On the contrary, Christ and many who followed him have entered upon God in the stillness of a burned out and lifeless wood.

The Passion narrative has always spoken to me. . . . I knew already from childhood that loneliness tastes very bitter. . . . Yet after years of having suffered from loneliness, it has become a part of me. Stillness, which initially was empty, has for me become filled with a sense of rest and serenity. It is in stillness that I have come to experience his presence. How much I appreciate at present a very still and serene chapel.

These considerations determine as well my vision as regards the Eucharist. Evidently, there is the aspect of coming together as a community of the faithful, and the celebrating together the memory of the resurrection of Our Lord Jesus Christ; but central to me is the preceding of Jesus Christ in suffering and self-giving for the coming of God's kingdom among us. This surely must instill in us a sublime stillness. How much we need to love him: he who has shown us his love to extremis.

I envisage that the Assumptionists as a group of religious who strive after the coming of God's kingdom are willed by God. Notwithstanding this, I do not really feel comfortable with community living as I experience it at the moment. In earlier writings, I have pronounced on reasons for this on the side of the community. I have, however, discovered also that the reason lies at my side as well. It is not so evident to analyze oneself, but community life has made me more aware of my own identity; and in the meantime, I am another year older as well. I like being alone. I like modesty (*ingetogenheid*) and calm. I desire very much also to make progress in a spiritual life. As a religious, I therefore wish for sufficient space for quiet contemplation. This does not imply that I want to turn away from people. I would like to cooperate at the great project of the Assumptionist Order: "The kingdom of God in us and around us." I assume that I will feel best at home in a small community in which one is prepared to live frugally. . . .

I experience it as valuable being able to pray together, talk together, and perhaps eventually work together with other community members. I do, however, not wish a community living that absorbs all time; which does not imply that I do not desire cordiality and outspokenness. I like much freedom. . . . I resent living in this large building amidst students.

I am much concerned about the third world and the terrible images that reach us from Africa and the other continents. There is, however, a great need as well for a new evangelization in our western countries. Considered realistically, in the last decades not a single new member has increased the ranks of the Assumptionists in Flanders, the Netherlands, or England [the congregation has not been present in the other countries within the United Kingdom]. When then at present a few young people have joined [one in England as well, which I did not know at the time], it would be odd to turn away from our region without further ado. I consider it valuable to cooperate in attempting to give new life to the Assumptionists in our western countries.

In more practical terms, I envisage as ideal the formation of a number of smallish communities in which a frugal lifestyle is pursued and which provide parish pastoral support. From out of these communities, other activities could be engaged upon. I would like to be part of such a community and contribute in the pastoral care. When I speak of pastoral care, for myself, I am thinking of celebrating the Eucharist, visiting the sick, preaching, adult faith initiation, publications, vocation pastoral, and spiritual guidance. Yet I don't envisage myself as parish priest. What I would best do for a living is unclear to me at the present time.

Reading this text at the present, that is, twenty-eight years after I wrote it, I note that the community at the Peda Sint-Augustinus in Leuven was in fact a small community, but there was no common pastoral engagement that bound the members together. The handful of men were all Assumptionists, but despite the emphasis on community living and the time spent together in the television room, and despite that they had known each other for several decades, they were men living besides each other and that each went their own way. I did not detect a passion for growing together in the relationship with Jesus Christ, with God. I did not perceive a common journeying towards God, towards holiness, towards greater care for each other, towards glory. Moreover, we lived in a large building amidst students, at a distance from other people.

At the time, Pater Edmund, the novice master, pointed the finger at me and quite rightly highlighted my speaking of wanting a great liberty, of liking to be alone. He put the question to me whether I did not think this places a rather great mortgage on the community in which I would come to live. The great question, he continued, is: "How much do I wish/will invest of myself in the community?"

It certainly was valid to critically play in upon my text and question/evaluate and probe into these matters. It was, however, the case that I gave a great deal of myself in the community. But sometimes I did not stay as long as others at common relaxation times after meals or in the evening. I wished to take time to work on the courses we were having and study other material besides, while others took it probably easier. I tried, moreover, to spend time at meditation and prayer instead of exposing my brain and thoughts to watching a game of football. The fact was that I was running as well as I could in the way that leads to becoming a well-informed spiritual person and a holy religious. As it became increasingly evident, I wanted and needed to live a religious life with a strong contemplative component; the others, unfortunately, could not accompany me on this journey.

# 18

## Among the Assumptionists (2)

A COUPLE OF weeks after we went to Hooidonk, the revalidation center of the Christian mutuality where we went as assistant caregivers, and a week after I wrote those pages of evaluation that I largely reproduced in the foregoing pages, we joined the week-long, shared retreat of the Flemish province of Assumptionists, which took place in the Abbey of Postel. The expositions of the retreat preacher were, according to my notes, quite theoretical and did not offer me new information. More interesting were the in-between conversations with the various paters. The following week, at the beginning of August 1992, in the context of the novitiate, Stijn and I joined a group of young people from Grimbergen to visit Taizé, a Burgundy village situated ten kilometers from Cluny. It is the place where an ecumenical community of brothers was founded in 1940 by Brother Roger Schütz (1915–2005), a Swiss Calvinistic preacher. Three times a day communal prayer takes place. Over the past decennia, increasing numbers of young people have visited the place to join in the prayer. They come and search for inspiration for their lives and usually stay a week, meeting together and spending time in silence or joining one of the groups talking about scripture. The Taizé community has, moreover, been organizing yearly mass gatherings of youth in various European cities.

I was quite reluctant to make the journey but went as was expected of me. It was the busiest time of the year: we joined about seven thousand others of various countries. Stijn and I put up our little two-man tent, as did the others of the group. For each meal, we had to queue for about three quarters of an hour. Prayers were held in various languages and much singing took place of the well-known Taizé songs so that prayer moments took a considerable time. We sat crowded together on the ground, while the heat was pretty stifling that week: a lot of sweating. We chose to attend the Bible-introduction groups: in the course of the morning and the afternoon, one of the Taizé brothers gave an introduction, after which we were asked to separate ourselves somewhat for half an hour of silent reflection around a few questions that we then discussed in smaller groups. We came to be part of a little group of six Italian girls; three Finnish ones among whom were twins, daughters of a Lutheran priest; and two Croatian girls. I participated also in other groups for discussion around the subject of prayer and our task as Christians. For the hours remaining, I took the opportunity to read under a tree with a beautiful view over the valley: the book I was reading was the Catholic catechism that had been given me by Pater Pastoor.

Taizé – common prayer

Stijn spent quite a bit of time socializing with the others of the group of Grimbergen. I was usually asleep when he returned late in the nights to the tent. I spend the evenings in quiet reading and prayer and got up early so as to participate in the early morning in the Roman Catholic Mass. On the Saturday evening, prior to our leaving, I went to the tree under which I had spent fruitful hours and stayed sitting there for a good while with several others, praying and constantly singing songs of praise. The entire week, I had Jesus in mind who did not worry much and who was constantly in conversation with others for teaching them about God. It was altogether an enriching week.

Having returned from Taizé, I wrote to Pater Provincial, that is, Pater Castro, formally requesting to be admitted to the pronouncement of temporal vows, for a period of one year, according to the Rule of Saint Augustine and the Constitutions of the Assumptionist Order. In this writing I reiterate much of the evaluation of July 20, which I have reproduced in an English rendering towards the end of the previous chapter. I mention in this letter once more my reservations towards some aspects of the community living as I had been experiencing it during the novitiate: a feeling unfulfilled as regards the living of a voluntary sobriety; the presence of about twenty students, which taxes or precludes the attainment of an atmosphere of serene modesty as could be expected in a house of religious; that a division of tasks would, in my view, be more community building and promote togetherness than the regularly sitting together for playing games; that it is in silence that we open ourselves for God's presence. I envisage, furthermore, in my letter:

Perhaps I am exactly being called to cooperate at a contemporary form of religious life that is centered upon Christ. Things that attract me very much in the Congregation of the Assumptionists are, among others: its internationality, the cordiality that characterizes it globally, and the alliance of the entire Assumptionist family (across its various branches). It is marvelous that I may belong within a religious order of which the objective is the spread of God's kingdom.

In the bosom of the Assumptionist Order whose only objective is the spread of God's kingdom, I wish to live the evangelical counsels, namely,

➢ the vow of purity so as to be able to direct thinking and acting completely upon God. As such, I wish to dedicate my life to the service of the gospel and our fellow human beings. Lived in joyfulness and serenity it is a sign and proclamation of the kingdom of God;

➢ the vow of obedience as a wanting to be available for God Our Father and for his Son Jesus Christ. As such, as a religious I wish to listen to the needs of the Church and the world and to engage myself within the order. This vow implies a trust in the superiors. Lived in faith and prayer it indicates a willingness to fulfill the will of the Father;

➢ the vow of poverty so as to witness that God is our true wealth and that he calls us to solidarity with the poor. It is a being available to the service of others and to deal with material things in the spirit of Saint Augustine. I desire to live a frugal life so as to enable a vital prayer life. It is a respect for God's creation and an attention to the problems of people worldwide. It is a protest against our society of over-consumption. It is a striving for the kingdom of justice and peace among the people.

After the novitiate, I would wish to commence studies for the priesthood. The Eucharist has to be the center of my life. In every Eucharist, Jesus is present in his offer and out of love he comes each time to us as broken bread and wine. The Eucharistic activity contributes in the liberation of the world from all evil.

I desire to be able to support people out of a thorough knowledge of scripture and to be able to offer them the sacraments. I would wish to obtain a well-informed view upon the problems of our society. I have in mind preaching and publications so as to turn people to God. I am willing to serve anywhere in the world, including our own Flanders. . . .

I received a positive response; and hence, on Sunday evening, September 27, 1992, at five o'clock, a Eucharist took place in the chapel of the Assumptionists in Halvestraat in Leuven, during which Stijn and I made our first profession in the hands of Pater Frans Houbey (1927–2003). Pater Frans, the former provincial superior, had been delegated by Pater Castro, the present provincial superior, to lead the service since Pater Castro had only days before undergone surgery to his neck. More than seventy people were present: several of the Flemish Assumptionists, a number of nuns, the family of Stijn, Peter Helsen, Gaby (our cook), Sister Christine (a nun who lived in a nearby flat and who regularly called in), Pater Wim Slangen (of the order of the Holy Cross, whom we knew through the GNW), Piet Willems and his wife (someone who kept a lifelong association with the order), as well as my family. After the Mass, we all went to the refectory where a cheese table had been prepared.

Most likely, Pater Aloïs Steegen (1907–94) and Pater Karel Maurissen (1926–2009) would have been present as well. They were Assumptionists who stayed at the Our-Lady-of-Lourdes Nursing Home in Erps-Kwerps. Every Sunday, Pater Castro, Pater Pauwel, or I drove to the nursing home to collect them for the Eucharist in our convent, some aperitif in the common room, the main meal, some cake and a cigar for Pater Aloïs to follow it.

Pater Karel had had a stroke some years earlier and he had lost his voice almost completely so that it was difficult to catch what he was saying. Pater Aloïs had dementia and he was a handful for the nuns of the nursing home. He was hiding things under his bed, for he thought the nuns were stealing everything, and he was preparing his escape. Once or twice he got away and the nuns found him in his pajamas near the parish church. At times, he was convinced that someone was in the bathroom. He proved it to me: slowly he opened the door and stealthily looked in the mirror above the sink. "There he is!" he cried out to me. I next looked as well in the mirror, and this gave him another surprise, but the next moment he laughed as he realized it was me. In the Peda Sint Augustinus, a lift took us from the garage to the ground level; but the lift contained a large mirror and, hence, this as well caused Pater Aloïs to startle each time.

I was sent to attend philosophy classes at the CKS (Centrum voor Kerkelijke Studies), an ecclesiastical institute in Leuven. The venue was a modern-style building attached to the Dominican monastery in Leuven. The institute was organized by various religious orders and a few abbeys, which sent their students there, as well as the Archdiocese of Mechlin-Brussels, which sent its seminarians there. Since the Flemish Assumptionists had been founding members of the institute so as to help provide a formation in Dutch, they were keen for me to attend it. As I would find out, though, the standard of teaching was not of a sufficient level to provide a satisfactory formation. In view of the fact that I had already graduated with a science degree, a program was devised that compressed a two-year course into one year. Two seminarians would accompany me in this adapted program. The institute normally ran but half of the courses of the two-year program; the following year they ran the other half of the courses.

For the three of us, some of the courses that were normally not provided that year were given to us separately. For a number of courses, we joined the larger group that was taking the two years.

The best course we attended was that in psychology; anthropology was reasonably well given by a youngish Jesuit; the other courses were not up to standard. I well remember the classes by a Redemptorist priest on Christian Ethics to the smaller group and on Religious Experience with the larger group. Apart from the fact that very little ground was covered, a discussion ensued with me in the larger group on the topic of Marian apparitions that were only seen by a few privileged ones even when others were standing by that did not share in the experience such as is the case, for example, at Medjugorje. The priest eventually denied that it was possible on the grounds that the only way that information could reach people is through the senses. In the process, he seemed to do away with apparitions whatever. He was an older man, and I was too tensed about it or felt to prohibited to point out that his arguments were plain rubbish: I had in mind that imperceptible signals could reach a dumb television and produce images on its screen; how much more should it in principle be possible for our human brains; moreover, if the apparitions are of a divine origin, no distance needs travelling since the divinity is everywhere even within us and not merely without.

Another course the three of us were to attend was taught, or supposed to be taught, by a Dominican doctor in theology on concepts of God, especially on Saint Thomas Aquinas. To our surprise, as soon as he walked in for the first class, he confided to us that he had accepted giving this course but actually could himself no longer believe in God. He still led the Eucharist in the convent but informed us that he would rather not say the Our Father, and he was desperately searching for hints of God's existence. It was, in fact, totally unfair to us. I cannot remember we received any proper classes from him. At one point the poor man fled the classroom after less than half an hour, whereas two hours were planned, so as to escape obstinately-disagreeing students defending their faith in God. For our evaluation at the end of the year (given that there was no material for us to study), we were to write an essay explaining the reason why we believed in God. In short, a number of long-serving theologian-religious of high repute at the institute were unfit to instruct us in view of their dried-up faith. One of the two fellow-students with whom I contested these priests of dubious faith or none was Paul Van der Stuyft, a seminarian who had formerly been an architect. Since then— and about twenty-eight years have passed since—we have kept a bond of friendship.

At the CKS and at our Assumptionist convent, I heard rumors of some flirting participation in Agape Meals: that is, a meal of sharing food, of fellowship, prayer (for example, the Our Father, and spontaneous prayers), and perhaps scripture readings. It is a meal that traditionally has been practiced by Evangelicals and Methodists. It is intended to be distinct from the Eucharist, which is in memory of the Last Supper. When it was apparently being promoted by radicals at CKS, it was obviously meant as a form of anarchism against the Mass, its sacramental aspect, the Eucharistic Prayer, the faith in the real presence, and against an ordained ministry. Coinciding with this, I think that a radical, female pastoral worker of the parish in which our convent was located managed to get the ear of some in our Assumptionist community for going along this avenue with her as an experiment. I became increasingly distrustful of being in the right environment for progressing on my spiritual journey towards and with God.

In cooperation with the same female pastoral worker, Stijn organized an entertainment evening for the youth of the parish in our refectory. I kept well away from it: it was a loud affair with disco music and dressing up as various characters. It became obvious to me that if this is what they wanted to accommodate, they could not support a journey towards greater communion with God and service flowing from it as envisaged in the traditional religious rules for monastics.

A number of other things added to my disappointment with and distrust of the Assumptionists of Leuven. At the basement level of the building was located the main kitchen, a kitchen and television room for the students, the garage, and a number of cellars. In one of these, a small cellar room in which beer crates, wine bottles, and various aperitifs were kept on a shelf, I happened to notice a black bin bag stowed away in the back. I thought, "Surely not!" but yes, lo and behold, it was the bag full of good, warm clothes and fur boots that I had donated about a year and a half earlier for giving along with Madame Mertens on her journeys to Medjugorje. All my clothes had been sitting in the closed-off bin bag for so long: what a pity and disappointment, for they could have been serving people for getting through the harsh winter in Croatia. I asked Pater Castro about it; he answered that he had kept the clothes behind so as to give them in due course to Pater Corry who was helping with the foundation of a new monastery in Romania. I felt it nonetheless as somewhat of a betrayal of the pressing, good cause for which I had intended them.

My disappointment was increased by an episode concerning postage stamps. At the time that I had entered the convent, Brother René lay dying of terminal cancer. So, we took turns at his bedside soon after my arrival. The Brother died and left a collection of postage stamps, which he had shown us while still alive: the bulk of the collection were Belgian stamps and Vatican stamps. Pater Castro mentioned the option of selling them and the proceeds be given to the missions, which the Brother would have been happy with. They had no idea, though, of its worth. I proposed that I could help with this: I had collected stamps in my youth and had bought stamps from a policeman in Deurne who had known Frans, my stepfather, and who did a lot of buying and selling of stamps. I looked him up and presented him with the collection. He was willing to give it the best price possible: in Belgian francs, the currency at the time, he offered one hundred and fifty thousand BF; that would have been roughly two thousand five hundred pounds sterling. I promised him that I would let him know within a few days whether the Assumptionists accepted the offer. I reported back to Pater Castro, and he promised that it would be decided at the upcoming meeting of the provincial council. As it happened, not the upcoming but a couple of meetings later, they eventually decided that they would keep the stamps as a memorial of the Brother. Why did they waste my time and the time of the man I visited? At present, when but a few elder Assumptionists are still around, it can be wondered what has happened with these stamps; and whether at the time the money that the stamps would have raised could not have been useful for some good cause? As with most of my material goods, I left most of my own collection to my brother, Walter, who was collecting stamps, when I entered religious life; the remainder went to another Assumptionist who collected stamps.

Rather unrelated to all this, I recall of this period a few visits to family. At times, my memory badly failed to serve me, especially when I just could not remember a name: it happened, among others, when visiting my sister, Jenny. I visited for an afternoon, and during the visit Jenny called me a number of times by name in the conversation. All the time, I could just not conjure up her name. For sure, I could not ask my sister, "What was your name again?" I was sweating, trying to recall her name. It was terrible; but I think that it went unnoticed. Only on the way back home did I recall her name. That entire afternoon, I had been unable to call her by name. It was as a selective blackout.

All the while, Moemoe was still in the nursing home *Bloemenveld* in Wilrijk, Antwerp. I still visited her every two or three weeks; either I drove the car of Pater Castro directly to the nursing home or took the train to Antwerp and the bus to Wilrijk. On the occasions that I had to pass through Antwerp and had some time on hand, I would visit the Beguinage of Antwerp and its small church. I enjoyed the peacefulness and the feel of the sacred, medieval building: it was a place where I could sit, pray, and reflect.

I decided that after the single-year philosophy at the CKS I would not be studying theology at the institute nor at the University of Leuven, even though the latter place could have led me to an STB in two years. I did not think either of these places would be helpful for the development of my life of faith, nor the Assumptionist community in Leuven.

I informed Pater Castro that I did not want to continue in Leuven. A seemingly good theological institute existed at Brussels that was organized by the Jesuits, namely l'Institute d'Études Théologiques (IET) de Bruxelles (dissolved in September 2019). The Flemish Assumptionists, however, did not favor my studying across the language border while they were organizing the Flemish-speaking CKS institute. Moreover, my staying with the French-speaking community of Assumptionists was not so evident either given that it was the charismatic Maranatha community. I was not keen to go stay with them, and the Flemish Assumptionists were uncomfortable about them. Pater Castro proposed to make contact with the English provincial of the Assumptionists in London about possibilities there. The latter replied favorably, informing that a very similar institute to the IET apparently existed in London, namely, Heythrop College, which was likewise supported by the Jesuits and which was a college within the University of London. An Assumptionist community located at Brockley, south of the river Thames would be able to receive me. They were three priests and had one temporary professed Assumptionist in formation who was studying at the college. Pater Castro approved of it as a possibility. Another possibility was taking up study in northern France and stay at a local community there. I asked whether I could enquire but he preferred to do it himself since he was going to attend a meeting of superiors in Lille, in northern France, within a fortnight and it would be the ideal occasion to ask around then: he would obtain a university prospectus and so on.

A substantial evaluation that I wrote between May 12 and 17, 1993, and that I gave the heading, "Glory to the Father, to the Son, and also . . . to the Holy Spirit" illustrates where I was at the time in my continuous searching:

> It is becoming more and more evident that I desire to spend a life in stillness. I recognize a strong contemplative element within me. It is in stillness, in the expansiveness of a harmonic creation that we can obtain feeling for the divine. I surmise that I will only be happy when this aspect of my life is being given its place.
>
> I wish, nonetheless, to make myself of use: to cooperate for a just world and proclaim Jesus Christ. Otherwise, my life would remain fruitless. In this context, the third world is often in my

thoughts. I consider doing a work that would be useful such as, for example, teaching or plain manual work, and doing it as one nourished by silence. People should be able to sense that I know myself to be in his presence. As regards proclamation; this can occur in every conversation that takes place. A systematic proclamation will certainly require a theological formation. Such formation will require much time over a period of several years: even if it would be merely for obtaining an officially recognized qualification. One does, however, not undertake a study just for the certificate obtained at the end but so as to enrich oneself, out of interest. As regards such proclamation, I consider potentially the writing of a book or the addressing of a group when the occasion presents itself: for example, as a catechesis. For engaging upon systematic proclamation, it is necessary to have a message that one wants to communicate; but such message is received by oneself only gradually. This requires a keeping in touch with one's source; it requires that one keeps one's spirit turned towards the divine and one's ear to the people.

Evidently, all aspects of one's life are required to form a continuum: prayer, contemplation, activity, proclamation, daily living; it needs to be one encompassing whole. One's entire life has to be enveloped in an atmosphere of serenity. Possibly, some people may wish to confide in such a one and talk about the problems of their life.

These are the principles upon which I wish to focus my life; I desire to bring this into practice and to make it real as good as possible. If possible, I would, moreover, wish to be a minister for the celebration of the faith; in the Eucharist and in the sacraments.

My present situation is that I find myself within the religious congregation of the Assumptionists and that I pronounced temporal vows. I have so far been living two and a half year within the community at Leuven. Now, to what extent can life within the Assumptionist Order, as I have come to know it, be brought into agreement with what I have outlined above? When I chose the Congregation of the Assumptionists about three years ago, it was a choice that was justifiable. What spoke to me particularly when I struck up an acquaintance with the congregation was the emphasis placed upon the equilibrium between the prayer life and apostolic outreach. It is expressed, for example, in the Rule of Life with a citation from Père d'Alzon: "Contemplation and action belong together for us; they are focused upon the same goal: cooperation unto the growth of the kingdom of Jesus Christ." Other elements that spoke to me are, among others, an emphasis upon the wish to be wholly catholic at the center of the Church; the strong international dimension; and the mutual allegiance among them. In another document that aims to synthesize the congregation's spirituality, the following citation of d'Alzon is highlighted: "The life of an Assumptionist needs be a life of prayer and modesty in the presence of God." It is a sentence that corresponds to what I expressed earlier [as regards envisioned principles for my life]. In this same document, Père d'Alzon is described as an apostolic contemplative. But surveying the spirituality and way of living of Père d'Alzon and of the Assumptionists in their entirety, I arrive at the perception that contemplation is considered as a springboard (or should be considered) for action and that it is not possible to speak of a contemplative pole that is developed in equal measure to the apostolic aspect.

Père d'Alzon lived from 1810 to 1880. He fervently resisted the trend that came along with the French Revolution; a revolution that was framed by the Enlightenment, which emphasized the own capacities of the human being. It was not without reason that the revolutionaries turned against the clergy, who for centuries had exploited the people and kept them under strict control. A result of this was that in the wake of the revolution God himself was neglected and hardly received any attention.

Père d'Alzon firmly opposed the actions and intellectual inheritance of the French Revolution, which he obviously envisioned too much in black and white contrast. Nonetheless, he rightly and meritoriously aimed to bring the recognition of God back into society. He approached this task by going hard at it with his full, southern, temperamental force. As such, I read that in his hurry he knocked over the chairs in the church as he sped along. My impression is that unawares he was under the influence of the Enlightenment, which (as mentioned) emphasized the own capacities and own activity of the human being. It is true that Père d'Alzon left a number of spiritual writings. . . . He saw, moreover, the need for congregations in which prayer and action go hand in hand. However, in my assessment, he has been unable to liberate himself from the great movement that possessed his time. These various factors have been influential for the spirituality of the Assumption. As advocated by d'Alzon, an Assumptionist is required to work as hard as four or even as one hundred men.

I have concluded that at the community of Leuven this expresses itself in a religious opinion and in a view upon life that stresses social engagement inspired by the Gospel; albeit, in contradistinction to the time of Père d'Alzon, one is rather embarrassed by the mystical aspect of religion.

It appears to me that it is at the core of the Gospel that Jesus wants us to be free and happy; and that we would open up to his spirit, the spirit who inspired him: the Holy Spirit; so that we, in our turn, would bear fruit. We are to turn others to him so that they also may be happy and free.

In our days, a significant impulse to Christianity stems from the Pentecostal movements whose members commemorate the coming of the Holy Spirit upon the apostles. These are known as the charismatic movements. They sing lengthy, attractive hymns so that one readily feels taken up by the entire gathering, which pervades enthusiasm. Even though I appreciate these movements, personally, I look for stillness for opening up to the Holy Spirit. It is, nonetheless, significant that the Assumptionist province of South Belgium experiences a revival under the impulse of the charismatic movement, namely, the Maranatha community started by Père Muthien.

During the past year, I have felt an increasing desire to make progress spiritually, to turn towards God so as to be liberated in body and spirit. It is a desire for stillness and serenity, a trying to be open for the Holy Spirit. This year, I have been placing emphasis on study and have felt a great need for prayer. I want to live in accordance with a well developed inner serenity that would allow me to be continuously in touch with our source, the Holy Spirit.

Out of the community, however, comes a summons to spend more time on the common activities: on social activity of any sort. Constantly, I am being called to the exterior. In these past years, I have experienced that this creates a tension.

I no longer wish to stay within the community at Leuven. I do not experience within it any support of the source of my faith; on the contrary. As such, last week I made inquiries at the new community in London. Regrettably, here as well I did not find the pursuit for modesty and for an environment in which it is possible to open up to the Holy Spirit. I have weighed the advantages and disadvantages; for hours and days I have labored over it. At one time I thought it better to leave the Assumption; at another time I thought it was better to stay. I have begged God Our Father for clarity, I prayed, and I have placed myself before him. I have arrived at the following scenes of the Gospel:

➤ Jesus going into the desert, where, despite the temptations of the devil, he nonetheless directs himself continuously to God, his Father, without giving in to sin,

➢ Jesus, who after a period of public life, goes up the mountain together with two beloved disciples, where he is transformed and where God speaks to him,

➢ Jesus descending from the mountain with his disciples and returning among the people; subsequently, he lives together with his disciples, shares meals, and sleeps with them in one house; he proclaims the Word and he admonishes others to do likewise; he washes their feet.

I do no longer wish to stay within the community at Leuven. I have decided that I will not go to London either. Perhaps I can still inquire in France? Perhaps in Lille?

Furthermore, I consider it indispensable to have each year a few weeks retreat at another place, perhaps with a few very good friends; to go up the mountain so as to be nourished by his overwhelming presence.

What I did not report in the above reflection is that the foregoing week I not only visited the Assumptionist community in Brockley, London, but also had an interview at Heythrop College, University of London, with two lecturers of the theology department: Dr. Marie Isaacs and Dr. Tom Deidun. My knowledge of English seemed acceptable, but Dr. Deidun advised me to study the language all my waking hours prior to the course starting. They advised that I would be informed within days whether I could be accepted to studying for the Bachelor in Divinity course; but before leaving the building, the registrar, Annabel Clarkson, advised me already that they just had given her the feedback that I would be accepted if I would choose to apply.

Just two days after completing the here quoted reflection, I went to visit Pater Jef in Borsbeek since I had chosen him as my spiritual director. We spoke for more than two hours, and I informed him of everything written above. I found that he could not quite understand or, rather, get a feeling of the issues I raised. In the afternoon he received my confession. I then went to visit the cemetery in Borsbeek where my parents were buried; I visited Moemoe in the nursing home in Wilrijk; and I went to the church in the Beguinage of Antwerp. I knew I had to make a final decision in that church as whether, yes or no, to stay any longer with the Assumptionists. I prayed for two hours in the presence of God. I begged him for the Holy Spirit. After some time, I came to the consideration that it actually did not matter whether I stayed within the congregation or not. What matters is living as good as possible in agreement with Jesus' spirit. Yet I considered that it would be profitable to remain for the time being within the congregation. Possibly, my presence could be a support to them. I also reflected that, at some future time, I might be able to offer guidance to other religious. As such, I left the church with the intention:

➢ to renew, after all, my vows for another year and to reconsider the matter in a year's time,
➢ to give it, after all, a go in London and to try cooperate at forming a community,
➢ and to make a yearly retreat of three to four weeks in solitude.

In the meantime, I was still having lectures at the CKS in Leuven. On May 24, for example, we discussed the aspect of time in our course on anthropology: how to imagine the time dimension of reality and how to envisage reality? With this as a starting point, it led me to fantasize with a text of the physicist Sir Arthur Eddington (1882–1944) in mind; it was, moreover, close to Pentecost:

Sailing upon the water

Is the totality of reality not as an interminable ocean that contains an enormous quantity of water? And is it not so that the reality known by us and that becomes visible to us at each moment can be imagined as a wave on the water surface, as the froth on top of the dynamic waters?

Strictly speaking, we belong with our body and our transience to this froth on the waters. Besides this, I wish here to evoke the image of a little boat that bobs on top of this ocean and that has us at the helm. At the back of our little boat hangs a bottle of coloring matter. Many other small boats are around that each carry a bottle of coloring matter: each a different color. Above the ocean, a wind blows from variable directions. This wind is called superficiality, lust, egoism, and so on. When we let ourselves be led by the wind only, we will sail now in this direction, then in that one; and the color carpet drawn by the bottles behind our boats will only be an arbitrary, non-artistic conflation of colors. In the ocean, however, in this animated reality, a dolphin swims. It is a beautiful animal and it is called Holy Spirit. When we would get round to putting our hands into the water and to looking what is taking place under the surface, we can grasp the dolphin by his fin. This noble animal desires this and is, therefore, always within in our reach. It swims in a steady direction. Putting our hands in the water is praying. It is required of us, moreover, to keep one hand at the helm: that is, we need to work as well. When we keep hold of the dolphin and are guided by him, the little boats around us will be invited as well to sail in the same steady direction. They will perhaps also put their hands in the water and let themselves be guided by the dolphin (for it is a dolphin that can be at several places at the same time). And, you should see then the magnificent color carpet that is being formed on top of the water. When we come to leave our small boat and end up in the water, we will have a beautiful view from out of the depths.

> The dolphin leads us then to a place under the water, where
> he belongs. It is a place around which many others have been
> gathered. We will be able to treat one another there to warm af-
> fection. And the Lord of the house, he kindly grants it to us.

It was disappointing and odd that Pater Castro failed to obtain
any sure information about the possibilities for study in France.
During his recent visit to Lille, he would have spoken to some
people; but when I questioned him, he could not provide any
details whatsoever. They (?) would sent some university prospectus about the programs available, perhaps; he was not sure. It
seemed quite amazing to me that having two temporally-
professed young men among their ranks after decades and one of
them being requested to take on theological studies, the superior
failed to obtain some adequate information about possibilities; if
only he had given me a free hand, I would long have made contacts myself. The way to France seemed now more or less closed
off; and Heythrop College, London, could not be kept hanging
too long since places were limited. I had to make my decision on
the basis of the information I had in hand.

Exactly one week later, on May 31, 1993, I received a letter
from Fr. Tom O'Brien, one of the three Assumptionists of the
community in Brockley, London, at Saint-Mary-Magdalen RC
Church, in response to a letter I sent:

Dear Bob,

Thank you very much for your letter. We enjoyed your short
stay with us and met the following weekend to discuss your
coming to stay with the community. We were all in favour. We
also felt happy with your decision to come to England to study
and live with us at Brockley. I had intended to write the following week, but we had a much unexpected surprise. On the

Thursday, Brother Jim told us that he had decided to leave the Assumption and in fact would be leaving Saturday morning. It was more than a surprise since the previous weekend he had been asking to renew his vows.

Jim's departure shook us all considerably. It left me devastated. It is now just over a week since he left, and since we received your letter for which I thank you. Since Jim has made a complete break with the Assumption, he will not be returning. There was little time to discuss his plans for the future or to understand how he came to his decision, as he left for America two days later.

This would mean that you would be an only student here with us and not have a confrere. You may, therefore, want to rethink your decision to study at Heythrop. From our point of view, we would welcome your presence. We found your prayerfulness and contemplative spirit a strength for our community. It is also our intention to have people interested in religious life living with us so you may not be alone for long if you still decide to come. . . .

I will write to your Provincial, Father Arnold, to explain the situation. Once again, I underline that we would be very happy for you to live here and study at Heythrop and would give you every support in this.

Please pray for us at this difficult time and pray for Jim. . .

Yours in the Assumption,

from Brendan, Michael and myself.

Tom O'Brien, a.a.

Some weeks afterwards, I completed the single-year philosophy at the CKS and passed with distinction. In the meantime, Paul and a few others had been informing the cardinal of what went on there. As a result, the cardinal would the following years be sending his few seminarians elsewhere, independently from the religious institutes. The CKS would be closed down not too long afterwards.

I did not want to end up with no place to study so that I continued in the road I had chosen, namely, the road to London and Heythrop College. It was clear that if I did not take things in hand myself and would rely on the lackluster approach of my superiors nothing would come of it. From France, as far as I recall, I heard no more. As such, I must have confirmed my coming to London to Fr. Tom O'Brien and have asked about availability of English-language courses, for I received a reply on July 4, 1993:

Dear Bob,

Thank you for your letter which arrived Thursday. We are very happy you still want to come and study at Heythrop and live with the community in Brockley. . . .

I will investigate local Language Schools to see what courses are being offered during the summer. You will live in the presbytery in the room that Br. Jim had before he left. . . .

Yours fraternally in the Assumption,

Tom

In the meantime, we were well into the summer. Pater Edmund, Pater Valère of the community in Zepperen, Stijn, and possibly Pater Castro and one or two others from Zepperen would go for two weeks holiday to France. It was not obligatory for me to join them, and I requested to go for a few weeks quiet, solitary retreat instead. Pater Pauwel suggested the Abbey of Rochefort to me, for the ancient abbey Our Lady of Saint Remy had been restored (from 1887 until 1948) by Trappist monks—that is, Cistercian monks of the strict observance—coming from the Trappist Abbey of Achel, known as the Achelse Kluis, in the

Campine region of Limburg, right at the Dutch border. The abbey of Rochefort would be located in peaceful surroundings and a number of old monks would still be Dutch speaking. It seemed a good place for me to go and make my first retreat. Hence, I wrote to the guest master, *le Père hôtelier*, and asked to come and stay from July 3 until 21. As it happened, the first weekend of July, the church of the abbey was being re-consecrated after substantial alterations and the guesthouse was, therefore, fully booked. I could come, however, from July 6 until 21.

In preparation for the retreat, I went to the bookshop and looked for a spiritual book in English, given that I was planning to take up study in London. I was browsing the bookshelves when I noticed a book lying on the ground at the bottom of the shelves with the front cover down; the back cover was made-up by the picture of a face. I picked it up and found that the front was not too clean; one corner was cracked. It was a large book, namely, volume two of *The Collected Works of St. Teresa of Avila*, translated by Otilio Rodriguez and Kieran Kavanaugh, two Carmelites. It contained *The Way of Perfection*, *Meditations on the Song of Songs*, and *The Interior Castle*. It was in English, as I was looking for; and it seemed suited reading for my imminent retreat. The cover, as said, did not look too nice, and it was not cheap either: 520 Belgian francs; but I decided to buy it regardless. As I gave it to the lady at the counter, she looked at its poor state. I explained it had been lying on the floor. She said she would give me a reduction, if I cared to buy it.

By train, bus, and walking, I found my way to the abbey situated about a mile from the town center. At the time, the porter was Frère Gérard van Bavel (1914–96) and *Le Père hôtelier* was Dom Jacques-Emmanuel Voisin, a former Jesuit and lecturer in mathematics (and future abbot of the monastery). Père Jacques-

Emmanuel showed me the room at the first floor: natural-stone walls, exposed wooden beams, a square wooden table with desk lamp, a cupboard, a bed, a sink, and a window looking out upon some nearby trees. Toilets and showers were at the end of the corridor. A key was given that allowed access to the cloister that led to the church, and a key for the garden—it was, rather, a small park with large trees and shrubs, a large pond, and hedges all around—for the exclusive use of the retreatants. Between prayer

Our-Lady-of-Saint-Remy Abbey, Rochefort – Side chapel containing the Blessed Sacrament

moments, it was there that I read daily in my book of Teresa of Avila. It was a privileged time. I spoke as little as possible with the other guests. Along the side of the abbey, along the other side of the hedged guests' garden, was a path that led into a wood and near the end of this stood, elevated along the path and reached by a flight of steps, a large crucifix. I prayed in front of it with arms raised. A little further, the path made a sharp bend of nearly 180 degrees, so that one could return by a path higher up the wooded slopes of the valley. This path led beyond the abbey; and returning by a lower path on the other side of the abbey, one could make a full circuit. I walked it daily, very slowly, in silence.

Here is a reflection written on the fourteenth, during that first retreat:

Beauty as a criterion of truthfulness

The idea of beauty is a reaction that we experience at the observation of a certain given. In science, beauty is considered a criterion for the plausibility of the veracity of a theory. This featured, for example, in the introduction of a term that provided symmetry to the electromagnetic equations, resulting in a more exact theory. It appears that when a proposed natural law is in greater alignment with the idea of beauty, it has a greater claim upon veracity. Furthermore, it seems that the more beautiful a natural law, the more encompassing it is. Hence, the more a natural law comes to meet the idea of beauty, the more representative it is of reality, the more in alignment it is with the truth concerning reality.

Would what is applicable to the material aspect of reality not be applicable as well for the totality of reality? Would it not be applicable for us as human beings?

It appears likely to me that to the extent that people, considered in their entirety, come to meet the idea of beauty, they are in greater alignment with the truth concerning reality. As consciously aware beings, such people will be more aware of truth than others are.

Now, who are the people that appear to me to correspond best to the idea of beauty? I hold it to be those people who are most free and who are turned towards the divine. The people who are most free are those of whom their entire personality constitutes a continuum: people of whom their inner feelings, thoughts, external conduct, speech, and actions are in harmony with each other. When they turn towards the divine and are grateful for their existence, I hold them to fulfill the idea of beauty. Assumedly, they are happy people.

As exemplary of such ones, I am thinking of Francis of Assisi, Teresa of Avila, Bernadette Soubirous, Mahatma Gandhi, and a number of unknown men and women in the street. Each of these fulfills to certain extent the idea of beauty. These are the people whom we must contemplate upon for turning towards the truth. These are the ones to whom we must turn for advice.

If we accept that beauty is a valid criterion for the level of correspondence to the truth, it appears in my assessment that it is not irresponsible for us as human beings to have faith in and to turn towards the divine.

From the Gospel I learn that Jesus Christ completely fulfilled the idea of beauty. As such, I believe in what is written: "He is the way, the truth, and the life." At the core of his message is that he wants to make people free, and he wants us to turn towards God, Our Father.

May his kingdom come, on earth as in heaven.

One week later, on July 28, 1993, that is, two months before my temporal vows were to be renewed, I formally requested this:

Reverend Pater Provincial,

With this letter, I request to be admitted in September for the renewal of my temporal vows for the period of one year.

Almost one year has passed since I pronounced my first vows on September 27, 1992. During the past year, I have dedicated myself to a single-year-study-program philosophy, prayer, and every two or three weeks a visit to my grandmother. Other activities have been limited.

This year, I have obtained the insight that Jesus Christ wants to deliver us in body and mind, and that by means of the Gospel he invites us to follow him. By opening ourselves in prayer to the Holy Spirit, we learn to command our spirit evermore in God's hands, to commend ourselves evermore to his mysterious presence among and in us. Along the small piece of road that I travelled in the past year, I have tried to let myself be guided by the Holy Spirit. It is obvious to me that I still need to travel a long way. According to Augustinian spirituality, we have to make progress upon this road by means of a community-living of prayer and being active. Christ has gone before us on this road of withdrawing at times in stillness and of living together while keeping before his eyes the realization of God's kingdom within and without us.

As it is, so far, I have experienced the living of faith within the community not as constructive and encouraging but rather as destructive and discouraging. I feel this particularly during the offices at which my official guide, Edmund J., or Stijn read to us. At those times, I have often had the feeling that the reading [a chosen comment upon scripture or about the faith] was but intended to moralize, to reproach, and to make level with the ground. I do not intend to speak badly, but I indicate how I, personally, have experienced it. . . .

Jesus Christ invites us upon a way of deliverance. A way along which we want also to help others turn to Our Lord Jesus Christ so that also they may be liberated and so that God's kingdom of peace, of justice, and of love may come among us. It is a way along which we need to commit ourselves with all our heart, all our soul, all our mind, and all our strength, and along which we grow in love for God Our Father and our neighbors (after Mark 12:30).

I desire to live a life focused upon God and to dedicate myself in celibacy, in a life of poverty, and in obedience to God Our Father, to the Son, and to the Holy Spirit. I also want to try this again for one year in community, more concretely within the community at London, and this according to the Assumptionist spirituality. Although I do not expect to find there an ideal situation, I am of the opinion that there is a great need for communities in which one tries to advance towards God. Such communities are as yeast in the dough and are able with his grace to encourage others in living this life.

As such, I request to renew vows for one year according to the Rule of Saint Augustine and the constitutions of the Assumption. . . .

Robert Govaerts

It was rather disconcerting that not long before I set out for London, a postcard arrived from France. It was sent by a few young Assumptionists at the community in Lille, asking when I would join them as they were expecting me. In reply, I informed them that some misunderstanding was involved, for I was set for London; I had not received any prior communications from France whatsoever.

Early August then, I joined the community in Brockley, London. The three priests of the new community were serving the parish of Saint Mary Magdalen. The parish church stood at the corner of the street; along one side of it was found the presbytery, which was the first house in the row (the second house had been bought up by the Assumptionists as well and Father Tom slept there); beyond the corner, on the other side of the church, was situated the Catholic primary school of the parish. During the first weeks I visited parishioners at their home: among them, Leon and Blanche, an elderly Flemish couple who had lived and worked in Nigeria. On Sundays, during one of the masses, I helped with the children's liturgy, that is, while the Liturgy of the Word took place. Community prayer-moments took place in the church in the morning and the evening. On Monday evenings, we met in the living room for reflecting upon the Gospel of the following Sunday; and on Saturday midday, we met so as to speak about the documents on the Assumption's spirituality produced by the superior general and advisers in Rome. Besides this, I made my way through a few recommended academic books in preparation of the theology course: namely, *Introduction to the Old Testament* by J. A. Soggin and *The Origins of Christianity* by Schuyler Brown.

In September, I was attending an English Language Course at SOAS (School for Oriental and African Studies). The course itself was quite boring and I did not learn very much because the tutors didn't follow us closely enough. What was interesting was the group of fourteen people that I was part of: Thailand, Republic of China, Japan, Qatar, Austria, and Italy. The young Muslim woman from Qatar appeared to have five children; she was wealthy and she spoke of her maid. She told me that in her country women were not allowed to speak to men; nevertheless, we talked for a few hours. Although she was a very believing woman, it did not make sense to her at first that I wanted to remain unmarried and without children because of my religious conviction. The Austrian girl that was in the class wanted to take up study at Heythrop College. She was following the same program as seminarians in her country and had chosen London for continuing part of her study program. She wants to become a hospital- or prison chaplain, and she is hoping that church policy would change so that, one day, she would be allowed to become a female priest. The Italian girl in the class was a Marxist. In short, it was an interesting sample of humanity.

On September 27, 1993, I renewed my vows for another year at the end of the weekday Mass in the hands of Fr. Brendan O'Malley (1934–2008) at Saint Mary Magdalen's, Brockley.

A week later, I officially began the Bachelor of Divinity course at Heythrop College, which was during the first year that it was located at its new campus at Kensington Square in London. I liked the campus, located as it was in the building owned by the Religious of the Assumption; the community was living in other buildings at the same site, which were spread around a central private garden to which we had access. It also meant that we had regular access to the Maria Assumpta Chapel. On Wednesdays a college Eucharist took place, which was very well attended; on the other weekdays a lower key Eucharist took place around lunch time. At other times, I would regularly enter the chapel between lectures. The degree was of the traditional type: Biblical Studies (Old and New Testament), New Testament Greek, Church History, Systematic Theology, and Philosophy of Religion. As optional modules I chose: Church, Ministry, and Sacraments; Christian Ethics; and Revelation (with texts of Karl Rahner and Karl Barth). The course ran over three years and was given through taught lectures, seminars, and essay writing (usually of two thousand words) that were evaluated in one-to-one tutorials. The lecturers included a few Jesuits (given that Heythrop was originally a Jesuit study house), other religious priests, diocesan priests, nuns, ministers male and female of other denominations, and lay people.

It was an interesting course, but it took a lot of time travelling up and down from Brockley: between two and a half- and three hours daily. I took the train from Brockley to London Bridge and then the underground to Kensington. Regularly though, because of bomb scares, underground stations were temporally being closed so that I had to follow other routes.

Initially, on days that no lectures took place or in holidays, I would obviously stay at Brockley; but midday meals at Brockley took a lot of time and were much centered on Eileen, the cook who came in most days around lunch time. Moreover, my room was next to the playground of the school, and it was very noisy when the children were out. Add to this that during the day, when the others were out, the heating was turned off. So, after a little while, I started to go into college from early morning until quite late at night, well passed the rush hour. I went first to the college chapel and studied in the library when I could. I followed the same practice on days that only a morning- or afternoon lecture took place, and even on days when no lectures took place or during holidays when the library was open. I often moved between the library and the chapel.

For the project of the new community in Brockley, a letter was produced by members of the English province in which as objectives are mentioned the cultivating of silence, a real community life, and living as closely as possible to the Assumption spirituality. Notwithstanding these objectives, when I stayed during the day at Brockley and was present for the midday meal, we sat at table for at least an hour chatting: often, just little talk with Eileen. When I did sometimes say something, it tended to be received with a disapproving comment from Father Michael. Moreover, under my room, a meeting room was located where almost every evening people were coming together; and Fathers Brendan and Michael were playing music for most of the time. Therefore, soon after my taking up study at Heythrop, it was becoming obvious to me that I was searching for a life that the Assumptionist spirituality could not offer me.

End December, 1993, I wrote a few words on a piece of scribbling paper in my continuous efforts towards discernment:

A program:
> stillness, serenity, an un-hastened life
> a spiritual life, prayer
> to testify of my faith in Jesus Christ with words and deeds
> to study and to write down why believing (dialogue with the unbelieving)
> means of living          (third world?)

At the end of the year, I returned for a week to Belgium. I do not remember anything of that week, but I have noted down that, surprisingly, I managed to visit a few times the Beguinage of Antwerp. At each visit, I sat for a couple of hours in the quiet Saint Catharine's Church, which was as a coming home to me. At the entrance to the beguinage, I saw advertised that they sold there the book *750 jaar Begijnen te Antwerpen* (750 Years of Beguines in Antwerp). I bought it with the intention of reading it in the underground of London, but I started it immediately and read it straight through.

Back in Brockley, as it appeared to be their custom, each of the three priests took a day off during the week. Outside of term time, on his day off, Father Tom invited me a few times along to visit places: Hampton Court Palace, Dulwich Picture Gallery, Horniman Museum, Saint George's Cathedral at Southwark, and the nearby war museum. Father Michael was more curious: On his day off, he did not want to speak with me at all it seemed. Once, when I just came out of my room, he as well happened to come out of his room, with an ice cream in his hand. I probably greeted him, saying "Good morning." I don't think he paid any attention, for he did not return the greeting and did not look my way; instead, he quickly walked across the landing and slammed the door of the living room behind him (which was right beside

Greeting parishioners after Sunday Mass at Saint Mary Magdalens's, Brockley. Father Tom is pictured on the left; Father Brendan is at the foreground with Father Michael besides him, partly hidden; and I am at the right.

the door of my room). The next moment, the television would be on, more than audible from my room. I was still more or less standing in the door of my room while this whirlwind passed. The fact was that I also lived in that house, and it made me feel unwelcome. Somewhat later, when Father Brendan had entered the television room, I heard them laughing. On the one hand, they wanted to foster community living and to inspire newcomers to join them; but on the other, when it is his day off, Father Michael found it too much even to acknowledge my presence. It appeared to me as very immature behavior.

On Sundays, we often had to wait for Eileen who did her shopping for the community at Sunday midday. We waited together in the living room with an aperitif before she came in and started the cooking. I just suffered these times. I remember that regularly on Sunday after the meal was at last done and the others went for a lie down, I went out for a little walk and went around the local cemetery; at those times, I felt totally empty and quite unhappy. In the meantime, I was trying to keep up with my coursework and essay writing in English.

As it happened, I more and more avoided being in the house even on Sundays. After Mass, I walked to the Horniman museum and sat in the garden with my military flask for water, a few sandwiches, and some material to write my essays, which I wrote straight in proper so as to hand in the next day. I got back home by the time it started to get dusk.

The community meetings at Brockley continued on Saturdays at midday; in February I still led some of the discussions around a few pages of the document entitled *Passion for the Kingdom*, in particular, the pages dealing with the religious vows. At the end of one of the meetings, I asked that a Mass be said in honor of Saint Rita of Cascia in thanksgiving for my family.

On March 6, 1994, I wrote to Pater Castro a lengthy letter, updating him of what stirred me interiorly and how I saw my way forward:

Hi Pater Castro,

. . . What has become clearer to me—or rather, what imposes itself—is the need for inner stillness. I wish to live a life from out of a deep inner silence. . . . I wish to open myself to God's presence and to be guided by the Holy Spirit, so that I may be free in body and mind and bear fruit for others. By reading a book of Teresa of Avila as well as by Paul's letters, I have come to the realization that we need to try to be temples for Christ's presence in us. This is presently central also in my reflection on and experience of the Eucharist. Central to the Gospel is for me, moreover, that Jesus wants that we would open ourselves to him and to the spirit in him, the Holy Spirit. As such, we will glorify the Father, the Son, and the Spirit and attain a being free in body and mind, and happiness; and as such, we will try to help others turn towards Jesus and his message. I consider, moreover, that we give witness when people notice that we are happy and are being nourished by the Holy Spirit. The Holy Spirit cannot be kept for ourselves but will express himself in our life and actions. As for me, I still have to make a lot of progress on this road and it is an enduring journey throughout our life.

This envisioning affects all aspects of life, which is as it should be.

I experience an increasing need to avoid all unnecessary talking. I would wish that I only have to speak in relation to our activity, for the sake of God and the good of others: when it is needed to do so. I wish, moreover, to travel on a road of detachment of all that is superfluous. In this manner, I want to make progress in the spiritual life and eventually to bear fruit for the greater glory of God and the good of others.

As you know, we meet in the community here a few times a week; on these occasions I have spoken about a need for inner silence: a being in the world but not of the world, as John expresses it. One cannot understand it and does not consider it as belonging to the spirituality of the Assumptionists. It is perceived as belonging to the contemplative life. It is true that these are aspects of the contemplative life, but I do not consider them as a goal as such. The glorification of God and prayer are themselves indeed a goal; but eventually, I want to be able to approach other people and spread God's message. I have attempted to speak about this once more in community when we discussed the religious vows. In the Congregation of the Assumptionists, however, these are solely considered in their social context, as concerning community living. Eventually, Father Tom could envisage the point I wanted to bring across and said that this search for serenity, for harmony with God, to which the vows can contribute, may indeed be absent in the Assumptionist spirituality; that perhaps it should have to be looked at.

I do not find in the Assumptionist Order, neither as it presents itself presently nor in its spirituality, this striving towards serenity, to a spiritual ascent, to an opening up for the Holy Spirit so that he can bear witness through us. Nonetheless, I wish to give this absolute priority in my life. . . .

I do not think that the coming summer I will renew my vows; in the foregoing, I have tried to outline the reasons for this.

. . . Even when I tried to set these thoughts aside, it has not been possible to do so; on the contrary, daily and at night these considerations present themselves. I cannot find rest in the Congregation of the Assumptionists. I do not know what God plans to do with me.

I intend to continue my theology studies this year and probably the coming years as well. I hope it will become clearer what presents itself to me. In any case, I wish to place my life in service of God and to witness of his presence through the Spirit: perhaps as a more eremitical life, I do not know; I will aim to be attentive to what is happening in the religious domain. Perhaps I can contribute something as regards dialogue with those who do not believe.

For the coming time surrounding Easter, I have as yet not made plans. . . .

United in prayer to God, Our Father, Our Lord Jesus Christ, and the Holy Spirit; and to Holy Mary, our mediatrix,

Bob

About a month later, I spend some days in Leuven and had a conversation with Pater Castro about my letter. By that time, Stijn, who had joined around the same time as me, had already left the order.

Now, as to what concerns spiritual guidance, I had written to the Carmelites in Kensington as early as September of the foregoing year, that is, shortly after my arrival in Brockley, enquiring whether they could provide this for me. I did not hear from them at first, but about mid October a reply came in the form of an apology: my letter would for some weeks have been lost in the post and only just have arrived to them. Father Ronan Murphy (d. 2006) sent the belated reply and would be willing to meet me. Kensington Church Street, where their convent and parish church is located, was near to Heythrop College and, as such, I went to meet Father Ronan a few times after college. Throughout January, trying to be helpful, I wrote several pages of thoughts about myself for the conversations with Father Ronan. He was a kind man but very busy, as it appeared. I remember that mid April, that is, after I wrote the foregoing letter to Pater Castro and subsequently visited, I sat down with him at a kitchen table in their convent. Shortly after I sat down, the telephone rang and he had to answer it. Five minutes later, he returned. I told him that it was not given me at the time to see full clearly into my future but that I was thinking of continuing my theological studies in the hope that things would become clearer along the way. The telephone rang again; so for a second time, he disappeared for some minutes. After he reappeared, he was soon called out again to deal with some matter. I thought by myself, "This does not work." After he returned the third time and time was moving on, he asked me what my age was and that it was time I would come to a clear decision: either I join the Carthusians or live in an apostolic community; I needed as well to decide whether I want to become a priest or not: if so, I needed to go to a diocese. His advice was that if I cannot see clearly in this, it would not make sense to continue my study, for one cannot study two more years just for oneself or for pleasure. But as it was, I certainly was not confident that he understood my struggles or that he had made the effort to read my pages that I had handed him some months earlier. So, having left him, that day and those following, I brooded and pondered.

Sounding another note was the first-year tutor for the Bachelor of Divinity course, Sister Jenny Dines. She was, in addition, lecturer in the Old Testament and taught us about the Psalms. She was living in a small community in Bethnal Green, a London parish served by the Assumptionists. At some point, I must have informed her of my decision to leave the Assumptionists. She found that I was a gifted and diligent student; obviously very interested in the course; and therefore, if at all possible, I should continue for the degree.

Perhaps it was around May that a visitation was planned to the English province of the Assumptionists by Father Marcel, a Canadian Assumptionist whom I had met in Leuven and had joined on the trip to the south of France. He came as an official visitor, sent by the general counsel of the order so as to interview the various members of the English province. During the days of his sojourn in London, he would use Brockley as his base. Prior to his stay, Father Michael made clear to me that I did not belong to the English province and that it would be unfair to them if I tried to speak with Father Marcel, since he came for them. It was a pity for it might have been worthwhile to speak with Father Marcel, since he would have had a good view upon the Congregation of the Assumptionists in all its internationality. They obviously spoke to him about me, but I did not speak with him and he did not invite me to do so.

In effect, it is the Assumptionists' fault that I found it necessary to leave them. As far as I know, since then, not a single person has joined the Flemish or English group; or if someone did make an attempt, they did not stay for long.

As regards myself, I would have to step into the unknown. In the meantime, I kept writing notes long and short, often in Dutch, sometimes in English. On June 20, 1994, the following short note in English:

One could say, "Why would Jesus have been the only one?" Why hold a Christian belief instead of another religious belief?

But look at Jesus' message. He has wanted to bring us to fullness [of life in God]. I go to Jesus because he wants to make me free and happy, and he shows that we can trust in God: that he is there.

Where else would I have found this? He wants to lead me into the full light, and I believe in him.

After the academic year was finished, I still went for a couple of weeks into the college and sat in the library, the chapel, or the common rooms; a few times, I visited a museum. On my return to Belgium, I had to leave one suitcase at Brockley, which I planned to pick up at my return to London; I was at the time already resenting that I would have to sit once more at table with them before I would get my suitcase back. Having returned in Belgium, I stayed a few weeks with the community in Leuven; I paid a few visits to family. I visited Jenny, my sister—our difficult reunion of years before had given way to much love—Sven and Karen, her children; Walter and Sonja, my brother and sister-in-law; and Steven and Liesbeth, their children. Sonja was at the time already more than a year under medical house-arrest: she could only move with crutches because of a sport injury at her knee, which had already three times been operated upon. I visited Emma, "de Moemoe"; and Uncle Eugène would have looked me up. After all that, I was able to stay for three weeks at the Our-Lady-of-Saint-Remy Abbey near Rochefort, which provided me a welcome retreat.

# 19

## Twenty-four years: 1994–2018 (1)

WHEN I LEFT the Assumptionists, it was the summer of 1994. Twenty-six years have passed since. It is not my intention to give a comprehensive account of all these years, but I will attempt to give a fair idea in the next two chapters up to 2018, focusing here and there on a particular memory.

Towards the later part of my first academic year at Heythrop College, when I was still living with the Assumptionists, I left the house in the early mornings—the background to this I have set out in the foregoing chapter—and on arrival at the college would first visit the chapel. After a couple of weeks, I noted that a few people met in the morning in the organ loft for prayer. These were two female PhD students in theology who wished to pray Morning Prayer together. They asked me to join them. One of them was Ivana, a married, female priest of the Hussite Church, a church that broke away from the Catholic Church in former Czechoslovakia; the other was Vicky, who was staying at the student hall for girls on the campus and who was doing a PhD on the theme of holiness. Ivana bought me a second-hand copy of *The Way of a Pilgrim*, written by a nineteenth-century Russian peasant. His life story introduced me to the Orthodox practice of the Jesus-prayer, that is, the quiet, incessant repetition of the prayer "Lord Jesus, Son of the living God, have mercy on me, a poor sinner," which is an adaptation of the blind beggar Bartimaeus's cry for help as found in Mark's Gospel (Mark 10:46–48 and parallels). The pilgrim hears in church during the liturgy the words written by Saint Paul to the Thessalonians, "Pray without ceasing" (1Thessalonians 5:17). Wanting to heed the Apostle's command, he reads in his Bible, and as he journeys along, he asks the advice of a starets, an old monk who becomes his spiritual guide. The holy man introduces him to *The Philokalia*, a collection of texts written between the fourth and fifteen centuries by spiritual masters of the Orthodox Christian tradition, first published in Greek in 1782 and later translated into Russian and other languages. The starets dies not very long afterwards, but the pilgrim obtains a second-hand copy of the book and aims to learn from it the art of ceaseless mental prayer—and his deceased starets still guides him along in dreams to the right texts for him to read in the book. Ivana had a compendium of *The Philokalia* in English, and I borrowed it from her. The complete collection of texts is translated in English in five volumes (volume five may still not be available). Soon afterwards, I bought and read volume one; many years later, I obtained volume two, which is largely dedicated to works by Saint Maximus the Confessor.

After I left the Assumptionists, Gina, a mature Chinese student from Hong Kong, soon wanted to make our friendship more intense. We adopted the custom of going to Mass in Saint Mary of the Angels, a parish where Fr. Michael Hollins was parish priest and where Fr. Anthony Baxter, one of our lecturers resided as well. So, I walked often on Sunday through Regents Park with Gina to Mass, and we often ate together at college and in weekends. Gina wanted more than friendship, but I rather felt being forced into something I did not really want, though for some time I went along. We spent some holidays together: to the convent of the Poor Clares in Arundel and to Belgium. We got on very well, but she did not accept or understand the vocation I was trying to discern and pursue. I found it extremely difficult, for I did not want to hurt her, but I had to go my own way. After Heythrop, we would still be in touch a few times. Looking back, for sure I was spiritually too undiscerning to recognize the hand in it of the old deceiver, the devil. If I had, I would have been able to take a firmer stance and have spared ourselves much misery.

In the meantime, I had asked Father Anthony, who taught Christology at Heythrop as well as an optional course on faith and revelation, to meet for spiritual direction. Considering my options, he mentioned Quarr Abbey, a Benedictine Abbey on the Isle of Wight, as worth exploring. Towards the end of the course, we were expected to write an extended essay of 8,000 words. We could approach any of the lecturers with the request to be the tutor for this essay, who would then help us choose a suited topic to write about. I asked Father Anthony, and the topic I wrote about was "Our Relationship with Jesus Christ." In this essay, I focused on the letters of Saint Paul.

As regards accommodation, my stay at Mrs. Treacy's flat lasted only a few months. The woman did not like me to be in the room that I rented from her. When she found I was inside—sometimes, she would peep through the keyhole to find out— she would slam doors, and she told me that it was not normal that I was studying in the room during the day. It became untenable at the time that I was preparing for exams, so that I left; for some time, I was given shelter in More House, a Catholic student chaplaincy, which is owned by nuns of the Congregation of Our Lady, who are Canonesses of Saint Augustine. During the third and final year of the course, I was allowed to stay in the convent of the Carmelites in Kensington, since Fr. Ronan Murphy knew me. I usually joined them for Morning Prayer, breakfast, and supper. On one occasion, though, when they needed as many rooms as possible for some visiting Carmelites, I had to vacate my room. Father Ronan put me up in the bathroom. Looking back, it is no exaggeration to say that all through my various studies, accommodation has been somewhat of a trial.

Despite everything, I completed the BD course in 1996, obtaining upper-second class as a result. Returned to Belgium, I stayed initially with the Assumptionist community in the presbytery of my home parish, that is, Saint-Jan-Berchmans Parish, in Borsbeek. Mid July, I went for a stay in the Abbey of Rochefort. Subsequently, I rented a top-floor studio-flat in the Van den Hautelei in Deurne.

I wanted to live a life of stillness, simplicity, and prayer. Pater Filip Deploige of the Saint-Jacobus Parish in Borsbeek helped me to move in. From the Assumptionist convent in Leuven, I obtained a desk, a metal bed-frame, and a few other items of furniture. On a low cupboard, I placed the statue of Our Lady of Banneux that had come from my parents' house. It was a time of intense searching of a way forward. First of all, I tried to obtain a part-time cleaning job: everywhere I asked but without result. I was at the time plagued with a swollen knee and this did not help either. It certainly was not the easiest time.

Not very long after my return to Belgium, Moemoe entered her last days. Uncle Eugène said that she refused to receive the last rites, or the sacrament for the dying, from the chaplain of the nursing home. Since it was clear that she had not long to live, I decided to ask Father Lieven—who received my own first confession some years earlier—whether he was willing to visit Moemoe with me, and if *she* was willing, to give her the last rites. He readily agreed, and I borrowed the car used by the priests of the parish and drove him to the home. When the old ex-missionary with his long, grey beard and constantly-shaking head entered the room where she lay, holding his prayer book, priestly stole, and ointment in hand, she immediately realized why he came to see her. She made efforts to sit upright, and we left Father Lieven with her alone in the room. She made her confession; though, as he told me afterwards, he could not make out the barely audible words;

Sitting at the desk, I drew an image of Our Lady of Banneux after the statue that I had in front of me.

but her willingness of doing so being there, he gave her the absolution and administered the final rites of the dying. I thanked Father Lieven that he had been willing to do this. She soon lost all consciousness; and the next day, or the day afterwards, she died. She had been born on April 14, 1897 and died on September 23, 1996.

Under my top-floor studio stayed, at first, a young woman and often her boyfriend as well; after she moved out, a young fellow moved in who was on drugs and who probably was a drug dealer; music all the time. During the night he worked at McDonald's. A number of times, when he pulled the door behind him in the evening, he did not turn off his music so that it went on all night. I lived with earplugs all the time. The fellow was not contrary, and he once invited me in his flat: we talked about faith. During the day, I tried to be elsewhere. I spent a lot of time in the cemetery of Borsbeek; not because I was mourning, but because it provided me benches where I could sit quietly. My preferred spot was near the Mount of Calvary—consistent of a large statue of Christ crucified with white statues of his mother Mary and of the Apostle John standing at the foot of the Cross, just as it is often found on Belgian cemeteries. I said the Divine Office there. At eight in the evening, the guardian of the cemetery and his wife, who lived in a house by the entrance, would close the gates of the cemetery, but getting used to me sitting there, they kindly told me that I did not have to be out at eight on the dot and that they would only close it when they did not see me around anymore. I was welcome to stay as long as there was some light, but I always left before eight so as not to inconvenience them. Apart from the times that I was searching at various places, I hardly spoke. It was a time of writing numerous little spiritual reflections. A little note of January 9, 1997 is this (translated in English):

> It is frightening to know that my choice of life, the way that I take, depends upon a few thoughts, in fact, upon arbitrariness. But I may believe and have to believe that Jesus Christ will nonetheless be with me and always remain close to me. He is with me and shall always be with me.
>
> God, how marvelous your ways are.
> How great you are.

A few days later, on Sunday, January 12, 1997, I expanded upon this thought:

Now and then, one hears people express their opinion that every-thing just had to be as it presents itself to us and that our lives develop in agreement with our predestination; that everything happens in accord with God's plan; and that eventually every-thing will turn out well. Personally, I very much doubt that this presentation of affairs is correct; despite the fact that people would like to find a sure foothold by entertaining such thoughts.

We, people, are part of God's creation: we are creatures, formed out of dust and ash. The entire created reality is called into existence by God out of nothing (*creatio ex nihilo*). Fur-thermore, the created reality is not only called forth at the be-ginning of time; as if started up by God, just as a watch is being wound up and subsequently left to run down: this is the vision of the deist. In actuality, God continuously calls forth the created reality; she is being upheld by him. God's creative activity is to be situated not only at the beginning of time; on the contrary, he is continually occupied with it: it is the vision of the theist. Accordingly, from our time-bound perspective, the created re-ality unfolds gradually and this thanks to God's enduring crea-tive activity, his enduring involvement (see also the cosmological proof of Thomas Aquinas).

We, people, are part of, object of, the creation, which unfolds itself, manifests itself, with time; and this while we occupy an active role. From out of our being situated, we are co-creators of reality. We co-determine the way the created reality turns out by our free expression of will. Hence, we are co-creative also of the way our own life turns out. This does not imply a denial that many other factors co-determine the continued de-velopment of our life, of other people's lives, and of the created reality as a whole.

Considered from our perspective, the future is not deter-mined. All the time, various options present themselves to us that require us again and again to opt for this or that. Continu-

building in which Mass was said on Sundays. Père Jean said, in addition, a vigil Mass at another church in Couthuin, namely at Surlemez (or, sur le mont), which formed a separate, well-populated hamlet; and on Sunday mornings, at Saint-Peter's Chapel, a private chapel of the count and countess (de Changy), who lived in a nearby castle. A good number of faithful liked to join in for the early Sunday Mass at this private chapel. I accompanied Père Jean to all masses, sometimes as well to the church in Huy. It was winter and the churches were cold; sometimes, some cleaning was required prior to the Mass, especially when pigeons had gotten in. A few times I went to do a bit of cleaning during the week in these places of worship.

Apart from this, Père Jean and I met to pray the Divine Office in the morning, at lunch, and in the evening. At midday, we were joined by Père Paul (Ludwig Nols), another monk of Leffe, who was parish priest at the nearby villages of Maneffe and Ottepe. We said Midday Prayer and then drove in Père Paul's car to a nursing home at Landenne run by sisters, the Résidence Saint-Charles, were we had lunch together with some other parish priests and the dean of those areas.

Once or twice, I dropped in at the meeting of Les Trois Fois Vingt, the group of senior parishioners—most were actually *quatre fois vingt*, that is, in their eighties—who met for playing cards and for company in a hall downstairs in the building that we lived in. And I visited parishioners in their houses or farms. Weekday masses were said for a handful of people in a room downstairs in the presbytery. Once a week, Père Jean organized a meditative prayer meeting in that same room. He had a selection of small pieces of paper on which was printed a prayer or a meditation, found in a magazine or wherever he had come across it. Holding about ten pieces of cards with the blank side up as a

fan of cards, he went round at the beginning of the meeting and
let each person pick one. Each in turn read his text and a little
moment of silent reflection followed in between; after each few
texts we sang a hymn. Here is a meditation that I found worthwhile to copy (with English translation juxtaposed):

Quelle beauté si nous pou-
vions chaque jour sourire
au Seigneur Notre Dieu.

How beautiful it is when we
know to smile each day to
the Lord Our God.

Que nous puissions Lui sourire car Il a créé tout
l'univers; le ciel et la terre;
toutes les créatures ; les
êtres humains. Dans sa
grâce Il nous a adoptés
comme ses enfants et tou-
jours Il veut adopter chaque enfant comme le sien.

May we be able to smile to
him because he has created
the entire universe, the
heaven and the earth; all
the creatures; the human
beings. In his grace, he has
adopted us as his children,
and always he wants to
adopt each child as his
own.

Que nous puissions Lui sourire en acceptant la vie tel-
le qu'elle est, même si elle
est difficile : chaque jour Il
nous tient dans Ses mains,
et chaque jour Il nous aime
jusqu'à la Croix."

May we be able to smile to
him in accepting life as it
is, even if it is difficult:
each day he holds us in his
hands; and each day, he
loves us unto the Cross.

Dieu nous a souri le premier,
à notre tour souriions Lui.

God had smiled to us the
first; in our turn, let us
smile to him.

Et avec Lui, par Lui, puis-
sions-nous nous sourire les
uns les autres.

And with him, through him,
may we be able to smile to
one another.

very poor singer and who was sitting next to me, found it needed to start every psalm just a word earlier than the others did and continue this throughout. It was done in pure maliciousness so as to annoy the choir leader, Brother DB, who sat next to me on my other side. I wondered about the energy required so as consistently not fall in with the rhythm set by the other monks. It upset all monks at various prayer moments. Brother T always took this wicked course of action when the abbot was absent. On one Sunday evening, when I was sitting at another place in the choir wearing an alb—so that I could go out and come back with the thurible (or censer)—Brother T and Brother DB, who was a strong singer but psychologically not so strong, were sitting next to each other. At some point, understandably, Brother DB could no longer take it and got up and banged the other one with his shoulders against the back of the stalls.

The first prayer service, the Office of Readings, took place daily at 5.30 in the morning. It started with the invitatory psalm, which was intoned by one monk in a certain tone, while after each stanza the others repeated the same verse. It happened that he did not mange to keep the same tone throughout; Brother DB trying to keep up the tone would angrily scream the verse at the top of his voice. True, the monk dragged down the pitch of the choir, but good heavens, it was no reason to be angrily screaming. Gregorian chant performed in anger is no longer an expression of praise to God but is an abomination. I did not want to be part of this and calmly put my book away and walked out of the church. The abbot had not been there; but afterwards he admonished me that I should not have walked out of the church; that it was an overreaction and that I upset Brother DB by doing so. I disagreed.

When the abbot proposed that Brothers T and DB be ordained to the priesthood, I expressed my reservations as regards Brother

T; the man was known in the abbey for psychologically abusive behavior. He was the major reason for the previous choir leader leaving the community. The abbot promised that both T and DB would undergo rigorous psychological assessment as to their suitability and that T would never be a priest outside of the abbey but always be a concelebrating priest at the abbey. I did not think this was a commendable justification for ordaining a man. Did the rigorous psychological investigation take place? I do not think it did. The abbot was acquainted with the Primate of Brazil, who flew in from Rome on the morning and performed the ordination of the two men he had never met and of whom he knew nothing.

Normally, after three years of simple profession, the monk makes a solemn profession in which he promises to live a life of celibacy, stability, and of obedience to the Rule and to the abbot. As I entered the third year of my simple profession, I wondered and prayed whether God wanted me to put my life in the hands of a man whom one knows to be grossly immature, self-deceived, and unreliable? The answer became more and more clear that God did not allow me to pronounce vows into the hands of such a man; under no circumstances: it would be an insult to his gift of divine freedom and to the gift of human life.

In the last months of my stay, it was one of those who had entered the abbey after me who caused some extra trouble to me. I was given the task, amongst others, to organize the washing-up roster. After each meal, two monks were to help with washing up, and a pin board on the wall indicated who was on duty. Wash-up was not really a heavy job: plates and cutlery and dishes were roughly cleaned in a sink and then put on a tray that went into a dishwashing machine that sprayed boiling hot water, detergent, and disinfectant onto it; then rinsed it; one opened the machine on the opposite side and waited till the steam got from the tray and then put things away. An older brother, Victor, who did his own thing, had usually started the job while the rest were eating. There were no problems with the roster, until Brother Christian—a big fellow of Barbados— got simply professed. He started to put very aggressive messages under my door whenever I had dared to put him on the roster for Sunday meals, or wherever I happened to put him on the roster at all. I must have mentioned it to the abbot who simply said that I was to try not to upset Brother Christian, who in fact was one of the abbot's favorites because he showed an interest in music. In effect, the abbot was a very weak leader, and Christian was a bully. The last months of my stay at the abbey, I received at least weekly messages under my door that tried to be as aggressive and intimidating as possible. Eventually I found out that a little after I set the wash-up roster, which was situated in front of the kitchen, Brother Christian would come and redo it, even though he had no right to do so. I decided to just let it be, given that the abbot would for some reason always be on the side of Christian, and I had mentally started to distance myself from life at Quarr. In fact, quite a few others of the younger monks were very reluctant to do their duty; eventually, I did as much as possible myself. How very self-deceived they were, for as Christ says, "the Son of man came not to be served but to serve (Matthew 20:28)."

I clearly recall the following silly experience that took place perhaps one or two years earlier. Through the abbot's connections in Rome, Quarr Abbey would be the community in which two Burmese priests would be received who wanted to learn the monastic life prior to introducing it in their own country. Prior to Fathers Pius and Gregory arriving, the abbot briefed us with the following ridiculous admonition. Since these Burmese priests would be small men, under no circumstances where we to tap their heads, for doing so is a most insulting thing to do. The monks looked at each other and it was said afterwards: "He must hold us for little schoolboys," and, "The abbot has seen too much of Benny Hill." Some days later, I was preparing the charcoal fire in the annex to the sacristy since I was that day responsible for the censer during Mass. As I was bent for heating the charcoal in the fire, while I was already dressed in a white tunic, for it was just before Mass, and while priests were passing along to the sacristy for getting ready, the abbot suddenly approached and tapped his hand on by balding head. I looked up and he stood laughing at me with Brother Christian beside him, and he said to the latter while pointing at me, "He is mad!" They both laughed me out in the face. I did not say anything.

I could fill dozens of pages with my experiences at Quarr but what I have said suffices. I left the abbey in July 2002; various others did the same. In the months and years after I left, some made their solemn profession and then left or were ordained and then left. In the time after my leaving, the abbot apparently stayed in a house on the Isle of Wight, for in the abbey itself he could not find peace. Brother John transferred to Ramsgate Abbey; Father Matthew to Pluscarden Abbey; T would leave the community and has been parish priest at a few places in the North of England (despite the abbot's assurances to me prior to his ordination), even though he hardly received any proper formation and even though, in my experience, he very much lacks integrity; DB left the abbey with the intention to marry; Christian apparently became more and more demanding until he left. Eventually, in 2008, the abbot resigned and he became chaplain to various communities of Benedictine nuns. He died in 2017, aged seventy.

One contact that was established during my last two years at the abbey and that I want to mention is that with Hugh Harrison,

Esq., a homeopath and craniosacral therapist who cofounded the Isle of Wight Natural Therapies Trust, of which the abbot was a trustee. Every few weeks Hugh visited the abbey to provide therapy to one of the monks who suffered from migraines and epilepsy. Since I was considering studying homeopathy, the abbot encouraged me to enquire with Hugh about available possibilities. Hugh was very helpful; he gave me a prospectus of the school of homeopathy where he studied, lent me some classical works on homeopathy, and directed me to some titles that were worth buying. Besides this, Hugh spontaneously gave me a full first consultation and some follow-up sessions. My constitutional remedy appeared to be Natrum Muriaticum (Cloride of Sodium); that is, I am susceptible to developing the Nat.-Mur. type of pathology. We also discussed some standard remedies that would be valuable for the abbey to have for those wishing to take them. Eventually, I decided that I would not take up a four-year study at the school of homeopathy but to keep my focus on faith in God, on spirituality, and on theology. Nevertheless, I kept seeing Hugh when he came to the abbey and we developed a bond of friendship.

Finally, I wish to recall Frère Denis Feignon. He was a young Frenchman who grew up on a farm and who had entered the seminary shortly after his parents split up but had not found peace in this pursuit. In virtue of some contact he had, he travelled to England and had been staying at another abbey. One day he arrived at Quarr Abbey. At first, he stayed in the guesthouse and helped out with some work in the grounds; subsequently, he decided to stay and entered the novitiate. Rather oddly, he seemed very interested in typing out variant versions of biblical texts in Latin—even though he had as yet not received any proper theological formation—and for this purpose was using an old word processor (It was prior to the time that any computers were available for use). He once invited me to his cell, wanting to show me what he was doing. It was rather eccentric that he divided his cell in two by hanging up the dustcover of his bed on a rope as a dividing screen. He had done away with the bed and slept on the floor. The word processor had been placed on a cupboard and he typed his texts standing. In our conversation, he seemed much inspired by the example of Saint Thérèse of Lisieux. Since the abbey did not hold French bibles, I lent him the rather old copy I had obtained from my time with the Assumptionists of *La Sainte Bible: Version nouvelle d'après les textes originaux par les moines de Maredsous*, published by the Abbey of Maredsous, Belgium, in 1949. Brother Denis very much appreciated this Bible and sometime later he decided that he wanted to enter the Abbey of Maredsous, which I thought a good move since he would be able to speak his mother tongue. Several months later, I sent him a Christmas card and letter, and I received a letter from him in reply at the end of January 2002. He sounded happy and settled at Maredsous. No further contact was maintained. On the internet I found that he died suddenly in 2011 as a monk of Maredsous, aged thirty-four. May he rest in peace.

My own journey led to Lampeter in Wales. As a dwelling, I found a caravan on a farm called Lluestnewydd at Bettws, four miles out of town. What brought me there is the fact that Lampeter is a university town where I started a PhD study. A few more words about this: while at Quarr, the idea grew that I wished to obtain greater insight into the relation between prayer, healing, and creation. Since Quarr had a religious bookshop, it received a leaflet from an author called Edward P. Echlin about his new book *Earth Spirituality: Jesus at the Centre* (1999). The book was obtained for me. In October 2001, Dr. Echlin gave a public lecture at Guilford (Anglican) Cathedral, which was near Wonersh Seminary, where I and another brother had to follow a few courses. I attended the lecture, and speaking with Dr. Echlin after it about my interests, he brought to my attention Professor Mary Grey, who was a friend of his. I contacted her, asking whether she would be interested to help me as supervisor for a study on the cosmic dimension of Christian prayer, and more specifically for a thesis on Christian prayer in the context of cosmic prayer. Her reply was encouraging; and in March 2002, I went to meet her at Sarum College in Salisbury, where she taught some modules. Besides this, she was professor of pastoral theology at the University of Wales, Lampeter. At Lampeter, she spoke to Dr. TO about my proposed project. They suggested making some deliberate choices of texts and made some specific proposals. I considered these and opted to focus on cosmic prayer in Johannes Eriugena (810—ca. 877). Hence, by March 21, 2002, I had presented a research proposal to the University of Wales to this effect. I presented the aim of the study as obtaining insight as to whether Christian prayer can be expressed in name of the total cosmic reality; and that some underlying matters that I wanted to probe were: What does the cosmic reality consist of? What is its true identity? And whether Christian prayer can contribute to personal and cosmic healing? Since TO was specializing in Eriugena, he would be involved as the main supervisor for the historical part of the thesis and Mary Grey as secondary supervisor for the chapters that would offer an appraisal of Eriugena in view of modern theology and science. When my proposal was approved by the university and given that TO was resident at Lampeter, it seemed opportune that I would take up residence there.

As soon as I arrived in Lampeter, I went to the local cycle shop and ordered a new bicycle that they would put together for me. It would allow me to travel up and down from the farm. I would officially start my study at the university in October, but I had already started work at it. In the last weeks of my stay at the abbey, I photocopied various books and articles that I found in the monastic library, and I ordered various books from my own funds through the bookshop of the abbey. At Lampeter I gathered more material and bought the main works of Eriugena. I spent time learning Latin and word by word tried to read texts of him in Latin.

In the meantime, I was looking for a job that would prevent my funds going down too quickly, even though the rent for the caravan was quite modest.

The way that led from the farm to the town had a descending stretch of quiet road; at some point it made a bend of nearly ninety degrees with hedges at the side. It was a beautiful, sunny day, and I cycled down the road at a good speed. At the said bend, I went to nearly the middle of the road; unfortunately, because of the hedges, I did not see the car just beyond the bend, coming from the other side. I pulled the brakes of my new bicycle. An important detail is that in Belgium and continental Europe bicycles are set up in such manner that the right-hand brake controls the back wheel and the left-hand brake the front wheel; my Scott bicycle, however, set up in Wales had it the other way around. I was thinking to get it altered so as to have it as I had been accustomed with, but I also thought that I would probably quickly get used to the new arrangement. On that morning I was caught out. As I pulled the brakes in the emergency, the bicycle did not behave as I would have hoped; instead, it threw me over the handlebars right in front of the car. I was extremely fortunate that the older man that was driving the car, Mr. McDonald, reacted very astutely. My head was right in front of the car's bumper, against it really, but I do not think it touched me. Mr. McDonald, and his wife who was sitting on the back seat, took me to the doctor's surgery in Lampeter, where they put my arm in a sling, for I had broken the collarbone; and I had a wound on my face and on my shoulder. An ambulance took me onwards to the hospital in Carmarthen. Not much was done in the hospital on that day: instead, I was kept sitting in the waiting room until nine o'clock at night; eventually, I was told to go home by taxi. At home I looked in a mirror and found that my face had become twice as broad. Over the coming days and weeks, I would be picked up by ambulance or by social transport for follow-up appointments. I telephoned TO, my supervisor, asking that he would look me up at the farm so that we could discuss my study and no time would be lost unnecessarily. The disappointment was that the man did not want to make the effort to visit me, even though he was an RC priest. Only more than a month or so later did I manage to go and fetch the bicycle; a farmer, whose farm was near where I had fallen, had put it for safe keeping in a barn on his farm.

On August 24, 2002, I noted: "This morning I saw a falcon (or a similar kind of bird at any rate) at only a few meters from the caravan on top of a meadow pole." I thought it very spectacular; never had I seen a large, wild bird of prey at close-up." I noted, in addition, around that time: "I consider that there is a spiritual realm which permeates all created reality. In this realm, there is silence, quietness. A forceful word is not heard there; it is a praying heart that finds entry there."

I struggled in the caravan at the farm. It was starting to get colder at night, but the gas fire did not have a pilot light, and I had great difficulty getting it on with one arm; another concern was that the caravan was not level since it had not been perfectly installed or had shifted slightly on its supports. So, unfortunately, begin September, I moved to a house in town where I rented a student room; it meant that with the arrival of other students, I had to endure quite a lot of student noise around me, which I definitely did not like. When I was well enough, I was allowed to start work in the vegetable-packing factory at the border of town: I had applied a few times till they eventually had taken me on.

Not so helpful was that TO would let me down in other ways, once I managed to see him in his office at the department. It soon became clear that he was not keen to work together with Professor Grey, who had a more liberal approach to theology. The first meetings with TO were in fact not very substantial and there was hardly a chance to discuss the topic of my study: either his car broke down so that he was late, or something intervened at the planned time of meeting, and so on. The first meeting at which I was invited to speak about my study was in November 2002. I had started reading Eriugena, and TO asked whether I found anything that would be of interest for my study theme. I did and ventured that his doctrine of the logoi certainly seemed worth exploring. To my surprise, after a few minutes, TO threw his arms in the air and said that I had a brilliant mind but that I was too philosophical for him. He therefore dismissed me and made it clear that he preferred not to continue as supervisor. He advised me to study an author other than Eriugena. It was pretty disappointing, for it was for the purpose of studying Eriugena with him at Lampeter that I was there. It was a non-reason that he gave, for I really had not said or done anything that deserved this. The only reason for my dismissal was that the man had just been appointed head of school; and since he had enough to occupy himself with, I was dispensable.

On the day that he dismissed me, in a very dismissive attitude, he sent me to have a talk with Dr. Oliver Davies. This was weird because at an earlier meeting TO had talked slightly of Davies as being superficial and as writing poor-quality books; and adding gesture to his words, he threw the book of Davies that the latter had gifted him in a corner. I must have asked Professor Grey to convene with Davies, and they thought that I could now only continue my thesis by looking at a variety of resources. On November 14, 2002, she sent me a note in which it was proposed that I look at pre-modern resources including Maximus the Confessor, Eriugena, and Hildegard; and next at contemporary resources. It was a renewed project that I, in fact, never managed to get into structure. I was still introducing myself into Eriugena; I was expected by Professor Grey to write in the first instance a lengthy introduction, which was of course a total waste of time and energy and more confusing than anything; and I was to start studying Maximus the Confessor, who was a Greek author and not Latin. Davies wanted me to read a tome on transcendentals; while Professor Grey wanted me to study various other resources.

In the meantime, I was working in Organic Farm Foods. I started cleaning every day in the factory, for it became clear that this study would take more time than anticipated. So as not to be caught out by a time-deadline, I changed as well from being a full-time student to being a part-time student.

Two friends from my time at the factory whom I gladly recall are Rev. James Chesseret, a Kenyan Anglican priest who worked many more dreadful hours than me to pay for the study fees of his wife Florence (Florence studied for an MA in pedagogy and James had earlier obtained an MPhil in theology), and Karim

Benhamza, a Muslim from Algeria who had been working on a PhD in economics at the university campus in Aberystwyth, but when his supervisor moved away from the university his study stalled and fulltime work for livelihood had overtaken; moreover, he had recently returned from his home country with a bride (Sophia) and they were starting a family in Lampeter.

On November 16, 2002, I wrote the following little reflection in my notebook:

A connecting link

The traditional religious institutes, or churches, have become diminished or obsolete because they fail to facilitate the possibility for human beings to be a connecting link between creation and God. Therefore, groupings that do encourage spirituality that enables human beings to be this link emerge and grow.

Hence, I believe that the decline of the churches or of religion has not its main cause in this or that aspect of culture of Western society. The main reason is metaphysical, namely, ignorance or denial of the human being and his place within the frame of wider creation.

I personally believe that a listening attitude is important. In most ecclesial assemblies there is usually a lot of talking, often by a person set up as a patriarchal figure, without the aspect of listening. We must learn to listen to created reality in meditation before we speak in its name to God. To listen is to some extent becoming one with.

Therefore, as (almost) a law of creation, or a cosmic law, churches have to disappear unless they take up their role within the frame of the cosmos.

The churches may disappear and humanity itself may disappear.

At the university, Dr. Davies was replaced with Dr. SO, an Anglican minister who had been a chaplain at Oxford. As Prof. Mary Grey had no expertise of ancient authors and of Saint Maximus in particular, she was unable to make corrections to the content of my chapters. Given this situation, she consulted with the head of department and asked to be relieved of her task as supervisor and to be replaced by SO as supervisor. Her contract with Lampeter also came to an end. Hence, from September 2005, SO became the sole supervisor of my thesis. Initially, he was encouraging and thought that given my degrees in science, I would be well-placed to include in my thesis modern-science resources, in particular, evolution theories and make a criticism of Richard Dawkins, and so on. I did this, and it became a major ingredient to my thesis besides Maximus. When I made serious work of this, SO made a U-turn and wanted me to leave the modern resources out and to look instead at the traditional re-sources, namely, Scripture, Plato, and Maximus. As I disagreed, he became quite confrontational. In the meantime, I had become fully aware that SO, whom I had been landed with, belongs to the Radical Orthodoxy Movement, which is known for its refutation of modern science. In fact, it became obvious that he had wanted me to include modern resources to serve his own purposes; he himself had focused in his own PhD study on Plato, Thomas Aquinas, and had drawn a contrast with Isaac Newton. When I did not follow obediently in his footsteps, he became annoyed. I read the article and the book he had written and found his view-points rather flawed; in discussion, moreover, he wanted to argue that animals did not suffer but that only human beings did so. In September 2006, I wrote to FK, head of department, that the situation had become untenable and that the man was not suited to supervise my thesis.

The result of the meeting that ensued between me, FK, and SO was that the latter would remain supervisor but would change his approach and that there would be more than one meeting once every half year. In the meantime, Dr. AA had joined the department and he was assigned as co-supervisor for the chapters on Saint Maximus. AA expressed satisfaction with the quality of my work on Saint Maximus and in particular that all my Greek translations were up to standard. Problems remained, however, with the supervision of the overall thesis and with the other chapters that would look at the more philosophical and scientific resources. As it turned out, SO would not enter into a constructive cooperation and my chapters remained unread.

I was as an outsider to the Department of Theology and Religious Studies. The people I had contact with were my work colleagues at the Co-op supermarket; and I had started to attend Mass once more at the Roman Catholic Church in Lampeter, Our Lady of Mount Carmel, so that I had some contact with a few other parishioners. Cycling and walking up and down from the farm at which I stayed to the Co-op or to the library, or running at various roads outside town, I often met a lonesome man along the road; sometimes he was sitting on a bench. We spoke and he invited me into his ground-level flat for tea. Ian had had an antiques shop at the border of town, but had not earned much from it. He did not have a television, only a few old books; a radio; a heavy, metal pole that had been the support of an old fence; and so on. He had no contact with family and lived a life along the sidelines of society, somewhat like myself.

The dwelling I had been renting at Gwar Coed Farm was significantly substandard, but eventually I found some more decent accommodation in a large room above the garage that belonged to a large house at the border of town. At last, I had no other noisy students living besides or under me.

Now sounding another note, when I had left Quarr Abbey it certainly was not with an intention to enter into a relationship; yet I had not excluded it. I had tried sufficiently a vocation of religious life in community and had left it behind feeling very much betrayed by it; neither did I feel called anymore to try join a diocese: I did not believe it worked out well for a single parish priest to live in a presbytery in a parish and be left to deal with all situations that presented themselves; I do not think it was what Jesus had intended. The idea of entering into a suited relationship was, therefore, in my mind; but it would have to be a lady who was prepared to live a life of prayer and faith, and to some extent, be supportive of stillness and the ideal of simplicity. It would have to be a loving relationship that would be supportive of both as regards faith and practical matters; as such, I perceived it as potentially very positive. I prayed about it and asked that God would guide it along: a solution had to be found. I knew it would involve challenges, and I hoped it would not detract from the relationship with God. There was a very specific moment, while I was walking with this in mind and while addressing God, at which I knew that this course would now be followed for better or worse; I hoped for the better.

I regularly entered the church during the day and found one day that a poster had been put up at the entrance porch. The poster introduced C.U.D., the Catholic Unattached Directory. Its aim was to assist single, practicing Catholics who wanted to find another practicing Catholic for friendship or perhaps even marriage. After registering, one would submit a little entry, introducing oneself and one's intention for registering. In return, one would receive a directory of various others from the opposite sex who had registered and whom one could contact. The practical arrangement was that one initially addressed another member, identified by a first name and a number, by placing a letter in a stamped envelope and this again in another stamped envelope addressed to C.U.D. who would pass the inner envelope on to the intended person. An alternative way of contact was possible by means of email.

Through C.U.D., I came into communication with Karen Shovlin from Lennoxtown, near Glasgow in Scotland. Having read my profile, Karen wrote to me on August 18, 2007. For some reason, her letter only reached me three weeks later; I quickly responded with a positive reply. She thought we sounded very similar, as she too enjoyed walking, quietness, and prayer. When I informed her that I had searched my way in religious life, further similarities were revealed. She too had long been attracted to a life with a strong contemplative element. She had been in religious life herself; in Karen's words:

> The order I joined was the Little Sisters of Jesus, based on the spirituality of Charles de Foucauld; (your story reminded me a little of him: the conflict between a contemplative and active life). I loved the contemplative side to the Little Sisters, and the active side that was involved: living in poor areas and taking manual work. I left . . . even a vow of obedience does not remove from us the responsibility we have for our souls before God. I had set my heart on living and dying in religious life; and when my brief sojourn (three and a half years) ended, I thrashed about in "the desert" for the next twenty years. . . . I have now gone back to basics, as the politicians say; I believe in the Mass, the Divine Office, prayer of any type, Our Lady, and love. At present, I feel as if I am emerging from my period

of darkness, discovering the real me, and coming to terms with my strengths, weaknesses, and motivations.

After a few more letters and a few phone calls, Karen came to visit me in Lampeter, Wales, for the days between October 20 and 24. She travelled by train and bus, and I had arranged for her to stay in a bed-and-breakfast in town. She arrived on the Saturday evening and on the Sunday morning we went to Mass. As it happened, that Mass was presided over by a rather eccentric priest

Karen, with Lennoxtown and the Campsies in the background (2010). The Campsies are a range of hills in central Scotland.

who supplied for the parish priest; and to add to the entertainment, a large group of Travelers descended upon the church for Mass with several of their children. The little church was packed—including the balcony at the back from where some of their kids caused hymnbooks to fall upon those sitting below—and it was pandemonium; yet it was still a prayerful Mass. Later in the day, Karen and I went for a walk. Our meeting of these days was at the start of a loving relationship. During that visit, I already mentioned to her during a day outing to the nearby town of Aberaeron that, all being well, I would probably ask her for marriage a couple of months later and that this would then possibly be for the late summer. At her leaving, I must immediately have written her, for already on the twenty-sixth Karen replied:

Dear Bob,

I received your letter today and wanted to reply immediately instead of my usual day of Sunday. I too need some time to come to terms with the great change my life has now taken since meeting you. I believe we can both, as you first said, go hand in hand towards the future and try to live a life as God wills. . . .

In my turn, I visited Karen in Lennoxtown, arriving at Hogmanay. I stayed in the spare room in her house, and met her elderly parents and her sister, Yvonne, with her family: namely, her husband, Paul McCready, and their children, Claire and Joe. Mid February, I visited again for a few days and asked her whether she wanted to marry me. The answer was "Yes." On the occasion, Teddy, her dad, remarked, "Did you have to come again all the way from Wales for that? Could you not do it on the telephone?"

Since Karen had a house in Lennoxtown that she was paying for by mortgage and since she had a job in Glasgow for Direct Line, a travel-insurance company, it seemed best for me to move initially to Scotland. Since she needed psychological support at the time, I decided to move to her house more quickly than was initially intended, even though it was inevitably somewhat unsettling as regards my study; I would stay in the spare room until we got married. Hence, already on March, 18, 2008, I moved to Lennoxtown and thus became a distance-learning student.

What I may not omit to mention is that a few weeks prior to my move, probably on a Monday after weekday Mass, one of the regular church attendees, Mr. Barry Swan, proposed to proofread the chapters of my thesis so as to help improve the spelling-correctness, and this at no cost to me. He informed me that he was a retired English-language teacher. I hesitated somewhat; but after he assured me that he had done this before for another PhD student in theology, I gratefully accepted his kind offer. In the months that followed my moving away from Lennoxtown, I did not manage to obtain any corrections from academics, but the large brown envelopes that I sent one after the other to Mr. Barry Swan, containing each time a chapter of my thesis, invariably returned corrected within days. He also telephoned regularly so as to discuss the corrections and to give encouragement. All together, he gave much of his time for me, and I will always remain grateful for the help he gave me. It was, in fact, extraordinary.

Karen and I married on August 9, 2008, at Saint Machan's RC Church in Lennoxtown. The presiding priest was the parish priest, Canon William Conway. Present as well as concelebrating priests were Paul Van der Stuyft, with whom I have kept in touch since the time that I met him during the single-year philosophy study at the CKS in Leuven; and James Tracy, who grew up in Lennoxtown as a contemporary of Karen. Brother David Hayes from Quarr Abbey, who was ordained a deacon and whom I kept in touch with for some time, was also there on the sanctuary with them and read the Gospel. In addition, among those attending the wedding were Sister Margaret Byrnes, RSCJ (Religious of the Sacred Heart of Jesus), who was PA to the principal at Heythrop College when I studied there, and Rev. Alexander Gorbenko, a Russian ordained minister of the New Church (or Swedenborgian -), which is a religious group that developed from various histori-

Wedding of Karen and me in Saint Machan's, Lennoxtown, 2008;
From left to right: Teddy and Sadie Shovlin (Karen's parents), Claire McCready (Karen's niece), Karen and I, Joe McCready (Karen's nephew), Yvonne McCready (Karen's sister, who acted as a witness), and Walter Govaerts (my brother, who acted as a witness)

cally related Christian denominations, influenced by the writings of Swedish scientist and Lutheran theologian Emanuel Swedenborg (1688–1772); I first met Alexander at a gathering of the Alistair Hardy Society in Lampeter at which we both gave a talk.

In the meantime, at the University of Wales, Lampeter, the vice-chancellor and the bursar both resigned after complaints of mismanagement forced them to do so. The university went into a crisis, and in the autumn of 2008, an interim vice-chancellor was appointed, namely, Mr. Alfred Morris. During that year, I received no corrections to any chapters from any supervisor. In December, SO sent an email in which he apologized, proposed a "dual approach" with AA, and asked me whether he could read some texts of mine over Christmas. It was too late for me; trust had been totally broken by then, and I did not accept the offer. Instead, begin December, I had taken contact with the vice-chancellor, Mr. Morris, about the lack of adequate supervision for my thesis. A few days after SO's email, I sent the vice-chancellor a follow-up letter, and sent photocopies to, among others, SO and AA. The Vice-Chancellor's Office advised me to make an official complaint to the university, which I did. I requested that contact with my postgraduate supervisor SO be kept to a minimum and that the examination would be fair and professional. In its response, the university seemed to want to give an impression of assurances that would come to meet my requests. In fact, around February or March, SO as well as the head of department, FK, and TO all transferred to Nottingham University.

Mid July 2009, I submitted my thesis, "Cosmic Prayer in Paul, in Maximus the Confessor and in the Emergent Christian Cosmology: Creation's Longing for Personal and Loving Communion with and within the Holy Trinity," and went to the viva examination mid November with hardly any academic corrections to my text. The only one who had gone through all my texts was Mr. Barry Swan. The thesis was considered of PhD level by the examiners but too lengthy and some minor amendments were asked for. Yet in the weeks following, we received no official communication from the university about the result, nor about the procedure of resubmission. Begin December, Karen wrote on my behalf to the new Head of Department, Dr. JW, requesting that we receive some communication from the university, but no acknowledgment of receipt of this letter nor any reply was made. Given that I could not obtain any communication about the result or the examiner's guidelines, I contacted the external examiner, Prof. Andrew Louth, directly and asked him whether he could give an indication when I would receive the guidelines from him.

Walter and Sonja at our wedding

Jenny and Salvatore (Torro) at our wedding

His reply was that he had sent them some time ago to the university. With this information, the next day, on December 16, 2009, once more, I made an official complaint against the Department of Theology and Religious Studies and wrote to the new vice-chancellor, Dr. Medwin Hughes—who had taken over when University of Wales, Lampeter, had become amalgamated with Trinity College, Carmarthen, so as to form a new university—but he did not acknowledge receipt or reply. Given that all the while I was without earnings, I started a temporary cleaning job on

December 19, 2009, in a NHS hospital, namely, Glasgow Royal Infirmary, through an agency.

Eventually, on January 19, 2010, JW sent at long last a letter to me that constituted a reply to the letter of December 3 and that was the outcome to the official complaint. The letter informed me that AA was appointed as mediator for further communications. Again some weeks later, on February 4, I received at long last the examiner's guidelines. A month later, I sent the amended text by email to AA; after which again silence for some weeks.

The entire situation at Lampeter, the uncooperativeness and the lack of communication affected my health. I was in hospital for investigation of some cardiac events between January 18 and 20 and again from March 18 until 26. As a result of the time lost from work due to my medical condition, I lost the cleaning job at Glasgow Royal Infirmary. Although it was but a temporal assignment, I wished to have been able to see it through and as such perhaps qualify for a more continuous employment.

Problems with the university at Lampeter were as yet not at their end. On April 19, 2010, AA advised that no further changes were necessary and to resubmit as soon as possible the thesis by email to the School Office, from where it would be forwarded to the internal examiner, Dr. AC. This advice about the manner of resubmitting was in agreement with the letter sent in January by JW, the Head of Department who had been chair at the viva examination. JW had asserted that the internal examiner was empowered to approve the final changes. As it turned out, this was not correct advice. A week or so after I submitted the amended thesis by email, the Senior Administrative Officer informed us that the internal examiner was not empowered to approve of the changes, and that two printed copies were to be sent to the Post-graduate Research Office, who would forward it to both the external and the internal examiner. Karen, my wife, pointed out the contradiction between the communications from JW and AA on the one hand and the subsequent requirement of the senior admin staff. In the end, however, the only option was to submit two soft bound copies of the amended thesis. I provided the two paper copies of the thesis and they arrived by courier in Lampeter on May 13, 2010. Lampeter acknowledged receipt of the thesis by telephone, but did not want to commit itself either by email or letter of acknowledging receipt of my thesis. No further communication was obtained until July 19, when the Senior Administrative Officer let me know that my thesis had been sent to the examiners and they were close to finalizing their reports. As it is, I never received those reports and was never informed what was in it. In October, however, the Administrative Officer informed me that the recommendation of the examiners was that I be approved for the degree of PhD by research; a recommendation which the university had, in fact, received some months earlier. The university was, however, as yet in no hurry to send me the PhD certificate.

The complaint that I had made against the Department of Theology and Religious Studies some time after my viva examination, which had been prompted by the fact that I could not obtain the examiners' recommendations nor any clear result or details about the manner of resubmitting the thesis, had not received a satisfactory answer; and given the further developments since, I took my complaint to the Office of the Independent Adjudicator for Higher Education (OIA) on May 25, 2010. In the Complaints-Scheme-Application Form, I was asked to summarize what I considered the university had done wrong:

There have been several mistakes and manners of ineffectiveness by university staff that has affected the whole period of my candidature for a PhD:

a) There has been a lack of proper supervision throughout my candidature: this started with the irresponsible and erratic behavior of Dr. TO; and I have highlighted problems with the fundamentalist attitude of Dr. SO who was unable to enter into an academic dialogue and against whom a complaint was issued on January 12, 2009;

b) The advice of the assigned supervisor has been ill-informed about the allowance of appendices, so that I was misled; this caused the necessity of resubmitting, further time-loss, and financial loss;

c) I submitted my thesis on July 16, 2009, and the viva was organized for November 16, that is, seventeen weeks later. This was well beyond the maximum of twelve weeks indicated by the university guidelines;

d) It has taken the university until February 4, that is, two and a half months, before they managed to send the examiners' guidelines and report. The delay is not with the examiners but again with the university;

e) There have been contradictory advice and further time loss before the university managed to advise me on the manner of resubmitting my thesis;

f) I have earlier complained about the unresponsiveness of university staff at Lampeter that has caused considerable distress.

Looking back upon this entire period and considering the entire sequence of events, it is plain that there was a good deal of incompetence as well as bullying behavior by various members of staff at the university from beginning to end. That said, it has been a mistake on my part wanting to put the pursuit of my study topic in the framework of studying for a PhD degree since this put me in the hands of the various people involved. Having left Quarr Abbey, I should have given absolute priority to my contemplative vocation, even outside of organized religious life, instead of running to another institute, even though it was a university. Among the people of the world, even those that are Catholic priests or ministers of other denominations or specialists on religion, and perhaps especially among all these, too many are servants not of God but of the devil. Looking back, I should have despised any postgraduate degrees, even though they are in theology, and have focused my life more on God. It would have made me much less vulnerable to people and have allowed progression on a spiritual path towards life in Christ and in the Spirit.

In various subsequent communications with the OIA, I defended my case, as did the university. A formal decision was reached by the OIA on January 27, 2011. All aspects of my complaint were found justified. A few weeks prior to this, a draft decision was communicated to me and to the university; and it is only after they received this draft decision that they sent me the PhD certificate in the post. I did not receive any accompanying communications about the result, no comments, by the examiners. The university still made efforts to dispute the decision, but it was judged to be unwarranted. The university had to offer me £2,500 in compensation: which was in fact a very modest sum. I was left with the choice to accept the offer or not; I accepted it since the entire episode had lasted long enough and I was not intending to go the route of employing lawyers. The university was also asked to take steps so as to ensure that in future it complies with its own procedures for investigating and deciding a student's complaint, and that it should offer consistent information to students about its guidelines for submission of a thesis.

In sum, I obtained the PhD certificate nearly two years after I completed the study; by then it had become irrelevant as regards career opportunities. It was never my intention to become a full-time academic for I considered that it would interfere with my vocation to a prayer life; but things could certainly have turned out differently than they did. When all was concluded, I asked the interior examiner, AC, whether he would be willing to provide me with a reference should I require one. He chose not to reply.

During and after my study, I produced a few writings for publication. The first articles in which I presented Saint Maximus and the idea of cosmic prayer were published in *De Numine*, which is the journal and newsletter of the Alistair Hardy Society for the Study of Spiritual Experience, a society with which I became somewhat acquainted because it was based at Lampeter and because the chairperson of the local members' group showed interest in my study and was supportive. A first article for *De Numine* was written after I presented its content at a conference organized by the society: "Transformation towards Jesus Christ according to St Maximus the Confessor," in *De Numine* 40 (Spring 2006). The second article was "A Dying Blackbird and Participation in Cosmic Prayer," in *De Numine* 48 (Spring 2010).

In the aftermath of my study, I published a few more articles: Two substantial articles closely related to my study are "Prayer and the Healing of Nature," published in *The Way* 49/4 (October 2010) and "A Transcendental that Calls for Recognition: The Longing for Loving Communion with and within God," in *The Downside Review* 455 (April 2011), in which reference is made to the tome on transcendentals that Dr. Oliver Davies advised me to read several years earlier—for clarification: transcendentals give expression to properties that, besides "being" itself, necessarily accompany being. In other words, all that can be said to have being (all that is) necessarily partakes also in each of these properties called *transcendentals*. They are called transcendental because they transcend all particularities in the order of being. One other article was "Prayer, Creation and Earth's People," written for *The Pastoral Review* 8/4 (July/August 2012).

Between 2006 and 2014, I wrote, moreover, twenty book reviews, most for *De Numine*, three for *The Pastoral Review*, and a few I placed at http://www.amazon.co.uk, including one in 2011 for the book, *The Brothers Karamazov*, (Penguin Classics) by Fyodor Dostoyevsky.

In addition to these articles and book reviews, I have produced two books: *Cosmic Prayer and Guided Transformation: Key Elements of the Emergent Christian Cosmology* (Pickwick, 2012), to which a foreword was kindly provided in friendship by Rev. Prof. David Jasper, an Anglican priest and professor in theology and literature at Glasgow University; and *St. Maximus as Spiritual Guide for Our World: An Evaluation* (CreateSpace Independent Publishing Platform, 2016).

Besides this, I did some odd tasks in and around the house in Lennoxtown. Eventually, the part-time job I found was as an early-morning cleaner at the Kirky Puffer, a Wetherspoon pub in Kirkintilloch, which is a few miles from Lennoxtown; I worked there from end 2012 until early 2014.

At home, Karen and I had started to put all small money coins and all money that we found lying on the street in a saving bank for the purpose of donating it to charity. While cleaning the pub, the pennies that I found increased significantly. At the time, we read in a Catholic newspaper an article about John Bradburne, who had died a martyr in Zimbabwe, where he cared for lepers at their Mutemwa colony. It became one of the charities to whom we could donate a little money from our coins. We pursued more information about John Bradburne and I wrote a little article about him entitled "A Man who Walked with Total Abandonment in the Way of God's Love," in *De Numine* 57 (Autumn 2014).

Next, from April 2014, I obtained an afternoon cleaning job (just two hours a day) in the main public library in Kirkintilloch, which also housed council offices and a consultation hub. My job was to go round the various toilets in the building and empty all bins. It took most of my afternoons, for I cycled up and down in all weathers; sometimes I supplied as cleaner in the nearby Auld Kirk Museum as well.

The best way to cycle between Lennoxtown and Kirkintilloch was a former railway track converted into a walking/cycling path lying largely parallel to the river Glazert and amidst some trees and uncultivated areas adjacent to fields. I cycled these few miles throughout the year. On my way back home, being tired, in the most inclement weather, it happened a few times that, suddenly, I would hear the quacking of ducks flying high above me in formation. It intruded my mindset as the sound from another world, as something unperturbed by weather and circumstances. Their energetic presence I found to be truly magical, and the sound of them immediately lifted my spirits.

From these years that I was cycling to and fro my cleaning jobs, I select two reflections noted down in August 2017 that I wish to share. The first was written on the eighteenth:

> As I read in Saint Augustine, one must not imagine that one will be nothing; instead, one will be either blessed or accursed. I have reflected much upon this and agree with it: the morally-neutral person does not exist. As Ruth Kluger in her book *Landscapes of Memory: A Holocaust Girlhood Remembered (2001)* describes: when Austria was under German occupation, some of the population in Vienna were sympathetic to the op-

pressed Jews while the majority were Arch-Nazis. And in Belgium under occupation, the population of Antwerp was divided in those who were white (resisting the occupation) and those who were black (cooperating with it). In the Balkan wars, the Serbs turned on their neighbors: a former neighbor would become a murderer. It is one or the other; there is no middle ground. In the Gospel according to Matthew, Jesus is attributed speaking of those on his right and those on his left, that is, those destined for salvation and those for everlasting burning (Matthew 25:31–46).

In every street, in every community, given certain circumstances, you will find enough people to staff a concentration camp. I have no illusion whatsoever about humanity.

The gate to life is narrow, the way of salvation is hard, and few find it (Matthew 7:14).

The second reflection was put down in a summarily written note of the twenty-ninth regarding past and present, a topic I often was thinking about on and off my bicycle:

As we progress towards and into God, past and present intermingle; all becomes present. Those whom we know, both dead and alive, become present to us: not only in memory but as living. We are part of a web of relationships that we can affect by our prayers, our thoughts, and our words.

At a more pragmatic level, given the Brexit-vote in the United Kingdom, I decided to go through the procedures for obtaining British citizenship. I obtained this on February 21, 2018. It seemed to make sense to follow this course, the more so since large part of my adult life has been spent in Great Britain. Nonetheless, I remain foremost Belgian in my personal background and identity. I hold both the Belgian and British nationality.

In the meantime, besides looking after her elderly parents, Karen did various part-time jobs as scheme manager for sheltered-housing living for older people; later onwards, she became parish secretary (a part-time job) at Saint Machan's RC Church, our parish church in Lennoxtown.

Then, after ten years of marriage, in September 2018, we resigned from our jobs, sold our house, and moved to Millport in the Isle of Cumbrae.

Karen and I during a holiday in the Yorkshire Dales in begin September 2017. Four times (in 2011, 2012, 2015, and 2017) we took a week's holiday in the area, when we rented a caravan at Howgill Farm near Skipton. The picture was taken near Burnsall in Wharfedale.

# 21

## A life along the side of the pond

IN 2013, AS I related, I was cycling up and down in the mornings to the pub in which I had a cleaning job. Before cycling back home, I would regularly pick up some groceries in a nearby supermarket. So also, on Wednesday, June 5, I went to buy vegetables, a few fruit yoghurts for Karen, and smoked mackerel for myself. The path I usually took back home was being surfaced with tarmac so that I returned by road. At a traffic light, where I have to turn into the road leading to Lennoxtown, I am standing beside a coach with darkened windows. I am wearing sunglasses, not because of the sun but rather as a protection against insects flying into my eyes. I hear knocking on the windows of the coach. At first I ignore it; but it endures and it makes me look up. I see no faces, at most a few vague outlines, but I see several waving hands. I wave back and smile. After the lights have changed and the coach and I have moved on, I still smile. In these waving hands, I found a sign of humanity. A passing, insignificant event amidst the busyness of the world, yet perhaps one that is worthwhile as a gratuitous sign of things that cannot be bought.

More than two months later, unrelated to the forgoing, I was listening to the news on the BBC World Service. Besides the violence in Syria between the Muslim Brotherhood and the government military forces, another news item upset me. The President of Ecuador announced that he ended the project protecting the areas of primitive rainforest in his country, because foreign governments had not been supporting the conservation fund. The day it was being reported on the news, August 16, 2013, he signed an agreement with oil companies that would allow them to start drilling in the forest. Such is the foolishness of people in the service of money and power.

The first months after we arrived in Millport, I provided holiday cover for the cleaner of the Garrison Building (a landmark in the center of Millport that houses the library, the doctor's surgery, a museum, and a cafeteria) in the mornings. In addition, I did an afternoon cleaning job in the local Cumbrae Primary School and Nursery as a supply worker replacing a member of staff who was off work long term. The first months, I only cleaned in the primary school building, but then also in the nursery. While cleaning there, my attention was drawn to a toy car since its lights were on. It was a yellow car sitting on a holder, with a blue, a red, and a green car besides it. Since it had not been placed properly on its holder, the lights kept being on. In the middle of the holder were the four respective remote controls of the cars. It reminded me of the little car with the turning wheel on its roof that made the wheels turn, a toy that I had encountered in my early childhood in the property that my mother was employed at as a cleaner. The one in the nursery where I was cleaning was its present day equivalent, I suppose.

A simple work that would allow earning some money for living and that would not impact on a life of prayer and stillness would be great. Unfortunately, in our noise-filled world this is not something evident. The desert fathers were able to live from making wicker baskets in their cells. Perhaps some artisan craftsmen and women still earn a living in this way, but I am not among them. Unfortunately, moreover, I have not had the privilege of finding a peaceful (cleaning) job—finding anything else suited, such as at a university, I no longer attempt or hope for. After the cleaning job in the primary school, from end August 2019 onwards, I started working weekly two days cleaning in Millport Care Centre, a local care center for people of various ages who suffer from physical disabilities, learning disabilities or autistic disorders, some with challenging behavior. The residents caused not really a problem as regards the cleaning job, and I am by now a well-experienced cleaner; but a man (and I suppose the same applies for a woman) who tries to work diligently in peacefulness and serenity seems, in my life-long experience, obstructed, virtually as a law of this world, from doing so by the various powers at play. A workday of eight hours cleaning was, moreover, rather too much for me: my health condition prevented me from continuing. As such, end April 2020 I gave up the job. By then, the coronavirus pandemic was around. In that circumstance, a contributing factor in my decision was that various staff members at that time were not observing precautionary measures, namely, the wearing of PPE and social distancing, although by then nursing homes were the places that most people were dying from the disease. Moreover, last but not least, as I entered this or that room, a movie could be playing on a television screen and often my attention was drawn to it for some instances: regularly, it were aggressive or horrid scenes that caught my eye. This happened more since most residents were being kept confined to their rooms as a precautionary measure to prevent eventual cross contamination with the threatening virus pandemic. I hated it that demonic scenes caught my eyes and entered my soul.

At least since my early twenties, I have desired for a life devoid of worldly speech, for stillness filled with Christ's presence, for serenity, for complete harmony, and for peace and joy. As it is, to large extent, I have failed to attain these. Karen and I are often still tossed about as a result of encounters with various people, including deceitful tradesmen and others.

The gate to life is narrow, the way of salvation is hard, and few find it (see Matthew 7:14). To attain life in Christ, in the Spirit, in God, the creature is to overcome a gaping abyss. It is possible only by the grace of God and in his mercy; and the creature is to cooperate with the gift of faith bestowed upon him or her. For sure, my cooperation has been insufficiently enlightened. For sure, I need to spend more time on prayer and stillness and be more cooperative with the Holy Spirit.

Nonetheless, we do the little that we do. Karen and I tend to pray the Morning Prayer from the Divine Office together at 7 a.m. and take, immediately before or afterwards, some time for quiet prayer or the private reading of scripture. On Sundays and, if possible, on solemnities, we say the Office of Readings to begin with, followed by quiet prayer, and we say Morning Prayer after breakfast.

Throughout the course of the morning, between 9.30 and 12.30, we aim to speak as little as possible; though Karen tends to have some more contacts and communications with people than I have.

On the days that it is possible, we say the afternoon prayer from the Divine Office together after the midday meal. Regularly, we let this be followed by a decade from the Rosary for a particular intention. In Lent, we have the custom to say two Stations of the Cross around midday instead.

Since we live on an island, our access to masses is somewhat restricted, but we do have a Catholic Church in Millport, namely, the Parish Church of Our Lady of Perpetual Succour, which is served by the parish priest of the church in Largs, the town opposite the island from where the ferry connection takes place. Mgr. Peter Magee, the parish priest, comes to say Mass on Sundays at 12.15 p.m. and on Thursdays. Obviously, from March 20 until mid July 2020, churches have been closed because of the pandemic and have only gradually started to reopen since for services and private prayer. In the positive, this period has let us discover a few places that offer a live stream of the Mass on the internet, that is, while the Mass is being said. Our parish priest has been very active in providing this, but we have, among others, also been appreciating the Masses broadcast from the grotto in the Lourdes sanctuary; Mass in English is said at the grotto daily at 4 p.m. British time (at 5 p.m. in France) and this not only during this period of the pandemic. Presently, Mass has restarted on Sundays in our parish church with various stringent safeguarding restrictions in place. Besides this, I think that in the forthcoming period we will continue to watch on our computer and participate spiritually at the Lourdes Masses during some weekdays at least.

For our evening prayer then, we aim to pray quietly together and each try do a little spiritual reading from 5 p.m. onwards; at 5.30 p.m., we say the Evening Prayer from the Divine Office together.

During our evening meal, we often listen to a CD. At the time of this writing, we are listening to Handel's *Messiah* conducted by Sir Malcolm Sargent in 1959.

At the end of the day, at 8.30 p.m., we pray Compline together as given in the Divine Office, introduced by a penitential rite and the hymn "O Maker of the World," and concluded by a chosen prayer to Our Lady, such as the Hail Holy Queen, the Prayer to Our Lady of Banneux, to Our Lady of Beauraing, or to Our Lady of Combermere. All the common prayers of the day are led by Karen on the even calendar days and by me on the uneven days.

After Compline, we usually read a book together. It is a custom that we started at my first visit to Lennoxtown in January 2008 and that we have kept up. We each take our turn at reading to the other; we each in turn choose the book. The books we have been reading recently are *Resistance Fighter* (2011) by Susie Howe, an HIV/AIDS nurse specialist who founded three Christian charities, including the Bethany Children's Trust; *Saint Silouan the Athonite* (1991) by Archimandrite Sophrony; and *St. Rose of Lima* (1968) by Sister Mary Alphonsus. The last is a book I had requested as a present for Christmas 2019. It did not disappoint us, for it offers a very captivating account of the saint's life. Reading about the remarkable life of Saint Rose (1586–1617), or of other saintly persons, and about their great zeal for God and for entering into communion with him offers inspiration for our own life of faith and for attaining greater faith. Presently, we are reading "The General Instruction on the Liturgy of the Hours," which is found at the front of the Divine Office books. On Sundays, we have sometimes watched a DVD on the laptop.

By these exercises and customs, we aspire to fulfill the scripture text that we chose as second reading at our Wedding Mass, namely, Colossians 3:12–17. The last two verses of this reading are: "Let the message of Christ, in all its richness, find a home with you. Teach each other, and advise each other, in all wisdom. With gratitude in your hearts sing psalms and hymns and inspired songs to God and never say or do anything except in the name of the Lord Jesus, giving thanks to God the Father through him."

As such, we envisage our marriage as a walking towards God hand in hand. Moreover, as expressed in the *Catechism of the Catholic Church*, no. 1642, which quotes from *Gaudium et spes* 48: " 'Just as of old God encountered his people with a covenant of love and fidelity, so our Savior, the spouse of the Church, now encounters Christian spouses through the sacrament of matrimony.' Christ dwells with them, gives them the strength to take up their crosses and so follow him . . . and to love one another with supernatural, tender and fruitful love." The catechism then quotes from Tertullian, *Ad uxorem* (To my wife): "How wonderful the bond between two believers, now one in hope, one in desire, one in discipline, one in the same service! They are both children of one Father and servants of the same Master, undivided in spirit and flesh, truly two in one flesh. Where the flesh is one, one also is the spirit."

Since we are called to be temples of God's indwelling, it would be most improper to expose ourselves to various banal texts, conversations or pictures. We have to be very guarded in our use of media. In view of our desire for the spiritual, the disadvantages of having a television far outweigh the advantages. Our home is thus one without it.

Obviously, we do not have children. I am well aware that should I have married someone with a child or should a child have been born to us, which might have happened, life would have had to be lived in a way that suitably encompasses that situation and things would have had to be different.

As regards telephone, I do not like it and find it very intrusive. At any given time, a telephone can ring, demanding that one drops at once anything one may be engaged with and makes a dash for it. It is enough to be just half-expecting a phone call to take away, to some extent, control over one's life; it impinges upon one's peace. One may desire to leave the world behind as much as is possible, but when that phone rings and one has to take the call, one is likely straightaway brought squarely back into the world. Yet, by necessity, we do have a telephone and broadband for internet; I even have a mobile phone since it comes out cheaper than using a landline and it has the advantage of mobility. Karen is more of a phone-person than I am and most calls in this house are for her; so, thankfully, I do not often have to answer it. But whoever the call is for, when that phone starts ringing, any conversation one may be having is likely ended. In my opinion, a phone is good for making a medical call or for arranging a meeting, and for any messages that can be left or received; beyond this, I do not normally use it. Nonetheless, I do recognize that it is kindness when family or friends make the occasional phone call. Regrettably though, very few people will send a letter or written card in the post these days, or even to a personal e-mail address.

Having spoken a couple of pages earlier about my few short-lived cleaning jobs on the island, a few words about Karen's jobs is called for. About six weeks after our moving, Karen started work as a caregiver in Millport Care Centre for two days a week. She liked the hands-on care and it recalled her earlier years as a nurse. But a thirteen-hour workday, often with plenty of exposure to television screens and other worldliness, did not suit. After half a year she found a part-time job as parish secretary based at Largs in assistance of our parish priest, just as she did in Lennoxtown. Besides this job, the care center management asked her to stay on as caregiver for one day a week, but this eventually became unsustainable. Her father, Teddy, having died in May 2019, aged ninety, she has been giving generous attention to matters regarding the care of her mum, Sadie, who since then resided in a nursing home. Sadie died only days ago, on August 14, 2020, aged eighty-five. May they rest in peace.

And what do we do for our yearly holidays? Even though we have had but a very small income, we managed most years to go for one week to a beautiful, somewhat secluded place as our holiday; the other years, we travelled to Belgium instead, where our visit includes meeting close family and friends and a little pilgrimage to one of the Marian shrines, such as Banneux N. D. or Beauraing. We have liked to go self-catering and our walking-and-reading holidays we have wanted to contain an element of spiritual retreat. As a general statement, it can be said that it is good to withdraw at times into nature, away from much of the human world: to a place where there is less human-produced noise, where the air is cleaner, where we can come to ourselves in the presence of God. Such physical separation is indicative of the

Picture taken during a visit of Karen and me to the Shrine of Our Lady of Beauraing with Rev. Paul Van der Stuyft in 2015

need for another kind of separation, namely, from the entire way of living that is prevalent around us. We need to live a life that is ruled by principles and objectives that are different from those of the world. On the journey towards God, we become separate from the lives of most people around us and from the common aspirations. It seems, however, that this present year Karen and I will not rent accommodation for a week's holiday; instead, we intend to take time on our Island of Cumbrae, which is very scenic and touristic.

We are surrounded by the sea and Karen has already twice seen porpoises when she was commuting on the ferry; I have once seen an otter, and seals can regularly be seen and heard. Sadly, as a result of the plastic age in which we live, the throw-away culture, and people's disrespect for God's creation, I heard on the radio that plastic is found in 100 percent of marine mammals from British waters examined by experts. Such is the work and world of Homo sapiens sapiens.

As intimated in the book of Job, God wanted to share his contemplation of the created reality with us. Accordingly, our purpose is to admire God's work and to glorify him for it. But when the earth's peoples will have become drowned in their own pollution and have destroyed much of the ecosystems, when the earth and its various non-human communities will no longer be able to support them, humanity will become extinct on the earth, and no new generations will contemplate the incoming waves, the seabirds in the intertidal zone, and the light display in the air when the sun sets behind the hill tops. These waves will still be there, and perhaps even birds will be around, and so on, but no longer will anyone from within the earth community look at it consciously aware and from there turn the mind towards the Creator of it. What a pity that many within the human species are

not less greedy and self-centered and more humble and apprecia-
tive of the created reality of which they are part. Christian faith
teaches us that the heavenly community will remain of which we
are to become part—even here and now—and that the angels look
on as well. Will earthly humanity go under while fighting for
what remains of the created world? Or will the counter movement
be able to stay the onslaught and allow survival of future genera-

The incredible gift of being able to contemplate the incoming waves —
an interface between heaven and earth; time and eternity; Kames Bay,
Millport

tions in some form? What role will epidemics and nuclear warfare
take on? What about the cancer of religious fanaticism? Or will
the human reproductive ecology, that is, the male sperm and the
female egg, be invaded by plastic microparticles and other pollu-
tants so that Homo sapiens sapiens will mainly produce severely
debilitated beings? Who will remain standing? At what point will

"You make the clouds your chariot" (Psalm 104:3b; Grail trans). View upon the mountains of Arran from Kames Bay. Wee Cumbrae is visible at the left.

the Lord visit the earth and gather the wheat in his granary and burn the chaff?

Humanity carries responsibility for the entire created world and for its own future; yet it is also subjected to influences and powers of various nature. In my reflection "Sailing upon the water," given earlier in this book, I envisaged humanity as bobbing on a deep ocean in which there are various currents underneath and winds blowing overhead. Taking this further, it is rightly perceived that the powers and influences that surround humanity stay not without but they submerge human hearts and minds so as to overtake them and to bring them into servitude. Saint Paul admonishes the faithful to stand firm. "Put on the whole armor of God, that you may be able to stand against the wiles of the devil. For we are not contending against flesh and blood, but against the principalities, against the powers, against the world rulers of this present darkness, against the spiritual forces of wickedness in the heavenly places" (Ephesians 6:11–12). And he explains what he envisages in speaking of the armor of God:

> Stand therefore, having girded your loins with truth, and having put on the breastplate of righteousness, and having shod your feet with the equipment of the gospel of peace; besides all these, taking the shield of faith, with which you can quench all the flaming darts of the evil one. And take the helmet of salvation, and the sword of the Spirit, which is the word of God.
>
> Pray at all times in the Spirit, with all prayer and supplication. To that end keep alert with all perseverance, making supplication for all the saints. (Ephesians 6:14–18)

The only salvific way out for humanity is conversion to God and prayer. The power in prayer in the Holy Spirit, who from of old has hovered over the chaotic waters so as to bring forth cosmic order and life (Genesis 1), I perceive as the only power that can preserve these. As envisaged in "Sailing upon the water," not by reliance upon our capacities but by adherence to the Holy Spirit can the created reality reach its purpose and goal in us.

> Come, O Holy Spirit,
> with your life-giving and healing power.
> That you may be present
> over your creation, over your people, over us.

About eight years ago, I visited the Assumptionists so as to recover a series of books that I had left with them. In the library of the convent in Halvestraat in Leuven, I saw various copies of the *Ecrits spirituels* of Père d'Alzon and requested a copy. During the years that I was with them, I had never had the opportunity to read it: all the classes and material that I received during my formation were in Dutch and largely came in the form of second-ary sources. A couple of years after my visit, when I intended to read it at last, I found that the hard covers and the paper edges had molded badly—decades in the moist atmosphere in the basement library of the Peda Sint-Augustinus probably did it not much good. I cleaned it up with anti-mould spray, but it reoccurred so that I decided it best to throw it out. Unfortunately, I never got to reading it. Though this intention fell through, I brought other reading material concerning the Assumptionists back as well from my visit, including a cartoon book translated into Dutch that presents the three beatified, Bulgarian Assumptionist martyrs, who were executed in the central prison of Sofia on November 11, 1953.

As regards the visit itself, peculiarly enough, it was again marked by their washing-up mentality. I had accepted to join them for the midday meal, and afterwards I participated in the cleaning-up tasks that followed it. I went into the kitchen; and since someone seemed required to do the washing up, I proposed to do it. But after only a few moments, the three priest monks that stood around with drying towels clearly expressed displeasure that it did not go quick enough. They talked among themselves which of them would continue at the sink and without speaking or looking at me took over. I left my place and, since I did not seem needed, left them to it. I went to say goodbye to the superior, Pater Castro. He kindly proposed to give me a lift to the station with his car since I was taking several books with me. I did not mind to go by foot but eventually accepted. It would have been odd not to have accepted the offer. Near the station, he lifted the heavy suitcase out of the boot before I had a chance. It was kind;

but as had become clear during this visit, I knew also that he had little regard for me. He was in a hurry for he had to drive quickly on to his many other tasks. As for myself, I found his and his *confraters'* hurry a waste of time; there are better ways of encountering God and of serving him. The separation between me and them seemed complete.

Besides this, a few years ago, I took contact with Quarr Abbey by sending a flyer of my book on Saint Maximus, addressed to Fr. Brian Gerard, an Irishman who had joined the community a year or so after I did and who is now the bursar of the community. He is the one person of all the newcomers who has stayed on in the abbey; he is as well the one who was able to nod approvingly to everything that flowed from the abbot's mouth. We had cooperated somewhat in an attempt to obtain coastal defenses for the abbey's eroding coastline. At the back of the flyer, I informed him and the community of my whereabouts; expressed my hope that presently, after the various upheavals at the abbey, life was now more peaceful and monastic; and asked for prayers. I never received a reply. With them also, the separation is complete. Even though, again, I am still interested to read about the Rule of Saint Benedict and about monastic life more generally.

It is a pity perhaps that I could not remain in a monastery. But being a monk is not a guarantee to holiness. Indeed, we need not be beguiled by their chant, their magnificent buildings, or their monastic outfit. It may suffice to remind of the sexual-abuse scandals by monks at the former Fort-Augustus Abbey in Inverness-shire, Scotland; at Saint-Benedict's School run by Ealing Abbey; at Ampleforth College run by Ampleforth Abbey in North Yorkshire; at Downside College run by Downside Abbey in Somerset; by monks of Douai Abbey near Reading, and various cases at their abbey school; at Belmont-Abbey School in Herefordshire; and at Buckfast-Abbey Preparatory School. In addition, we may be reminded of the alcoholic drinks sold by Buckfast Abbey: high in alcohol- and sugar content and sold cheaply. These vile drinks called "Bucky" are known as the scourge of Scotland; they are reputed to be very potent in causing aggressive behavior. What does all this tell us of the moral norms of monasticism, and of the state of monasticism in the Western contemporary society?

Each person has to work out his or her own holiness; has to find with God's help an own path towards living in the embrace of divine grace.

Looking back over the various ecclesial institutes and communities that I have passed along, it can be noted that the buildings are still there but that not many religious are left in them. The CKS (Centrum voor Kerkelijke Studies) in Leuven, where I was made to study philosophy by the Assumptionists, has closed down. The Assumptionists in the West have to large extent been reduced to a few old-age pensioners; the Assumptionist parish-pastoral-communities in Borsbeek no longer exist, for all those whom I knew there have died and there is no one to replace them. The community in Leuven has largely become the nursing home of those remaining of the Flemish region. The community in Brockley has long finished; Saint-Mary-Magdalen's Parish has been taken over by the Spiritans. Heythrop College in London were I studied theology has closed down, not because of lack of students but because of financial difficulties. The few monks of the once renowned Benedictine community of Quarr Abbey are now managed by a French monk of Solemnes who has become their superior. It would be good if in the long-term future the site would be able to serve as a place of Christian prayer and contemplation in some form, even if not Benedictine. The Trappist monks of the Abbey of Rochefort have become few as well. It is many years since I went on retreat in the abbey, but Karen and I visited it some years ago with Rev. Paul Van de Stuyft, and we attended midday prayer.

It is my view that radical change is needed in the RC Church as a whole for it to remain viable. And it is only viable if it can support people to live a life of faith in Jesus Christ; if it can support them on authentic spiritual paths towards life in God. A few elements that I envisage need improving or changing are touched upon in the following paragraphs.

The liturgy, to begin with, was renewed in the wake of the Second Vatican Council and was much simplified. Many priests, however, introduce into the Mass petty conversations at the beginning, middle, and end that do not belong to it. Much better would be if they keep to the prayer of the Roman rite: nothing more, nothing less. All too often, priests serve Mass with an air of inflated self-importance; people want to come to Mass for Christ, not for watching a showman. Sermons are intended to be elucidations of the readings of scripture and encouragements in the faith; they should not be used as occasions for obliging a community to listen to all kinds of personal obsessions and preoccupations or for various jokes; nor should sermons be used for imposing the faithful to a spiritual intrusion by an insistent emotional address.

The church deserves and needs a more spiritual and holier priesthood. To this end, I have come to the view that parish priests should be either married men or celibate men that live locally within the community of a religious institute. I do not believe that Jesus would have wanted for his church single priests in a presbytery. This does not imply that at present there are no holy and spiritual men among the clergy but that too many of them are not fit for the task, are not living an inspiring life, have addictions, or live in breach of their vow of celibacy.

If parish priests are not honorable, balanced, married men living with their families within the parish community then, ideally, they would be members of a religious institute and be living in a community in which they can find support. Of course, as shown above, many abuse scandals that have been happening have involved priests and monks living in religious communities. Situations as these have been allowed to happen because of the cover-up culture among the clergy, who have considered themselves as members of an elite group that is above the law. Clearly, signs that a certain religious is not living a dedicated spiritual life should have been picked up. And if they are not picked up, it indicates a systematic failure in a community that is supposed to travel together towards God. Given all that has emerged into the open in recent years, I would say that a spiritual malaise has taken hold throughout the RC Church and probably throughout other churches as well.

All those fulfilling functions within the parish should obviously be properly trained. Ideally, every parish should have a number of "priests" who have been ordained, that is, been prayed over and laid hands upon so that they are assigned to lead the Eucharistic service, administer sacraments, and preach the gospel.

Not many choose to be ordained to the permanent diaconate (*diakonia*, service). As the Catechism of the Catholic Church stipulates (par. 1570): "Among other tasks, it is the task of deacons to assist the bishop and priests in the celebration of the divine mysteries, above all the Eucharist, in the distribution of Holy Communion, in assisting at and blessing marriages, in the proclamation of the Gospel and preaching, in presiding over funerals, and in dedicating themselves to the various ministries of charity." In the celebration of the Eucharist, deacons would be on the sanctuary together with the celebrating priest(s) and be wearing a white tunic and a stole hung over one shoulder diagonally over the body. As it is, unlike priests, permanent deacons, who can be married or single, do not receive any remuneration for their services in a parish. This would appear to demonstrate once more that in actuality an unwarranted focus is placed on the priesthood and a concern to preserve its exclusive privileges. Women are not eligible to be deacons; even though, arguably, already in the early church, female deacons were around (see Romans 16:1 and 1 Timothy 3:11). A Vatican commission created by Pope Francis has recently been studying the role of women deacons in early Christianity but has so far not come to a consensus on the matter.

Besides the ordained ministry, religious life would be an integral part of the renewal. I believe that new ways must be sought for living out closeness between religious houses and parish communities; a coming together that respects the various charisms of the religious institutes. The here considered element of renewal is obviously only properly envisaged in combination with the envisaged idea of a renewed priesthood. Undeniably however, various religious communities make great efforts towards an inclusion of the parish community. Eventually, heaven allows for a great diversity but this within an intimate and divine unity.

If graciously designed and well-kept churches would be open throughout the day and be houses of prayer with various religious and lay people being present in prayer, they would express a promise of the Kingdom of God instead of carrying a notion of irrelevance and demise.

In addition to this, Jesus envisaged all those who believe in him to be brothers and sisters of each other; therefore, clergy who want to be called *father* are misled for it is not from God (cf. Matthew 23:8–9). Each person fulfilling priestly and other functions in a parish should simply be addressed by their Christian name, perhaps with or without the prefix *brother*. In formal address, the title *Reverend* could likely be envisaged as suited for those sharing in the priesthood.

The hierarchy of the RC Church says to have a great esteem for the vocation to the marriage but sees this as irreconcilable with priestly ministry. Hence—unlike the assessment of the other churches—a married man is deemed unfit to serve at the altar. Unfortunately, the unmarried men that have been serving as RC priests have shown themselves to be often more unfit. Why would a mature, suited, and devout married man not be able to lead the Eucharistic community, or be less acceptable in the eyes of God? And if the latter would be the case, why did God create all higher living beings, including humanity, as male and female? And why did he create sexual attraction, if he would not have found it very good (Genesis 1:27–28, 31; 2:18, 22)? Is—besides the celibate God-seeker living in a religious community—the devout married man not supremely suited to offer to God the fruits of the earth and the work of human hands and receive them from him as transformed into the Body and Blood of Christ by the working of the Holy Spirit, so that the Eucharistic community and the whole created reality may in turn be transformed into Christ by them?

I have touched earlier in the book upon some misgivings regarding the practice of the sacrament of reconciliation. A few more thoughts here are called for. I certainly recognize that this sacrament has a valid place in the life of a Catholic Christian. I also recognize that there are regional differences in how the clergy admonish the faithful to practice this sacrament. Certainly here in Scotland—though probably very rarely so in Belgium—some clergy strongly encourage the church attendees to undergo this sacrament regularly, and it seems to me that this is to some extent supported by the RC Church as a whole. At one level, it is arguably the case that it is a means by which the clergy try to justify their existence. At another level, it enables the clergy to exercise a position of power.

The traditional formula in the English-speaking world by which to enter upon this sacrament is "Bless me Father for I have sinned. . . ." So here we are expected to say what Christ did not want us to say, and this is a sin indeed if done in this awareness.

It concerns me that the RC practice of the sacrament of confession has been instilling people with a narrow-minded idea of sin and sinfulness: for example, a notion of ecological sin remains unmentioned. Moreover, the clergy, in their great enthusiasm for calling people to come to confession, risks a trivializing of sin. If a drunkard beats up his wife and frightens his children and makes their life a hell but afterwards goes to confession by a priest, he is alright. This sequence may repeat itself regularly. For the wife and the children the psychological and physical harm remains and the fear of it reoccurring. Not denying the power of Christ to forgive sins when a penitent comes to him in remorse and with a desire to better life, the question remains whether a priest has the right to give each man absolution and clear his conscience of the sins committed in such an easy way.

I want to add that sacramental confession, when overdone and with light penitence being given, quasi invites an experimenting with sin. Conceivably, in these circumstances the use of the sacrament can become, just as sin, an addiction that is part of the very sin.

The priesthood's own experience of the sacrament in conferring it to others and receiving it themselves for their own sins has obviously for many of them not done them much good; for we now know where many of the priests stand as regards their own sinfulness and moral behavior.

And last but not least, a renewed approach in all these areas could be significant in conquering the scandal of disunity among the churches.

As it is, I attend the RC Church in a critical and somewhat dejected mood, as one sidelined. But I still do attend it for I want to be associated with the communion of saints amidst whom Christ is. I attend it because the sacraments as means of grace stemming from Christ carry real value to me. I attend it because of Christ and for Christ despite all things. Salvation in Christ cannot be reached in isolation but only in a web of relationships with many others.

My impression is that living a spiritual life without any religion usually dissipates into insignificance. The RC Church is the one I am acquainted with, and none other appeals to me for joining them—admittedly, I would not want to deny that my knowledge of other churches is rather limited. Will any significant changes occur in the RC Church? I guess that the clerical powers will yet for a long time hang on to a status quo; but eventually, we must trust that the RC Church belongs to Christ and that he will take charge over it. Alternatively, it is not inconceivable that the remaining priests, the bishops, and the magisterium of the Church will take the RC Church in the West right to its grave, and that in its stead a new church will emerge from without that is a follow-up representation on earth—together with various other existent churches and Christian movements—of the One, Holy, Catholic, and Apostolic Church that is professed in the Nicene-Constatinopolitan Creed (issued in 381) and that is believed in as the ultimate Church that exists in God's presence. I consider that the present times are very much times of transition; we are moving towards a tipping point that lies just beyond, in the relative near future. Hopefully, transition is towards a church that is animated by the triune God, Father, Son, and Holy Spirit; that can lead multitudes of various backgrounds to living in God; and that thus would be a force for good.

Now, what about the vocation to a contemplative life? At all times of humanity there have been contemplatives. What is a contemplative? The *Cloud of Unknowing* (written by a priest of the latter part of the fourteenth century) gives an indication. The following extracts are taken from the Penguin Classics edition (1978), which features a translation into modern English by Clifton Wolters:

> 17. St Luke tells us that when our Lord was in the house of Martha . . . Mary sat at his feet. . . . What she was looking at was the supreme wisdom of his Godhead shrouded by the words of his humanity. And on this she gazed with all the love of her heart. Nothing she saw or heard could budge her, but there she sat, completely still, with deep delight, and an urgent love eagerly reaching out into that high cloud of unknowing that was between her and God.

> 27. First and foremost I will tell you who should practise contemplation . . . who should engage in this work . . . "Everyone who has truly and deliberately forsaken the world, not for the *active* life, but for what is known as the *contemplative* life. All such should undertake this work by grace, whoever they are, whether they have been habitual sinners or not."

> 75. And if they have come to believe that their conscience will not really approve anything they do, physical or spiritual, un-

less this secret love which is fixed on the cloud of unknowing
is the mainspring of their work spiritually, then it is a sign that
they are being called to this work by God; otherwise not.

Hence, as this text indicates, the contemplative life cannot be combined with any other aspiration; absolute preference is to be given it. The contemplative vocation demands a forsaking of the world. Obviously, the contemplative will have to be engaged in activities such as his state of life requires but really wants to have his or her mind turned towards God; any professional career that requires proper application of the mind will prove to be untenable. Even writing books in theology, when considered a purpose in itself, is in effect a hindrance for the more hidden work that is required of the contemplative.

A little classic of the devotional life called *The Practice of the Presence of God* by Brother Lawrence (whose real name was Nicholas Herman and who was a lay brother among the Carmelites of Paris in the seventeenth century) is at least equally elucidating as regards the contemplative life. At the time of writing, he was an old man of nearly eighty. The little book consists of four conversations and fifteen letters. I present an extract from the fourth conversation:

> As Brother Lawrence had found such an advantage in walking in the presence of God, it was natural for him to recommend it earnestly to others; but his example was a stronger inducement than any arguments he could propose. His very countenance was edifying; such a sweet and calm devotion appearing in it, as could not but affect the beholders. And it was observed that in the greatest hurry of business in the kitchen, he still preserved his recollection and heavenly-mindedness. He was never hasty nor loitering, but did each thing in its season, with an even uninterrupted composure and tranquility of spirit. "The

> time of business," said he, "does not with me differ from the
> time of prayer; and in the noise and clutter of my kitchen, while
> several persons are at the same time calling for different things,
> I possess God in as great tranquility as if I were upon my knees
> at the Blessed Sacrament."

Though he was busy with practical activities, his mind was not completely possessed by it but was habitually turned towards God and aware of his presence. Alas, I am far from having reached a state of repose in God as Brother Lawrence obtained.

A third author whom I wish to quote here is Thomas Merton (1915–68), a Trappist monk in the Abbey of Gethsemani, Kentucky, who became known as one of the greatest spiritual writers of the twentieth century. The lines I reproduce here are found at the end of his autobiographical essay "Day of a Stranger," dated May 1965 in its earliest version. The essay is taken up in a collection entitled *Thomas Merton: Selected Essays* (2013), edited by Patrick F. O'Connell. Merton describes his day at a time when he had started to live part of his day in a hermitage:

> I sweep. I spread a blanket out in the sun. I cut grass behind the
> cabin. I write in the heat of the afternoon. Soon I will bring the
> blanket in again and make the bed. The sun is over-clouded.
> The day declines. Perhaps there will be rain. A bell rings in the
> monastery. A devout Cistercian tractor growls in the valley.
> Soon I will cut bread, eat supper, say psalms, sit in the back
> room as the sun sets, as the birds sing outside the window, as
> night descends on the valley. I become surrounded once again
> by all the silent Tzu's and Fu's (men without office and with-
> out obligation) [these are various eastern poets and religious
> writers whose works he has on his shelves]. The birds draw
> closer to their nests. I sit on the cool straw mat on the floor,

considering the bed in which I will presently sleep alone under
the ikon of the Nativity.

Meanwhile the metal cherub of the apocalypse [that is, the
nuclear-armed plane] passes over me in the clouds, treasuring
its egg and its message.

This text illustrates that the contemplative God-seeker cannot
satisfactorily be engaged in any professional career that requires
his full attention. He or she has a persistent need and desire to be
quiet so as to enter into the presence of God. I experience this
need and desire as painfully acute in my life; all too often, stillness is not available.

It is only when one is a little quiet that one is able to notice
things. A few winters ago, for example, I was waiting at a bus
stop in Kirkintilloch. In the bus shelter two men were talking to
each other; one of them had a puppy on a lead. The little animal
lay under the metal bench. The man held the chain rather tight so
that the puppy held its paw on top of the chain, trying to ease the
pulling of the chain at its neck. Every time that the man noticed
the slightly increased tension on his hand, he turned from his
conversation and gave an annoyed pull at the chain. Eventually,
he gave the dog a scolding: "Stop doing that!" he shouted. The
man failed to observe his own little dog and thought that it was
getting itself all the time in a tangle with the chain. I felt pity for
that puppy, bound for life to its dull owner.

Regrettably, not all dogs that are around are as that puppy.
Many choose as their pet a strong, aggressive animal or a dog
with a screwed-up face; as a rule, they can rightly be perceived as
an expressive extension of their owners' sentiments and looks.

Should the contemplative cease looking at the created reality
around him/her and turn the gaze of one's spirit towards God?
No, the created reality is not to be left behind; a comfortable

escapism will not do. Rather, as we progress towards God, we will come to see the created reality as God sees it (compare my book *St. Maximus as Spiritual Guide for Our World*, pp. 290–96).

Since we moved to the Isle of Cumbrae, I have been seeing waterbirds that swim in the sea close to the shore even in inclement weather. I have seen that when a strong wave is nearly upon it that could potentially throw it upon the rocks, it quickly dives under water and appears moments later at another place in relative safety. When the wind howls and the rain lashes down, we move inside, yet these small creatures manage to live from moment to moment amidst the elements in their starkness. Awareness of this instills wonder, a sense of mystery.

The various species are marvelously adapted to living in their environments; nevertheless, harshness, chanciness, and cruelty are pervading characteristics of the created reality. Many individual creatures of the various species, including humanity, are being sacrificed in the grand project of life while the earth keeps turning. This sentiment was at the fore of my mind, for example, a few years ago when I found a little spider in the bathroom at Bencloich Road in Lennoxtown and wanted to put it outside. I caught it in the bug catcher and went into the garden. But when I opened the door of the catcher, it inadvertently slammed closed again, since I was not careful enough. The spider was out of it but lost a leg. It had not been my intention to hurt the spider and I was distraught.

The cruelty of fate reached a climax when on April 5, 1943—as I narrated in chapter four—hundreds of American bombs dropped over Mortsel, near Antwerp, hit not their intended target but fell on the allied town, on its schools, and on the girls working in the nearby Gevaert factory. Another of the many climaxes of the cruelty of fate is associated with Bhopal, where thousands died from poison gases issuing from a leak on December 3, 1984, at a pesticide factory owned by Union Carbide, an American chemical corporation. After the leak, the factory was shut and abandoned with its lethal pesticides still inside and thousands of tons of toxic waste were left dumped nearby, until those leaked away into the community wells. Union Carbide did not want to spend the money to clean it up. Since the gas leak happened, a great many babies born there have died and have been horrendously disfigured; and it continues.

The fourteenth-century anchoress Julian of Norwich is beloved for her *Revelations of Divine Love*, which she received in 1373. Her third revelation is well known for the idea that "nothing happens by chance or luck; everything is under the control of God's foresight and wisdom." (Taken from the Hodder and Stoughton Christian Classics edition, edited by Halycon Backhouse with Rhona Pipe, 1987) But say that to those of Bhopal; or to an African woman who daily has to walk several miles to try get some water for her bucket, while multinationals siphon off most of what is available for their own gain; say it to an African woman who has her child dying on her lap for lack of everything or is dying of diarrhea because the little water was infected; or say it to a girl sold into prostitution; or to countless others who have their own story of misery. While I acknowledge that in Christ many things will be transformed and taken up into divine life, Julian's revelation sounds grotesque in the light of reality as we know it.

And oh yes, what is the lesson from chaos theory? James Gleick's book on chaos instills the idea that complex systems pervade our reality and that we ourselves are a good example of it: a wildlife population, a biological organ, an atmospheric storm, a national economy, and so on are all examples. These complex systems, however, are seen to give rise to simple behavior; and complexity is now understood to observe laws that hold universally. When we look through a small window upon a complex system, it only reveals irregularity or chaos, but when we look more closely or from a greater distance, that is, from a different perspective, we may be able to discern regularity in the irregularity. In particular, complexity as seen everywhere around us and even within us often takes on a fractal pattern. Fractals are, as defined in the Merriam-Webster dictionary, "various irregular curves or shapes for which any suitably chosen part is similar in shape to a given larger or smaller part when magnified or reduced to the same size." Or, in other words, in a fractal each pattern is made up of smaller copies of itself, and those smaller copies are made up of smaller copies again, and so on. In natural systems, eventually, a limit is reached at which the fractal symmetry breaks down. In our own bodies, examples are the network of our veins, the network of tubular branches or bronchi in our lungs, the arteries in our heart, the nerves, and the pattern of neurons in our brains. The reason I mention this here is that the omnipresent fractal geometry clearly demonstrates that in systems of complexity we cannot assess what difference the smallest alteration can make; but it can be a crucial and complete difference. Imagine yourself landing with a parachute on a large carpet with a fractal pattern of various colors: the slightest difference in the way you are trying to steer-by would be crucial for whether you would touch down on the green, the brown, the blue, the white, or the black; and imagine that each color carries its own consequences for you and several others that are related to you in one way or other.

Each individual at the place where he/she is can make a difference for one's own individual existence and for the various systems of complexity amidst which we find ourselves. All that we think, say, or do does matter. More than anyone, the contemplative aims to discern who God is and, gazing into the cloud of unknowing, desires to attune every fiber of his/her existence to God's plan for him/her. Since God is ultimately the Creator of all systems that exist, it does matter; yes, paradoxically, despite our insignificance, it does, for all that is.

Dom Paul Delatte (1848–1937), the third Abbot of Solesmes and the first Abbot of Quarr Abbey while the Solesmes community was in exile, wrote in his *Commentaire sur la Règle de Saint Benoit* (1913):

> All things, in the measure that they participate in being, are bound to God, who is creator, providence, and final end. . . . The entire, immense, created reality speaks of God and is him obedient; it is to him a harmonious hymn, a unique glorification. "The Lord has made everything for its purpose" (Proverbs 11:4). Even moral evil cannot unsettle the plan of God. . . . Creation as a whole possesses in a true and special way a liturgical physiognomy. It resembles divine life itself: for the Holy Trinity is a temple where the Word, by its eternal generation, is a perfect praise of the Father, *splendor gloriae et figura substantiae ejus*; where the communion of the Father and the Son is sealed by the kiss of peace and the personal rejoicing that is their common Spirit. . . .
>
> Every being, every life, every created beauty, natural or supernatural, is an ontological praise of God. Formal glorification, however, is only rendered by the creatures of a rational nature . . . . The human being is taken up by the created reality, lifted up by it, and instituted as its priest, so as to let ascend, in his own name and in name of all beings, an intelligible praise towards God (pp. 149–50; my translation).

Much of what is said in this quotation of Dom Delatte, I confirm; but as you probably have guessed, the tenor of my own thinking and sentiment is rather more nuanced, more subdued perhaps. Those who are with God have joy unspeakable; this I believe. And the faithful are associated to the whole of created reality in their living, praying, and liturgical praise of God; this I hold as well. But surely, simultaneously, those who stand in the truth are distraught at seeing those who are in poverty, those who are homeless, those who suffer injustice, those who live in terror, and those who despair; they are distraught at seeing the annihilation by the human race of large sways of the created reality and of the various ecosystems so that eventually God's praise will be halted and higher creaturely existence on earth as a whole be seriously compromised. I wonder about the mysterious presence throughout God's handiwork of destruction, selfishness, malignity, cruelty, and evil. I render glory to God the Creator, yet am speechless and gaze in silence. I hymn his deity and desire stillness. Deity is at the yonder side of paradox.

The faithful who are sensitive to all these events and situations do not only let ascend an intelligible praise towards God but also let ascend the sentiments that are the other aspects of the cosmic prayer, namely, the groaning, the suffering, perhaps even the despair, as well as the mysterious longing for communion with the Holy Trinity and for transformation towards personalization with the Trinity (compare my book *Cosmic Prayer and Guided Transformation*, pp.134–35). To be fair to Dom Delatte, the monks who sing the Divine Office consciously give voice to most of these sentiments as expressed in the Psalms foremost. But regrettably, in my experience, many monks have been far from able to adopt such awareness and have been too narrow-minded to go far beyond the illusions of a certain triumphalism that justifies to them their blindness.

In the summer of 2018, when we sold the house in Lennoxtown and searched for a new dwelling, we prayed for a house that would be good for our souls. Given our experience with neighbors, we looked for something standing alone and that would be affordable for our very limited means. We found on one of the websites a very small cottage advertised in Millport. When we went in June 2018 for our weekly holiday, we stayed in a caravan in Millport and had a chance to have a look at the cottage we had seen on the website. It was accessed through a close and sat behind some tenement flats in the back-garden area. It was interesting but totally unsuited for us: it really was much too small and much work was required. Two months later, we saw on the website another cottage in a back garden in Millport. It was larger than the one we had seen formerly during our holiday. We went to see it. At first, we found that this one as well required too much

Our present residence

452

doing to it; and too high a price was asked for it. Ten days later, not having found any satisfactory alternative, we decided to go for it.

It is a little secluded. The old garden wall between the nineteenth-century houses that are situated at the front makes up part of the back wall of our house. All the windows and the door are situated along the other side of the cottage. It is an old wash house that has been extended and the former owner used it as a holiday cottage.

It can only be accessed from the street via the close of the tenement flats at the front.

The garden is for common use, but we have also a patio that is private. In the patio area are a few raised beds. When we arrived, these were well overgrown with out-grown bushes. Three lavender plants that were squashed closely to each other among other plants I have since spread out over the beds after removing some of the larger

The statue of Our Lady that we have erected in one of the raised beds of the patio

bushes. Amazingly, all through last summer, each day, fifteen bees at least were around it. This summer, several bees are again visiting it daily.

Before the winter, I needed a few wooden planks and went to Largs with the two-wheeled trolley that I inherited from Teddy, my father-in-law. I was not feeling well but set out anyway for the three miles towards the ferry. Not even fifty meters away, I met Sam, who a few months earlier had fitted double windows in

# Acknowledgments

Though this is an autobiographical work, several pages have been dedicated to my parents and to events surrounding their lives that predate my own life. The writing of this book, therefore, has only been possible with the assistance of various people. I wish to express grateful thanks to each one of them; they include the following:

Invaluable has been the help provided by various local-history groups around Antwerp. I wish to thank especially Mr. Eddy Smits, chairman of the local-history group De Kaeck in Wommelgem, and Mr. Frans Goris, who performed research for my benefit in the archives of the municipality about my grandmother Emma Van Kesbeeck. As regards the family Govaerts living in the area of Ranst, invaluable has been the information provided by local-history enthusiast Mr. Frans Schelfhout. In addition, very helpful for obtaining information about the farm of my grandparents in Vaartstraat has been Mr. Walter Van der Avert of the documentation center of Ranst. I was greatly helped by Chairman Mr. René Beyst of the local-history group in Aartselaar; by Mr. Eddy Beyens of the group in Hove; by Mr. Armand Akkermans, secretary of the group in Edegem; and by Mr. Walter Janssens, chairman of the documentation center of Borsbeek.

My grateful thanks are due to Ms. Gonda Fevez, administrative assistant of the district Wilrijk in Antwerp for some genealogical research and to Mr. F. Meunier, delegate civil servant of Schaarbeek, Brussels.

I was kindly helped by Rev. Dirk Op de Becq, parish priest for the churches in Wilrijk, and by Mr. Laurent Hollevoet, pastoral assistant at Neerland, Wilrijk. My grateful thanks to Ms. Vinciane De

Keyser, pastoral worker of Saint-Bavo Parish, Wilrijk, and to Rev. Fons Houtmeyers, parish priest of Saint-Rochus Parish, Deurne, for allowing me to consult the parish archives; as well as to Ms. Chris Ghielens, pastoral worker of the Parish of Saints Peter and Paul, Wommelgem, for providing me an extract of the baptismal register regarding my mother, Carolina Van Kesbeeck. I also thank Sr. Denise Van Deuren, archivist of the Sisters Annunciates of Huldenberg, for providing information about the primary school at Kandonk Laar, Wommelgem, and Rev. Paul Van der Stuyft for driving me towards Huldenberg, for helping me in my search with regard to Evere and Schaarbeek, and for welcoming me to stay with him during the days that I was doing research for this book.

Dr. Patrick De Voogt and Mrs. Denise De Weerdt have kindly helped with information about the family De Weerdt. I am grateful to Mrs. Maria Van Uffel (maiden name Van Kesbeeck) and Mrs. Louisa De Bruyn (maiden name Luyckx), both cousins of my mother, for providing me with information about the family Van Kesbeeck. Most kind has been Mrs. Vera De Raedt (maiden name Bellemans), daughter of my mother's cousin Leontine Luyckx. I am grateful to the late Mrs. Jeanne Van Kesbeeck (maiden name Van Hoeydonck), an aunt of my mother, for the conversation I was able to have with her about the past not long before she died, and to her grandson Mr. Steven Van Kesbeeck for a copy of the picture of the golden jubilee (which also Maria Van Kesbeeck and Louisa Luyckx have kindly provided).

I thank Mrs. Maria De Wever (maiden name Fret), and her daughter, Mia, for helping me with various questions regarding my mother's life. I also thank my brother, Walter, for helping me fill in some details about our parents' life and about his own career.

And last but not least, I thank my proofreader, that is, my beloved wife, Karen. Grateful thanks.

Deo gratias!

Printed in Great Britain
by Amazon